COMPUTER GRAPHICS

with 29 ready-to-run programs

Dedication:

This book is dedicated to all TRS-80™ owners.

Other TAB books by the author:

No. 1275 *33 Challenging Computer Games for TRS-80™/ Apple™/PET®*

No. 1276
$15.95

COMPUTER GRAPHICS

with 29 ready-to-run programs by David Chance

TAB BOOKS Inc.
BLUE RIDGE SUMMIT, PA. 17214

FIRST EDITION

FOURTH PRINTING

Printed in the United States of America

Library of Congress Cataloging in Publication Data

Chance, David.
    Computer graphics—with 29 ready-to-run programs.

    Includes index.
    1. Computer graphics. I. Title.
T385.C45   001.64′43   80-28652
ISBN 0-8306-9636-9
ISBN 0-8306-1276-9 (pbk.)

Cover art courtesy of Computer Graphics by Melvin L. Prueitt, Dover Publications, Inc.

Contents

Preface

If you aren't using graphics with your TRS-80 microcomputer you are leaving out the most fascinating aspect of your computer. Whether playing, experimenting or running a program, graphics opens hidden areas of your computer.

This book contains 29 programs that are tested and ready to run. Each program uses graphics. The first chapter helps you to get started. Several different program examples are given that you can experiment with. Chapter 2 shows you how to generate graphics patterns and the random and controlled movement of objects. Program examples illustrate INKEY$, PEEK and POKE.

If you are just learning about graphics, this book is ideally suited for you. The beginning chapters are written in layman's terms to avoid confusion. If you are already using graphics on your computer you might find the sample programs quite useful and you might still learn something you didn't know.

I might stress that if you are a beginner you should read the first few chapters carefully before running the programs contained in Chapter 3. This will give you a firm understanding about what goes on with each program.

Each program in Chapter 3 has a flowchart, plus notes on the changes you might make in the programs (to experiment). The notes will step you through each program line (unless the line is self-explanatory). Each program contains REM STATEMENTS to help you understand the workings of the program. The print statements are 38 characters long to suit the book's page width. Rewrite them to increase the readability of your program.

David Chance

Chapter 1
Getting Started

Getting started is one of the easiest things to do when working with graphics. The most advantageous programming aids you can have are called Video Worksheets (catalog number 26-2105). You can buy them at any local Radio Shack store. One side of these worksheets contains all the TAB locations, PRINT @ locations and the X and Y locations of your video display. These worksheets are invaluable when you want to set up a specific display containing many different locations. On the opposite side of these worksheets you'll find numerous spaces for program lines, your variable list and comments. All program lines can be kept neatly along with your variable list in the squares provided.

After you have a general idea of the graphic display you want, chart it down on the worksheets and at the same time fill in the necessary lines and variables.

If you are new at creating graphics for the TRS-80 you will soon learn that one thing you cannot create is an ordinary circle (other than the letter O and the zero). So if you're out to create a bunch of circles on the display, you've chosen the wrong computer.

There are, however, thousands of creations that can be made with the TRS-80. If speed of execution isn't a factor, you can always rely on the SET-RESET function. This is the best route if you're just learning about graphics. The video display has 6144 graphic locations arranged in a 128 × 48 matrix, that can be Set and Reset at your command. That many locations provide you with many different creations waiting for you to draw. Just playing with the TRS-80 will open up many new frontiers.

You can use the following functions to set up the display:
1. CHR$
2. PRINT@
3. STRING$

CHR$

The following program lets you examine the graphics codes:

```
10   CLS
20   A=0:REM PRINT @ LOCATION
30   FOR CODE=129 TO 191
40   PRINT @ A,CODE;CHR$(CODE)
50   IF A=896 THEN 70:ELSE A=A+128:REM SPACE TO
     EXAMINE CODES
60   NEXT:GOTO 90:REM END OF RUN
70   PRINT @ A+20, "PRESS ENTER TO CONTINUE";:
     INPUT X
80   A=0:CLS:GOTO 60:REM RESET A - CONTINUE LOOP
     OF CHR$
90   PRINT @ A+20,"PRESS ENTER WHEN FINISHED";
100  INPUT X
110  CLS:END
```

Line 20 starts the PRINT@ location at 0 (zero).

Line 30 FOR NEXT loop for graphic codes 129 to 191.

Line 40 prints the code and sets the graphic area.

Line 50 checks variable A before adding a space.

Line 60 the NEXT for continuing and end of program to Line 90.

Line 70 is for user to examine codes before clearing video.

Line 80 resets A to 0 (zero) and continues LOOP.

Line 90 terminates program when ENTER is pressed.

This program will let you more closely examine the graphic codes and lets you know just exactly where these blocks will be set on a line (horizontal lines 0 - 15). An example: Note that graphic code 131 produces a square block set at the top of the line, or at the top of a graphic cell (made up of 7 bits). Code 140 locates the square at the bottom of the line (or graphic cell).

What's the point? If you've created any form of graphic display using the CHR$ mode, you've probably found that to get the display you want, it can become quite tedious not knowing exactly where the graphic block will be set on a given line. By running the above program (and saving it on tape for future reference) you'll have a better knowledge of these graphic codes.

Naturally the CHR$ function is also useful for other purposes, but this is a graphics book and everything can't be taught here.

PRINT @

The PRINT @ statement is a very useful function when working with computer graphics. A total of 1024 PRINT@ locations are located on the video display—a more than ample amount. By following the video-display worksheet you can place characters exactly where you want them (unless you're a pro and know all locations by heart). You have to be careful not to let the characters fall to the next line when setting up a display. For example, PRINT @ 57, "COMPUTER", would put "COMPUT" on the top line, while the R to COMPUTER would fall to the next line. If you are working on a program that contains both graphics and characters (words) be sure to add the trailing semicolon, or you'll end up with a carriage return blanking-out part of your display.

You can achieve some very pleasing displays when PRINT @ and CHR$ are combined (combined as was the previous program). When placed properly, these two functions make large letters. It's very simple! Examine the graphic codes, chart each one on a video worksheet and zap(!). You have an instant bulletin board. If you have pre-schoolers, these large letters could be their road to learning the alphabet. The bulletin-board program could be constructed to print out sentences using the large letters. A FOR-NEXT loop would create a delay between words.

Your imagination is the only limit to the things you can do with a computer (any computer). If you don't know everything about your computer, playing with it serves as an excellent teacher.

STRING $

The STRING$ statement (or function) is something else that is very useful when creating graphics. The only drawback to using this statement is that unless you clear enough memory before you use it you'll end up with an OS ERROR (out of string space).
An example using the STRING$ statement:

```
10   CLEAR 64:CLS
20   A$=STRING$(64,43)
30   PRINT A$
40   GOTO 40
```

Line 10 clears just enough memory (string space) for the STRING$ statement in line 20. Of course if you were to see a number larger than 64, you would have to clear more memory.

Line 20 contains the actual STRING$ statement—STRING$(64,43). 43 is the character code representing the plus sign and 64 is the number of plus signs that will be printed by line 30.

If you were to change the character code from 43 to the graphic code 191 (for all bits on), the computer would print a solid bar across the top of the video. Using the short program above and graphic codes 129 through 191, experiment with the program.

CHR$, PRINT AND STRING$ (COMBINED)

Combining these three statements will give you an array of all the possible patterns on your display. For example:

```
10   CLEAR 1000:CLS
20   A$=STRING$(63,191)
30   B$=CHR$(149)
40   PRINT @ Ø, A$
50   PRINT @ 96Ø, A$;
60   FOR L=64 TO 896 STEP 64:PRINT @ L,B$;:NEXT
70   FOR R=126 TO 958 STEP 64:PRINT @ R,B$;:NEXT
80   GOTO 80
```

The above program would print a neat border around the outer edges of your video display. Code 149, (line 30) just turns on three bits of a line. Step 64 in lines 60 and 70 keeps the left and right lines vertical. Experiment with the program by inserting different values for A$ and B$, and you'll come up with some rather unusual displays. Be sure to add the trailing semicolon to keep from getting a carriage return.

The program VIEWER contained in this book will further your knowledge of the differences between, SET-RESET, CHR$, PRINT @, STRING$ and POKE. The program merely sets a display and shows the different operating speeds of each function. You'd be surprised at how slow POKE is compared to using CHR$, PRINT @ and STRING$ for the same program.

Chapter 2
Generating Game Patterns

You can generate game patterns in many different ways. The choice is entirely up to you. If you're concerned about the program's execution speed you should probably POKE your graphics; but, as was said in the last chapter, execution speed can be obtained from other functions. Besides, the old adage "if you don't know where you are POKEing *don't,*" is very true.

Your best bet would be to start with some other function until you become more familiar with the hazards of POKE (explained later in this chapter). We use SET and RESET extensively throughout the programs in this book. Why? So the reader can become more acquainted with its function. Thousands of games can be generated using the SET-RESET function. They won't be the fastest, but they'll be easier to write and handle. As stated earlier, you can also generate game patterns using the CHR$, PRINT @ and STRING$ function. In my opinion (and only mine) top execution speed comes from using the above functions. If you still are hesitant to believe me, and haven't done it yet, key in and run the program VIEWER, then see what you think.

Generating game patterns can also be done randomly. This is the trick to the program MOUNTAIN. Arguments placed within the program keep the RANDOM generation within certain limits. Always remember to place your arguments *before* the RANDOM statement, placing them afterwards will only lead you to a FC ERROR (Illegal function call). This means simply that the statements have gone beyond the set parameters that the computer and video display are capable of handling.

RANDOM MOTION

You might want to move an object randomly. For example, a program might contain some spacecraft that you want moved about the video screen randomly.) An example might be:

```
10   CLS
20   RANDOM
30   C$="<:<0>:>":N$="              "
40   A=410
50   PRINT @ A, C$;
60   FOR I=1 TO 50:NEXT
70   PRINT @ A, N$;
80   M=RND(2):ON M GOTO 90,100
90   IF A > = 440 THEN 40:ELSE A=A+RND(4):GOTO 50
100  IF A< = 380 THEN 40:ELSE A=A− RND(4):GOTO 50
```

Line 10 clears the video screen.

Line 20 seeds the RANDOM generator.

Line 30 of course is the spacecraft (C$). N$ must contain the same amount of spaces that C$ has or parts of the spacecraft will be left at different locations on the video.

Line 40 variable A is the starting PRINT @ area.

Line 50 prints the spacecraft at A.

Line 60 is a time loop before the spacecraft is blanked-out.

Line 70 prints N$ at A to blank-out spacecraft before variable A is changed.

Line 80 a random function either selects left or right movement of the spacecraft.

Line 90 has the argument placed *before* A is increased so the craft won't fall to the next line. If variable A is greater than or equal to 440, the craft will return to the beginning position and A is reset to 410.

Line 100 is the exact opposite of line 90, meaning the craft will be moved to the left.

Both lines 90 and 100 return (GOTO) line 50 to keep the craft moving.

If you've entered and run the preceeding program you should have noted that experimenting with the time loop, (line 60) lets you move the spacecraft at a slower or faster rate. You can also cause the craft to jump more or less by changing the RND function in lines 90 and 100. By adding several more lines and arguments, you can actually move the craft up, down left or right.

You are probably wondering now, what is the point of all these games? The point is that you can learn the many different ways in which your computer is capable of operating by just running several different games. Some games contain most of the functions that a computer has. And what better way to relax after a hard day than powering up a computer and running a game? Sitting in front of the T.V. watching reruns made two decades ago?

Back on the track . . . . . You can apply the same random motion with the SET-RESET function. Enter the following short program and run it:

```
100   CLS
110   RANDOM
120   X=64:Y=47
130   IF X< =0 OR X> +127 THEN 120:ELSE SET(X,Y)
135   FOR I=1 TO 10:NEXT
140   IF Y< =0 THEN RESET(X,Y):GOTO 120
150   RESET(X,Y):Y=Y-1
160   M=RND(2):ON M GOTO 170,180
170   X=X+RND(5):GOTO 130
180   X=X-RND(5):GOTO 130
```

Line 120 sets the area for X and Y to begin.

Line 130 tests X before setting X and Y (if argument is true X and Y will be reset to the beginning position).

Line 135 is a short loop to slow down the SET & RESET of the light block area.

Line 140 tests Y, if true, RESETS X & Y and goes back to the starting position (line 120). If RESET were left out of this line the block areas would remain light at different points, top of video.

Line 150 RESETS X & Y also desends Y, so block will move to top of video.

Line 160 almost exactly as line 80 in the last program, but selects (randomly) either left or right movement of the block.

Line 170 & 180 are for right or left movement of the block respectively and returns back to line 130, to keep the block moving.

With minor program modifications the light block could be moved up, down, along with the right and left movement. With the addition of more variables you could have more than one block moving around the video.

CONTROLLED MOTION

Once you have an object moving randomly on the screen, you take the program with the spacecraft and add another dimension to it, such as a guided missile.

```
10   CLS
20   RANDOM
30   C$="<:<0>:>":N$="            ":S=989:M$=CHR$(143)
35   PRINT@ S, M$;:FOR X=0 TO 127:SET(X,47):NEXT
40   A=410
50   PRINT@ A,C$;
60   FOR I=1 TO 50:NEXT
70   X$=INKEY$:IF X$="" THEN 140
90   PRINT@ A,N$;:M=RND(2):ON M GOTO 100, 110
100  IF A > = 440 THEN 40:ELSE A=A+RND(2):GOTO 120
110  IF A < = 380 THEN 40:ELSE A=A– RND(2)
120  PRINT@ A,C$;
130  IF X$< >"  " THEN 50
140  PRINT@ S, "   ";:S=S– 64:PRINT@ S,M$;
150  IF S=(A+3) THEN PRINT @ 25, "** A HIT **":FOR I=1
     TO 500:NEXT:GOTO 170:ELSE IF < > 349 THEN 90
170  PRINT@ 25,"       "
180  PRINT@ S," ";:S=989:PRINT@ S,M$;:GOTO 50
```

Note that you've made only a few minor changes. At line 30 M$ is for the rocket and variable S is the rocket's area.

Line 35 prints the rocket at S.

Line 70 is the INKEY$ function, " " meaning, press the space bar to fire.

Line 130 checks X$ to see if rocket has been fired.

Line 140 fires the rocket (that is, if the space bar was pressed). Prints a blank, descends S by 64, then prints the square? rocket again. And, while the rocket is moving in an upward motion:

Line 150 tests S, to see if at a certain point S will equal A+3 (A+3 is the center of the spacecraft, where the 0 is located). If it does, line 150 will prints "** A HIT **" @ 25, goes into a time loop, (so message can be seen) drops down to line 170 and recycles. If you miss the spacecraft, or S <> 349, line 150 returns to line 90. This causes the 'flutter' of spacecraft. If S does equal 349, S is reset and returns back to its starting position (989).

With several other modifications to the above program could provide more than one spacecraft, allow the rockets to fire in different directions and, of course, add scoring.

You can also use motion control to manipulate things other than rockets. An example might be moving words (horizontally) across the video screen.

Enter and run the following example:

```
10   CLS:PRINT CHR$(23)
20   A$="THEY"
30   B$="WENT"
40   C$=LEFT$(A$,2)+"A"+RIGHT$(B$,1)
50   D$=LEFT$(B$,1)+"A"+RIGHT$(A$,1)CHR$(94)
60   FOR W=64 TO 120:PRINT @ W,A$;:PRINT @W-1,
     " ";:NEXT
70   FOR W=128 TO 184:PRINT @ W,B$;:PRINT @
     W-1," ";:NEXT
80   FOR W=192 TO 248:PRINT @ W,C$;:PRINT @
     W-1," ";:NEXT
90   FOR W=256 TO 312:PRINT @ W,D$;:PRINT @
     W-1," ";:NEXT
100  GOTO 100
```

Line 10 clears the video screen and changes to the 32 character-per-line format.

Lines 20 through 50 contain the four words that are used.

Lines 60 through 90 sweep each word across the video screen from left to right. The statement PRINT @ W-1, " "; is used to blank-out letters to the left of the words. If that statement were to be left out, it would defeat the purpose of the program.

By adding a few more lines, you could have the words bounce off the right side of the video screen and return to the left side (inserting STEP-1 statements and change numerical contents of the FOR NEXT loops). You would also have to add a PRINT @ statement, W+1, " "; to blank-out letters on the right side of the words.

INKEY$

Just about the most common way to control objects on your video screen is to use the INKEY$ function. The INKEY$ function allows you to use just about any key desired to control an object. You must be sure to insert the INKEY$ statement within a specified line, however. For example:

```
10   X$=INKEY$:REM SETTING X$ TO THE INKEY$
     FUNCTION
20   PRINT @ 64,X$
30   GOTO 20
```

Obviously inserting the above lines in a program won't work! You could punch keys until your fingers fell off, and nothing would be printed at 64. The program runs so fast that all it would be doing is going from 20 to 30 and back again. What line 30 should have read was:

30 GOTO 10

This way you could press all the keys you wanted and each key pressed would be printed at 64. Anytime you are using the INKEY$ function you must have, X$=INKEY$ (X$ is only an example) located where the computer will recognize what X$ is for. Otherwise, you'll end up having problems with your program.

If you plan on making a program that will use the INKEY$ function and would print the letters at a specified area in order to create a word, you might try the following example:

```
10    CLEAR 500: CLS
20    A=64: WW=0
30    X$=INKEY$: IF X$=" "THEN 30
35    IF X$=" " THEN 80: ELSE IF X$="0" THEN 120
40    W$=W$+X$
50    PRINT A, X$;
60    A=A+1: WW=WW+1
70    GOTO 30
80    A=A-1: WW=WW-1
90    W$=MID$(W$, 1, WW)
100   PRINT @ A, "";
110   GOTO 30
120   CLS: PRINT @ 128, W$
130   END
```

This program example will receive whatever characters you press on the keyboard (excluding Ø, which ends the program). The up arrow backspaces a character to let you erase and change it. You can also insert spaces between words by pressing the space bar.

Line 10 clears 500 bits of memory for string space.

Line 20 variable A is for character placement, variable WW is used for backspacing only.

Line 30 starts the INKEY$ function.

Line 35 contains two arguments. The first one (up arrow) is for backspacing. When the up arrow is pressed control falls to line 80 where variable A is decreased by one (one for each time the up arrow is pressed) to blank-out the last character. Variable WW is decreased by one so that the length of W$ is decreased by one, this will keep the word, phrase or sentence up to date with what the user is inputting. The second argument in line 35 terminates the program and prints W$ (lines 120 and 130). You can use any character for the second part of that argument.

Line 40 W$ contains all characters input by the INKEY$ function.

Line 50 prints each character (except for spaces) starting at 64 and increasing by one space.

Line 60 increases variable A and WW by one (for character).

Line 70 recycles control back to line 30—the INKEY$ function.

The preceding program suits many applications; just be sure to clear enough memory for the string's length. You can add several other arguments to keep words, sentences, numerals or whatever in a neat fashion. You could also add a flashing cursor to precede each character by adding the following lines to the program just entered:

```
25   C=25
```

Change line 30 to read:

```
30   X$=INKEY$: @ C," ":: FOR T=1 TO 150:
     NEXT:PRINT @ C,CHR$(143);: IF X$="" THEN 30
```

And finally insert the next three lines:

```
55   C=C+1
85   C=C-1
95   PRINT @ C,CHR$(143);
```

This isn't exactly an excellent flashing cursor, but it will give you a general idea of what can be done. Line 30 controls the flashing rate with its FOR NEXT loop. Experiment with different values for the loop and come up with something of your own.

PEEK

You can create controlled objects or character movement using the PEEK command. If you have a TRS-80 memory map handy look it over and locate Keyboard Memory. Note that the decimal locations are from 14336 to 15359. Now enter the following short program:

```
10   CLS
20   K=PEEK(15340)
30   PRINT @ 128,K
40   GOTO 20
```

What this short program actually does is PEEK into the TRS-80 keyboard memory and print the value of the key being depressed at 128. You should receive the following values:

Up arrow = 8
Down arrow = 16
Left arrow = 32
Right arrow = 64
ENTER = 1
CLEAR = 2
Space bar = 128

Pressing a combination of the above keys will give you many different values. By adding arguments within a program for the values stated or a combination of them you could control many things on your video. For a further look at the PEEK function enter the program ARCHITECT and you'll soon discover what I mean by controlling.

As with the INKEY$ function the PEEK function must also be located where the computer will recognize it, or that one variable for PEEK will mean nothing. You can also PEEK into the video display memory and POKE the different values, as is done in one area of the program MAZE GAME. When the values are changed and checked by an argument, program execution could branch to another line, add scoring, or terminate the program. As with the other program examples, experiment with PEEK until you understand what is taking place and then make up a program of your own.

POKE

Although you should bear in mind the adage "if you don't know where you are POKEing don't;" my motto is, if you want to learn more about POKE, use it! Just like driving down an unknown road, you don't know what you'll find until you've taken the trip.

POKE locations on your video display are from 15360 to 16383 (decimal). Chart each location on a video worksheet and keep it for reference. This will come in handy later. The next program example will make a simple frame around the outer edges of the video display using POKE:

```
10   CLS
20   P=191
30   FOR X=15360 TO 15423:POKE X,P:NEXT
40   FOR X=16320 TO 16383:POKE X,P:NEXT
```

```
50   FOR X=15360 TO 16320 STEP 64:POKE X,P:NEXT
60   FOR X=15423 TO 16383 STEP 64:POKE X,P:NEXT
70   GOTO 70
```

Line 20 sets P to 191 for all bits on (graphic code).
Line 30 and 40 contain the 2 horizontal lines, top and bottom.
Line 50 and 60 contain the 2 vertical lines, left and right.

Be sure to insert the STEP 64 in the above two lines or you'll
end up having a white screen, instead of a border.

My advice when POKEing into your video memory for a
certain display is to write it separately from the rest of the
program. That is, if part of your program will use POKE
statements for graphics, leave out the rest of the program text and
work on the POKE statements either first or last. Put the entire
program together after you're sure both parts work. Nothing could
be worse than to finish a 100 or 200 line program, RUN it and send
the computer to another world because one numeral was miskeyed
in a POKE statement. The computer might automatically dump
your program and goes back to the MEMORY SIZE? question. Or
you might panic and press the RESET button frantically only to
discover that nothing can be done. You'll have to turn off the
computer and power-up again, losing every line that just took you
two days to put together.

I know this from a first hand experience. It happened to me.
So, until I learned more about POKE, I completed the POKE
statements separate from the rest of my programs. If you've never
experienced the above, enter and run the following:

```
10   CLS
20   P=191:X=15360:XX=16520
30   POKE X,P
40   X=X+64
50   IF X< >XX THEN 30
```

You should have a blank video with the question MEMORY
SIZE? in the upper left hand corner of the video screen. The
mistake was in line 20, XX=16520, where a 5 was accidentally
pressed instead of a 3 and the programmer didn't check over the
figures.

That error was self-induced so you wouldn't have to power-up
again, but the computer did dump the program and return back to
the MEMORY SIZE? question, which is just about as bad. Which all
goes to prove what was said earlier, if you had a long program in
memory, you would have lost the entire thing because of the
miskeyed number in a POKE statement.

Other than suffering from this uncertainty, POKE can be very useful when setting up a graphic display. Just be sure to check and recheck all of your figures before running it.

VIDEO DISPLAY

The TRS-80 video display has a 12-inch monochrome cathode ray tube (CRT). The CRT is scanned twice per second. The electronic beam travels from left to right, top to bottom. It has 1024 character locations (cells) full screen, or 512 character locations when using the 32 character-per-line format. There are a total of 16 lines, (horizontally—0 through 15) and each line contains 64 character locations (or 32 with the 32 character-per-line format).

The SET-RESET function provides 384 possible block locations per line. Giving you a total of 6144 possible SET-RESET locations full screen.

You can greatly prolong the life of the video display (CRT), by adjusting the brightness and contrast to a comfortable viewing image, but not bright enough to burn a permanent image in the CRT's phosphors. This must especially be remembered when executing a program that contains a lot of graphics. Programs such as these require you to adjust the brightness and contrast, but by all means, do not adjust them too high or you'll find yourself purchasing a new CRT.

To understand the technical side of the TRS-80, I would suggest picking up a copy of THE TRS-80 MICRO-COMPUTER TECHNICAL REFERENCE HANDBOOK (cat. no. 26-2103). It provides a lot of information about the internal workings of your computer, at a technical level, of course. This manual also covers different areas of trouble-shooting the TRS-80. Parts of the troubleshooting don't require you to be a technical expert, but if you don't know what an integrated circuit is, don't tackle it yourself.

SALES PITCH

If you are not into writing your own programs, you should be experimenting with your computer more until you can. Entering a wrong argument, after all, won't cause your computer to explode. There are useful keys to help you through the trial and error period. When caught in a continuous loop, because you've added a GOTO instead of an END, for example, you have the BREAK key. If that fails you have a RESET button and if all that fails to give results, you have the power switch. Or you could be running a graphics program, nearing the end of execution, and someone slips up behind you and presses the CLEAR key!

If you must submit to buying programs, you're better off with a book of them that you enter yourself. Like the ready-to-run versions all the program bugs have been removed, but, unlike the ready-to-run version, a book of programs help you learn more about what is taking place within a program. REM statements will step you through each line and, in the long run, you'll save a bundle. Besides, you can purchase an entire book of programs for the price of one ready-to-run program. You might consider TAB book No. 1275 *33 Challenging Computer Games For TRS-80™/Apple™/PET®*.

Don't misunderstand, this book will not and was not intended to teach you all there is to know about computer graphics, but if you'll take time to study the REM statements and program notes your knowledge of computer graphics should be greatly expanded. Soon you'll be able to create your own graphics programs. Learning to write your own programs is a great achievement. You'll be getting the computer to do what you want it to.

GRAPHICS PROGRAMS

Within the remaining chapters you find 29 pre-tested programs, ready to key-in and run. Each of the programs contains a flowchart, some changes you could make to customize the program, and program notes that will step you through every line within a program. You will be given a firm understanding of how each program works, through the REM statements or the program notes.

You can study each program and change it to fit your needs, if you wish, or leave them as is. Either way you should find hours of enjoyment and learning experience about computer graphics.

Chapter 3
Adventure and Competition

(OVER THE) MOUNTAIN

This program will draw a mountain with three peaks. Your mission will be to control a spacecraft (starting location bottom left corner of video) over these peaks and while doing so, pick up a parcel that the computer will automatically launch out of the first peak.

You will control your ship by entering thrusts (0-6) by entering the letter D first, you'll be able to descend. You can move right horizontally by entering a 0 (zero), but you haven't any commands to move your ship to the right. This will be done randomly by the computer. See Fig. 3-1.

To pick up your parcel, you will control your ship over the first peak (right before you reach the peak, the parcel will be launched). You will notice the ship has an opening in the bottom of it. This is the area for the parcel. The parcel must hit *exactly* in this opening. If it strikes anywhere else it will be treated as a hit to your ship.

After you successfully pick up the parcel you will have to maneuver over the other two peaks and finally descend (slowly) to the safety zone (bottom of ship must make contact with horizontal bar in safety zone).

I forgot to mention two other things:

• When your ship reaches a certain area, you will receive laser fire—don't get hit!

• Keep an eye on your fuel level, if you run out you lose complete control of the ship and it falls, straight down.

Program Notes

If the third peak is lower or equal to the second peak, the computer will print "let's try again", as the second peak must be lower than the third.

Line 425 contains the argument for the laser attack.

Line 429 checks if you've been hit.

Line 434 is the INKEY$ function. This is used so that the user doesn't have to press ENTER when inputting a thrust.

Line 435 contains the VAL function for A$, so the computer can interpret your thrust.

Lines 500 - 550 are for your descent moves.

Lines 600 - 620 determines the laser attack.

Lines 800 - 850 *drop* your ship when fuel supply reaches 0 tons.

24

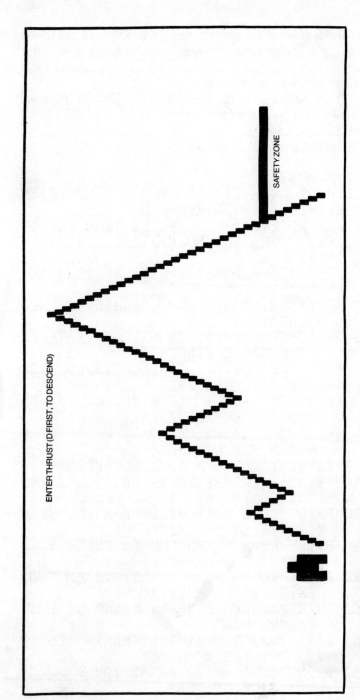

Fig. 3-1. Sample run of Mountain.

Incidentally, if you pass the parcel area and don't pick up the parcel, you'll still have to continue to the safety area. After reaching this area, the computer will advise you to try again (with the amount of fuel you have left).

If you think the fuel supply is too low, line 15 can be increased to a higher number. As written, the program provides at least 1200 tons (an ample amount).

See Fig. 3-2. for the flowchart.

Program Listing

```
5 REM PROGRAM TITLE: OVER THE MOUNTAIN
10 CLS:PRINT:HT=0:R=0:U=0
15 FL=RND((1000)*2):IF FL< 1200 THEN15
20 PRINT"OVER THE MOUNTAIN"
30 PRINT
40 PRINT"YOUR MISSION WILL BE TO PICK
      UP A PARCEL"
50 PRINT"WHILE YOU ARE GOING OVER THE
      MOUNTAIN."
60 PRINT"THIS MOUNTAIN WILL HAVE THREE
      PEAKS, THE FIRST"
70 PRINT"PEAK (LEFT SIDE OF VIDEO) WIL
      L HAVE THE PARCEL"
80 PRINT"YOU ARE TO PICK UP. AT THE SE
      COND AND THIRD PEAK"
90 PRINT"ARE LASER CANNONS, WHICH WILL
      BEGIN FIRING WHEN"
100 PRINT"YOU REACH A RANDOM POINT."
110 PRINT:PRINT"PRESS ENTER.....";:INP
      UT X:CLS:PRINT@64,;
120 PRINT"YOUR SHIP WILL BE MOVED UP B
      Y ENTERING THRUSTS"
130 PRINT"FROM 1 THROUGH 6, ENTERING A
      0 (ZERO) WILL MOVE"
140 PRINT"YOU HORIZONTALLY. TO DESCEND,
      ENTER A 'D' THEN A"
150 PRINT"NUMBER BETWEEN 1 AND 6. YOUR
      PARCEL MUST HIT"
151 PRINT"EXACTLY IN THE OPENING LOCAT
      ED AT THE BOTTOM OF"
152 PRINT"YOUR SHIP. AFTER YOU SUCCESSF
      ULLY PICK UP THE"
```

```
153 PRINT"PARCEL AND GO OVER ALL THREE
       PEAKS, YOU MUST"
154 PRINT"SLOWLY DESCEND AND HIT THE SA
       FETY ZONE, ANYWHERE"
155 PRINT"ELSE WILL INDUCE AN ERROR AN
       D YOU'LL HAVE TO"
156 PRINT"START OVER."
160 PRINT"ALSO KEEP AN EYE ON YOUR FUE
       L LEVEL, TO RUN OUT"
170 PRINT"WILL BE CERTAIN DEATH !!"
180 PRINT@832,"PRESS ENTER.....";:INPU
       T X$:CLS
190 REM SET MOUNTAIN
210 REM KEEP HEIGHT OF MOUNTAIN BETWEE
       N 47 AND 12
220 REM PEAK MOUNTAIN AT 3
230 REM INPUT ALL MOVES AT 0
240 Y=47:X=10:P=3:I=1
245 H=RND(40):IF H < 20 THEN245
250 SET(X,Y)
260 Y=Y-1:X=X+1
265 IF R=1 THEN320:ELSE IF R=3 THEN360
270 IF Y<>H THEN 250:ELSE X(I)=X:Y(T)=
       Y
280 SET(X,Y)
290 X=X+1:Y=Y+1
295 IF R=2 THEN340:ELSE IF R=4 THEN380
300 IF Y<>H+5 THEN280
310 H=H-10:R=1:I=I+1:GOTO250
320 IF Y<>H THEN250:ELSE X(I)=X:Y(I)=Y
330 H=H+11:R=2:I=I+1:GOTO280
340 IF Y<>H THEN280
350 R=3:GOTO250
360 IF Y>=12 THEN250:ELSE X(I)=X:Y(I)=
       Y
370 R=4:GOTO280
380 IF Y<>47THEN280
385 IF Y(2)<=Y(3)THEN PRINT@20,"NO GOO
       D, LET'S TRY AGAIN";:FOR LL=1TO12
       00:NEXT:R=0:CLS:GOTO240:ELSE GOSU
       B390:X(8)=X(3):X(7)=X(2):Y(5)=Y(2
```

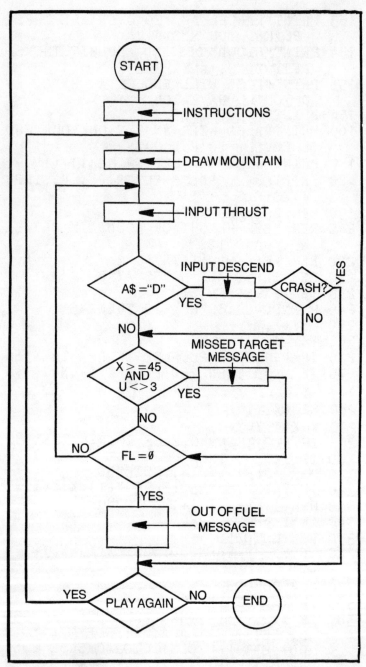

Fig. 3-2. Flowchart of Mountain.

```
        ):X(9)=X(1):Y(6)=Y(1):FOR Q=X(3)+
        27T0126:SET(Q,Y(3)+27):NEXT:PRINT
        @887,"SAFETY";:PRINT@952,"ZONE";:
        GOTO400
390     X=8:Y=47:M=46:J=0:RETURN
400     SET(X,Y):SET(X-2,Y):SET(X-1,M):SET
        (X-2,M):SET(X,M):SET(X-1,M-1)
410     PRINT@0,;
420     PRINT"ENTER THRUST (D FIRST, TO DE
        SCEND)";
422     IF X>=45 AND U<>3 PRINT@64,"MISSED
         PARCEL PICKUP !!";:RESET(X(1),Y(
        1)):GOTO434:ELSE IF X>=45 PRINT@6
        4,"                          ";:GOT
        O434
423     IF X>=23 AND U<>1 AND U<>3 THEN GO
        SUB1000
425     SET(X-1,M-1):RESET(X-1,M-1):IF J=1
        THENX(3)=X(3)-1:IF X(3)<=0 THEN X
        (3)=X(8):ELSE SET(X(3),Y(3)):RESE
        T(X(3),Y(3)):PRINT@984,"LASER ATT
        ACK !!";
427     IF X(2)>=126 OR Y(2)<=0 THEN X(2)=
        X(7):Y(2)=Y(5)
428     IF X>=50 THEN X(2)=X(2)+1:Y(2)=Y(2
        )-1:SET(X(2),Y(2)):RESET(X(2),Y(2
        )):ELSE PRINT@984,"
        ";
429     SET(X-1,M-1):RESET(X-1,M-1):K=RND(
        5):IF POINT(X,Y)=0 OR POINT(X,M)=
        0THEN700
430     IF U=3 THEN434:ELSE IF X>=20 AND X
        <=45 THEN PRINT@64,"LAUNCHING PAR
        CEL.....";:RESET(X(1),Y(1)):X(1)=
        X(1)+1:Y(1)=Y(1)-1:IF Y(1)<=15THE
        N Y(1)=Y(6):X(1)=X(9):ELSE SET(X(
        1),Y(1))
431     IF X>=20 AND X<=45 AND POINT(X-1,M
        +1) GOSUB1100:GOTO410
432     IF POINT(X+1,M) OR POINT(X+1,Y) TH
        EN860
```

29

```
434 A$=INKEY$:IF A$=""THEN 422:ELSE IF
    A$="D"THEN GOSUB500:GOTO410
435 C=VAL(A$):IF (M-2)<=4 OR (Y-1)<=4
    OR (X-2)<=0GOSUB500:GOTO410
440 K=RND(2):RESET(X,Y):RESET(X-2,Y):R
    ESET(X-1,M):RESET(X-2,M):RESET(X,
    M):RESET(X-1,M-1):FL=FL-ABS((C+M)
    -(Y+M)):IF FL<=0 FL=0:ELSE IF U=3
    AND P=1 THEN RESET(X-1,M+1)
450 PRINT@920,"FUEL LEFT:";FL;"TONS.";
    :IF FL<=0 THEN800
455 IF M<=5 OR Y<=5 THENGOSUB500:GOTO4
    10:ELSE IF X>=120 THEN GOSUB390:G
    OTO400:ELSE Y=Y-C:M=M-C:IF C=0 GO
    SUB1150:GOSUB460:GOTO470:ELSE X=X
    +K-2:GOSUB460:GOTO470
460 SET(X,Y):SET(X-2,Y):SET(X-1,M):SET
    (X-2,M):SET(X,M):SET(X-1,M-1):IF
    U=3 AND P=1 THEN SET(X-1,M+1)
465 RETURN
470 IF Y>=10 AND Y<=14THENGOSUB600
475 FOR L=1TO55:NEXT:IF K<>2 GOTO435:E
    LSE IF M<=7 OR Y<=7 GOSUB500:GOTO
    410:ELSE 410
500 PRINT@0,;
510 GOSUB460:PRINT"ENTER DESCEND
                  ";
520 SET(X-1,M-1):RESET(X-1,M-1):A$=INK
    EY$:IF A$=""THEN520
525 PRINT@920,"FUEL LEFT:";FL;:C=VAL(A
    $)
530 RESET(X,Y):RESET(X-2,Y):RESET(X-1,
    M):RESET(X-2,M):RESET(X,M):RESET(
    X-1,M-1):FL=FL-ABS((C+Y)-(C+M)+K)
    :IF FL<=0 THEN FL=0:GOTO800:ELSE
    IF U=3 AND P=1 THEN RESET(X-1,M+1
    )
535 IF X>=120 OR Y>=46 THEN GOSUB390:G
    OTO400:ELSEY=Y+C:M=M+C:IF C=0 THE
    N GOSUB1150:GOTO540:ELSE X=X+K-2
540 SET(X,Y):SET(X-2,Y):SET(X-1,M):SET
```

30

```
             (X-2,M):SET(X,M):SET(X-1,M-1):IF
             U=3 AND P=1 THEN SET(X-1,M+1)
545 FOR S=105TO127:IF POINT(S,37)THEN
    GOTO1200:ELSE NEXT
550 A$="":RETURN
600 REM COUNTER ATTACK
605 IF J=1 THEN SET(X(2)+1,Y(2)):SET(X
    (2),Y(2)):RETURN
610 SET(X(3)-1,Y(3)):SET(X(3),Y(3))
620 J=1:RETURN
700 HT=HT+1
710 PRINT@0,"DIRECT HIT !!
             ";
720 PRINT@64,"YOU'LL HAVE TO START OVE
    R !!";
725 IF HT>=2 PRINT@128,"YOU'VE BEEN HI
    T";HT;"TIMES !!";
730 FOR LL=1TO1900:NEXT
740 R=0:U=1
750 CLS
760 GOTO240
800 PRINT@0,"YOU ARE OUT OF FUEL !!
             ";
805 FL=0
810 RESET(X,Y-1):RESET(X-2,Y-1):RESET(
    X-1,M-1):RESET(X-2,M-1):RESET(X,M
    -1):RESET(X-1,M-2)
830 SET(X,Y):SET(X-2,Y):SET(X-1,M):SET
    (X-2,M):SET(X,M):SET(X-1,M-1)
840 IF Y>=46 Y=47:ELSE Y=Y+1:M=M+1
850 IF Y<>47 THEN810
860 CLS:PRINTCHR$(23)
870 PRINT:PRINT:PRINT:IF U=3 AND P=1TH
    EN 890
880 PRINT"C R A S H !!!"
890 PRINT
900 PRINT"ARE YOU READY TO TRY AGAIN";
910 INPUT A$
920 IF LEN(A$)<>3 THEN940
930 GOTO10
940 PRINT"MAYBE SOME OTHER MOUNTAIN ??
    "
```

```
950 GOTO950
1000 SET(X(1),Y(1))
1010 U=1
1020 RETURN
1100 PRINT@0,"YOU'VE MADE THE PICKUP !
     !          ";
1105 PRINT@64,"
     ";
1110 FOR LL=1TO1000:NEXT
1115 PRINT@0,"
     ";
1120 U=3:P=1
1130 RETURN
1150 X=X+3
1160 RETURN
1200 IF U<>3 AND P<>1 PRINT@0,"TRY AGA
     IN !!          ";:FOR L=1TO1200:
     NEXT:R=0:U=1:CLS:GOTO240
1205 PRINT@0,"CONGRATULATIONS !!
     ";
1210 PRINT@64,"YOU ARE IN THE SAFETY Z
     ONE";
1220 PRINT@128,"AND MADE THE PICKUP !!
     ";
1230 FOR L=1TO1200:NEXT
1240 GOTO860
```

GET THERE FIRST

Is exactly what must be done to win at this game. The game board will be made up of 16 squares; the top four will have your playing pieces, while the bottom four will have the computer's (Fig. 3-3).

The object of the game is to get all four of your pieces in one column; if you start for column 2 all four of your pieces must end up in that column (2,6,10,14) to win. Once you have moved a piece you cannot change it.

To give you a better idea of the game, here is an example: It's your move:

FROM 1 TO 6 Then the computer moves. If the computer doesn't block you, your next move should be:

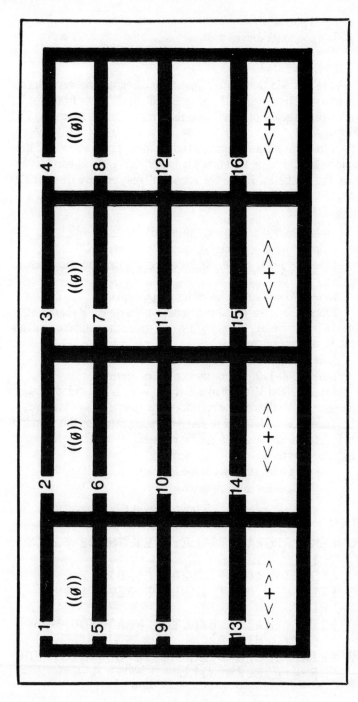

Fig. 3-3. Sample run of Get There First.

FROM 3 TO 10

The computer moves next.

Finally, if all works out, your final move will be:

FROM 4 TO 14

And you win that round. Just remember, whichever column you choose, stick with it. If you select column 3, move from 1 to 7, don't skip a square or you'll lose that round (that is from 1 to 11, skipping 7).

If there is a time when you cannot move enter a zero and the game will end in a tie (but that's not winning). Oh yes, don't try to cheat the computer. Either the round will only end in a tie or you'll lose.

Program Notes

Lines 320-360 draw the game board.

Lines 370-400 read the data for the squares area.

Lines 405-460 place all numbers (yours and the playing pieces).

Lines 470-485 set variables for proper squares.

Lines 490-570 are self-explanatory. Variable RR changes the players' order of play. If you go first one round the computer will go first the next round, and so on.

Lines 640-735 input your moves.

Lines 1000-1100 are for the computer's moves.

Lines 1200-1340 test to see if you won. If you did it prints a message; if not, the routine returns to the computer's next move.

Lines 1345-1440 test to see if the computer won the round; if not it defaults to a tie or returns for you next move. These lines also check for cheaters.

The remaining lines are self-explanatory.

See Fig. 3-4 for the flowchart.

Program Listing

```
10 REM PROGRAM TITLE: GET THERE FIRST
   !!
20 CLS:DIM A(20),S(20),C(20)
25 PRINT@15,"GET THERE FIRST !!"
30 PRINT
40 PRINT"THAT'S EXACTLY WHAT YOU MUST
   DO TO WIN."
50 PRINT"THERE WILL BE 16 SQUARES, YOU
   R 4 PIECES WILL"
```

```
60  PRINT"BE IN THE TOP FOUR, THE COMPU
    TER'S WILL BE IN"
70  PRINT"THE BOTTOM FOUR. HERE'S WHAT
    YOU MUST DO,"
80  PRINT"FIRST: YOU WILL BE ASKED TO I
    NPUT A NUMBER BETWEEN"
90  PRINT"1 & 5, IF CORRECT YOU'LL MOVE
    FIRST, IF NOT THE"
100 PRINT"COMPUTER WILL MOVE FIRST."
105 PRINT:PRINT"PRESS ENTER";:INPUT X:
    CLS:PRINT
110 PRINT""SECOND: WHEN YOU MOVE A PIEC
    E YOURS EXAMPLE:''
120 PRINT"YOU MOVE FROM 1 TO 6, THAT M
    EANS YOU'LL HAVE A PIECE"
130 PRINT"LEFT ON 2, 3, & 4. THE NEXT
    TIME YOU MOVE, MOVE"
140 PRINT"3 TO 10 (IF THE COMPUTER HAS
    N'T BLOCKED YOU)."
150 PRINT"SO, IN SIMPLE TERMS, EITHER
    YOU OR THE COMPUTER"
160 PRINT"MUST HAVE ALL FOUR OF YOUR P
    IECES IN ONE STRAIGHT"
170 PRINT"COLUMN TO WIN. REMEMBER NOW,
    AFTER YOU HAVE MOVED"
180 PRINT"ONE OF YOUR PIECES YOU CAN'T
    MOVE IT AGAIN, SO BE"
190 PRINT"SURE WHERE YOU ARE MOVING IT
    BEFORE YOU MOVE IT !"
200 PRINT"NOTE: IF YOU FIND YOU OR THE
    COMPUTER CANNOT MAKE"
210 PRINT"A MOVE, WHEN ASKED: FROM? EN
    TER A 0 (ZERO)."
280 PRINT
290 PRINT"THIRD...DON'T JUST SIT THERE
    READING PRESS ENTER"
300 PRINT"AND GET THE GAME STARTED";:I
    NPUT X:CLS
310 REM DRAW PLAYING BOARD
315 RANDOM
```

```
320 FOR Y=0TO24:SET(9,Y):SET(10,Y):SET
    (118,Y):SET(119,Y)
330 SET(35,Y):SET(92,Y):SET(63,Y):SET(
    64,Y):NEXT
340 T=0:H=0:XX=0
350 FOR X=10TO117:SET(X,T):NEXT
360 T=T+6:IF T<=24 THEN350
370 REM SET AREAS FOR SQUARES
380 FOR I=1TO16:READ A(I):NEXT:N=1
390 DATA 6,19,34,48,134,147,162,176,26
    2,275,290,304,390,403
400 DATA 418,432
405 REM PLACE THE NUMBERS AND PIECES
410 FOR I=1TO16
420 PRINT@A(I),N;:N=N+1:NEXT
430 Y$="((0))":C$="<<+>>"
440 M$="       "
450 FOR I=1TO4:PRINT@A(I)+67,Y$;:NEXT
460 FOR I=13TO16:PRINT@A(I)+67,C$;:NEX
    T
470 REM PROPER SQUARE ?
480 FOR I=1TO16:S(I)=I:C(I)=I:NEXT
485 FOR I=13TO16:C(I)=1:NEXT
490 REM WHO GOES FIRST
500 GOSUB510:NS=RND(5)
505 IF RR=2 THEN560:ELSE IF RR=1 THEN
    570:ELSE 520
510 PRINT@709,"
                        "
515 PRINT@709,;:RETURN
520 PRINT"SELECT A NUMBER BETWEEN 1 &
    5";
530 INPUT NA
540 REM PRINT AT ONE AREA
550 IF NA<>NS THEN570
560 GOSUB510:PRINT"YOU GO FIRST":RR=2:
    GOSUB1500:GOTO630
570 GOSUB510:PRINT"I GO FIRST":RR=1:GO
    SUB1500:GOTO1000
630 GOSUB510
640 PRINT"FROM";
```

```
650 INPUT F:IF F=0 THEN1000:ELSE IF F=
    OO THEN1450
655 IF S(F)=0 THEN630
670 GOSUB510:PRINT" TO ";
680 INPUT TT
685 IF TT<1 OR TT>16 THEN GOSUB740:GOT
    O670
690 IF S(TT)=0 THEN670
695 IF C(TT)=1 THEN GOSUB740:GOTO630
700 IF H>=1 AND ABS(S(F)-S(TT))>13 THE
    N GOSUB740:GOTO630
710 PRINT@A(F)+67,M$;
720 PRINT@A(TT)+67,Y$;
```

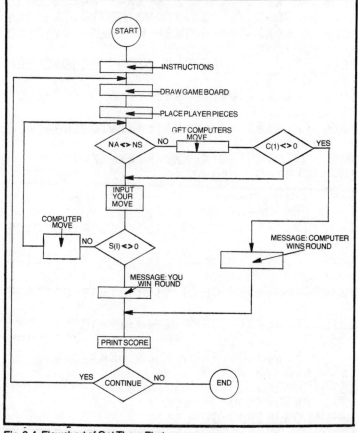

Fig. 3-4. Flowchart of Get There First.

```
725 REM IF H=0 THEN S((TT)-4)=0
730 H(H)=F:S(F)=0:S(TT)=0:H=H+1:GOSUB5
    10
735 GOTO1200
740 GOSUB510
750 PRINT"ILLEGAL MOVE, TRY AGAIN";
760 FOR JJ=1TO1500:NEXT
770 RETURN
1000 REM COMPUTER'S MOVE
1010 J=RND(16)
1020 IF J<=12 THEN1010:ELSE IF C(J)=0
     THEN1010
1030 IF XX=0 THEN1040
1035 IF XX>=1 THEN K=K(XX-1)-4:GOTO105
     0:ELSE IF XX>=1 AND K(XX-1)>=1 AN
     D K(XX-1)<=4 THEN K=K(XX-1)+12:GO
     TO1050
1040 IF J=16 THEN K=J-5:GOTO1050:ELSE
     K=J-3
1050 FOR I=1TO4:IF K=S(I) AND S(I)<>0
     THEN 1450:ELSE NEXT
1070 PRINT@A(J)+67,M$;:PRINT@A(K)+67,C
     $;
1080 C((K)+4)=0:K(XX)=K:XX=XX+1
1090 C(J)=0:C(K)=0
1100 GOTO1345
1200 REM CHECK FOR USERS WIN
1210 IF S(1)=1 THEN II=1:IT=13:GOTO125
     0
1220 IF S(2)=2 THEN II=2:IT=14:GOTO125
     0
1230 IF S(3)=3 THEN II=3:IT=15:GOTO125
     .0
1240 IF S(4)=4 THEN II=4:IT=16
1250 FOR I=IITOITSTEP4:IF S(I)<>0 THEN
     NEXT:GOTO1000:ELSE NEXT
1300 REM USER WON
1310 GOSUB510
1320 PRINT"YOU'VE WON !!!"
1330 GOSUB1500:GOSUB510
1340 WN=WN+1:GOTO1550:REM PLAY AGAIN ?
```

```
1345 REM CHECK FOR COMPUTER WIN
1350 IF C(1)=0 THEN R=1:RT=13:GOTO1390
1360 IF C(2)=0 THEN R=2:RT=14:GOTO1390
1370 IF C(3)=0 THEN R=3:RT=15:GOTO1390
1380 IF C(4)=0 THEN R=4:RT=16:GOTO1390
1385 GOTO630
1390 FOR I=RTORTSTEP4:IF C(I)<>0 THEN
     NEXT:GOTO630:ELSE NEXT
1400 GOSUB510
1410 PRINT"YOU'VE LOST THIS ONE !!"
1420 GOSUB1500
1430 GOSUB510
1440 LO=LO+1:GOTO1550:REM PLAY AGAIN?
1450 REM TIED
1460 GOSUB510:PRINT"TIED !!":TI=TI+1:G
     OSUB1500:GOSUB510:GOTO1560
1500 FOR LL=1TO2000:NEXT
1510 RETURN
1550 REM OUTPUT STATEMENTS
1560 PRINTTAB(5);"TIED";TI TAB(15);"LO
     ST";LO TAB(25);"WON";WN

1570 GOSUB1500:GOSUB510
1580 PRINT"READY TO PLAY AGAIN";
1590 INPUT P$
1600 IFP$=""NO'' THEN 1615

1605 IFRR=2 THEN RR=1:RESTORE:CLS:GOTO310
1610 IFRR=1 THEN RR=2:RESTORE:CLS:GOTO310
1615 GOSUB510
1620 PRINT""COULDN'T STAND TO LOSE,COULD YA
     ?"
1630 GOSUB1500:GOSUB510
1640 END
```

CHUTE

This program simulates skydiving. You must control your parachute so that you can land exactly on a given target.

You must keep in mind, like the real thing, this target isn't going to stay still and wait for you. Just like you are drifting around in the sky, the target will move left and right (Fig. 3-5).

The object of the game: at the exact moment FEET TO GROUND equals 0 (zero), the FEET FROM TARGET must also equal 0 (zero). After three attempts (missing every time) the computer will print a message, CLOSEST FEET OBTAINED. This will give you something to work after—try to beat that distance.

Don't worry about the chute failing to open, that wasn't included in this program. Incidentally, if your line happens to become blanked out by the target, simply hold down the right or left arrow key (for movement) and your line will re-appear.

See Fig. 3-6 for the flowchart.

Program Notes

Line 20 the CLEAR statement is used because of the string length involved for the target. You can adjust this statement accordingly if your memory is limited.

Line 210 contains the variables for the areas the target starts out, and sets the string statements for the target and the users line.

Lines 220 and 230 print the target.

Lines 240 GOSUB 800 is for print at statements.

Line 250 and 260 blank out the target for a split second, while line 280 selects (randomly) either left or right movement of the target. Left or right movement of the target is limited so the target doesn't fall to the next line of the video display. Also each random movement of the target is checked so it doesn't land on the user's line, it will over-step one way or the other.

Lines 320 and 330 are for the PEEK statement in line 265. For left or right movement of the users line (parachute).

Line 350 variable D is the argument to see if the user's line is equal to the target (centered).

Line 360 variable MM is for the feet before reaching ground. You can change this variable to a higher number to add more excitement to the simulation.

Lines 500-630 provide left movement of the target line. Arguments are contained within this line for key closure, to ensure that user will be able to move his/her line.

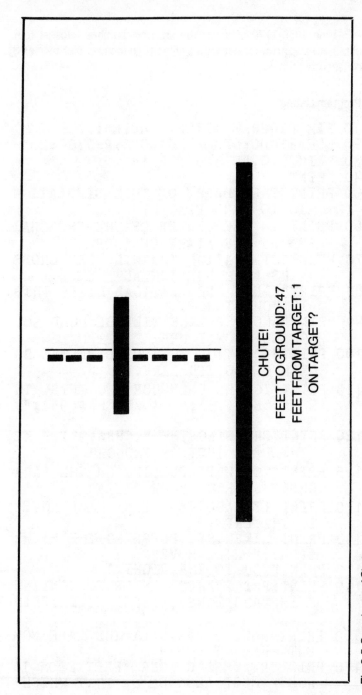

CHUTE!
FEET TO GROUND: 47
FEET FROM TARGET: 1
ON TARGET?

Fig. 3-5. Sample run of Chute.

Line 1050-1170 pick out the smallest number (closest feet obtained) and prints it out with a short time loop, if user misses 3 consecutive times.

Program Listing

```
10 REM PROGRAM TITLE: CHUTE !
20 CLEAR1000:DIM P(50):CLS:P=1:GG=2
30 PRINT@20,"C H U T E !"
40 PRINT
50 PRINT"THE OBJECT OF THIS SIMULATION
       IS TO LAND EXACTLY"
60 PRINT"IN THE CENTER OF THE CROSSHAI
       RS. AT THE START OF THE"
70 PRINT"SIMULATION YOU WILL SEE CROSS
       HAIRS (ONE HORIZONTAL"
80 PRINT"LINE, ONE VERTICAL LINE) THIS
       IS YOUR TARGET."
90 PRINT"ANOTHER LINE WILL BE USED SO
       YOU'LL KNOW YOUR"
100 PRINT"POSITION THIS WILL BE THE BR
       OKEN OR DOTTED LINE."
110 PRINT"YOU'LL ONLY USE TWO KEYS, TH
       E  ";CHR$(93);"  &  ";CHR$(94);".
       "
120 PRINT"PRESSING THE ";CHR$(93);" KE
       Y WILL BE JUST AS THOUGH"
125 PRINT"YOU WERE PULLING ON THE PARA
       CHUTE  CORDS, YOUR CHUTE"
130 PRINT"(THE DOTTED LINE) WILL MOVE
       TO THE LEFT."
140 PRINT"LIKEWISE, PRESSING THE ";CHR
       $(94);" WILL MOVE"
150 PRINT"YOU TO THE RIGHT."
155 PRINT:PRINT"PRESS ENTER TO CONTINU
       E INSTRUCTIONS";:INPUT X:CLS:PRIN
       T
160 PRINT"NOW, AT EXACTLY THE SAME MOM
       ENT 'FEET TO GO'"
170 PRINT"REACHES 0 YOUR 'FEET FROM TA
       RGET' MUST ALSO BE 0, THAT WHICH"
```

42

```
180  PRINT"YOU WILL HAVE LANDED IN THE
     CENTER OF THE CROSSHAIRS"
190  PRINT"(TARGET). YOU MUST KEEP IN M
     IND ALSO THAT THE"
191  PRINT"TARGET ISN'T GOING TO STAY S
     TILL AND WAIT FOR YOU,"
192  PRINT"IT WILL BE CONSTANTLY MOVING
     (AS IT WOULD IF YOU"
193  PRINT"WERE USING A REAL PARACHUTE)
     ."
194  PRINT
195  PRINT"PRESS ENTER TO JUMP";:INPUT
     X:CLS
200  REM SET CHR$ FOR GROUND TARGET -
     REAS - USERS LINE
210  V$=CHR$(149):A=32:B=416:H=207:H$=S
     TRING$(35,140):C$=STRING$(40,32):
     J=30:K=414:L$=CHR$(145):MM=50
215  REM PRINT GROUND TARGET
220  FOR Y=ATOBSTEP64:PRINT@Y,V$;:NEXT:
     FOR CH=JTOKSTEP64:PRINT@CH,L$;:NE
     XT
230  PRINT@H,H$;
235  FOR Q=0TO127:SET(Q,24):NEXT
240  GOSUB800:REM FOR PRINT STATEMENTS
245  REM DELETE GROUND TARGET AND MOVE
     IT
250  FOR Y=ATOBSTEP64:PRINT@Y," ";:NEXT
260  PRINT@H,C$;
265  T=PEEK(15350):REM KEY CLOSURE FOR
     USER MOVEMENT
270  M=RND(2):ON M GOTO280,500
275  REM MOVE TARGET RIGHT
280  E=RND(2):IF A>=45 THEN 500::ELSE A
     =A+E:B=A+384:H=H+E
285  IF A=J THEN280
290  FOR Y=ATOBSTEP64:PRINT@Y,V$;:NEXT
300  PRINT@H,H$;
310  FORKK=1TO015:NEXT
315  REM MOVE USERS LINE FOR KEY CLOSUR
     E
```

43

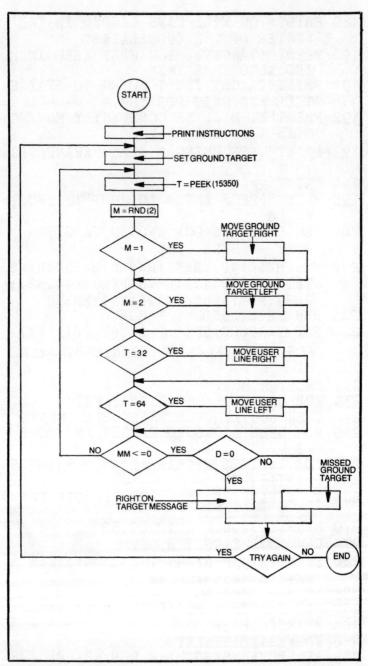

Fig. 3-6. Flowchart of Chute.

```
320 IF T=64 THEN FOR CH=JTOKSTEP64:PRI
    NT@CH," ";:NEXT:J=J+1:K=K+1:FOR C
    H=JTOKSTEP64:PRINT@CH,L$;:NEXT
330 IF T=32 THEN FOR CH=JTOKSTEP64:PRI
    NT@CH," ";:NEXT:J=J-1:K=K-1:FOR C
    H=JTOKSTEP64:PRINT@CH,L$;:NEXT
350 D=ABS(A-J)
360 MM=MM-1
370 IF MM<=0 MM=0
380 PRINT@U+142,D;
390 REM D FOR FEET / MM FOR MILES
400 PRINT@U+78,MM;:IF MM=0 THEN900
410 GOTO250
490 REM MOVE TARGET LEFT
500 E=RND(2):IF A<=20 THEN280:ELSE A=A
    -E:B=A+384:H=H-E
510 IF A=J THEN500
520 FOR Y=ATOBSTEP64:PRINT@Y,V$;:NEXT
530 PRINT@H,H$;
540 FOR KK=1TO15:NEXT
550 FOR Y=ATOBSTEP64:PRINT@Y," ";:NEXT
560 PRINT@H,C$;
565 T=PEEK(15350):D=ABS(A-J)
570 IF T=64 GOTO320
580 IF T=32 GOTO330
590 MM=MM-1
600 IF MM<=0 MM=0
610 PRINT@U+142,D;
620 PRINT@U+78,MM;:IF MM=0 THEN900
630 GOTO270
800 REM SET AREAS FOR PRINTOUTS
810 U=601:V=U+64
820 PRINT@U,"C  H  U  T  E  !";
830 PRINT@V-2,"FEET TO GROUND:";
840 PRINT@V+60,"FEET FROM TARGET:";
850 PRINT@V+130,"ON TARGET ?";
860 RETURN
900 REM ON TARGET ?
910 IF D=0 PRINT@V+143,"YES !!":GOTO95
    0
```

```
915 REM MISSED BY D FEET
920 PRINT@V+143,"NO !!";
930 PRINT@V+185,"SORRY...YOU'VE MISSED
    THE TARGET !"
940 FOR KK=1TO1200:NEXT:P(P)=D:P=P+1:I
    F P>=4 THEN 1050
945 GOTO960
950 PRINT@V+185,"THAT IS EXCELLENT, RI
    GHT ON TARGET !!"
955 P=1:GG=2:REM TO START COUNTERS OVE
    R
960 PRINT@V+251,"ARE YOU READY TO JUMP
    AGAIN";
970 INPUT J$
980 IF J$="YES" THEN CLS:GOTO200
990 PRINT@V+251,".AFRAID  OF HEIGHTS AR
    E YOU ???           "
1000 GOTO1000
1050 REM CHECK FOR CLOSEST FEET
1060 REM OBTAINED SO FAR
1070 G=0:I=1
1080 IF P(I)<=P(I+1) THEN1130
1090 F=P(I+1)
1100 P(I+1)=P(I)
1110 P(I)=F
1120 G=1
1130 I=I+1:IF I<=P-1 THEN1080
1140 IF G=1 THEN1070
1150 PRINT@V+251."CLOSEST FEET OBTAINE
     D =";P(GG)
1160 FOR KK=1TO2000:NEXT
1170 GG=GG+1:GOTO960
```

ALL TOGETHER

This animated race-car game lets you be in the driver's seat. There are a total of three cars in the race, yours (left lane), computer's (center lane) and a pace car (right lane). The pace car will continue throughout the race, unless it runs out of fuel or crashes. If you don't want to leave it titled as a pace car, you can just give it a number.

The race runs from the bottom to the top of video screen. The first car to finish 100 laps will be declared the winner. If you happen to run out of fuel before the race is finished, the computer car and the pace car will continue (Fig. 3-7). See Fig. 3-8 for the flowchart.

Program Notes

Lines 255 and 256 set variables for placement of cars, laps and fuel.

Line 280 is the completed cars.

Lines 290-310 print the cars, unless they're out of fuel.

Line 320 blanks the cars' last position.

Lines 325 and 330 check boundaries, increase laps, and decrease fuel amount. You can change the decrease in fuel amount to a random amount if you wish. Example: line 325 BF=BF−5 change to BF=BF−RND(5).

Lines 335 and 340 move the computer car and pace car.

Line 345 receives your key closure.

Line 350 moves your car right.

Line 360 moves your car left.

Line 370 checks position of your car and wraps it around when it reaches the top of the video, counts your laps and decreases your fuel amount.

Lines 400-450 check for an accident off course.

Lines 460 and 470 speed up the computer car and pace car.

Lines 480 and 485 check for a blown engine.

Lines 560 - 670 check for collision, fuel, laps and take a car off the track if fuel = 0.

Program Listing

```
10 REM PROGRAM TITLE: ALL TOGETHER
20 CLS:PRINT:PRINT
30 PRINT"ALL TOGETHER IS A RACE GAME T
      HAT PUTS YOU"
40 PRINT"ON A WILD RACE COURSE. JUST L
      IKE THE REAL THING"
50 PRINT"YOU ARE ONLY VULNERABLETO:"
60 PRINT"RUNNING OUT OF FUEL."
```

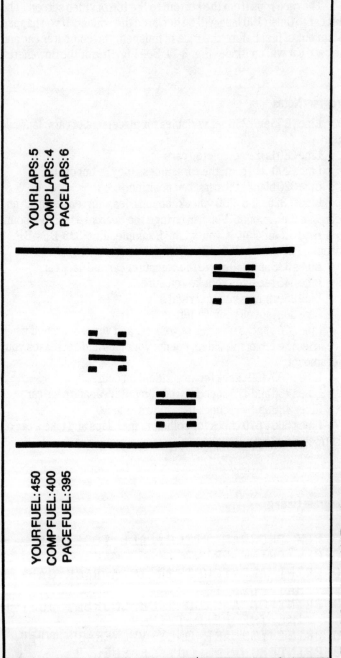

YOUR LAPS: 5
COMP LAPS: 4
PACE LAPS: 6

YOUR FUEL: 450
COMP FUEL: 400
PACE FUEL: 395

Fig. 3-7. Sample run of All Together.

```
90 PRINT"BLOWN ENGINE."
100 PRINT"AND CRASHING."
105 PRINT
110 PRINT"A PACE CAR IS USED THROUGHOU
    T THE RACE (TO ADD ACTION)."
111 PRINT"YOUR CAR IS IN LEFT LANE, CO
    MPUTER'S CAR CENTER LANE"
115 PRINT"AND THE PACE CAR IS IN THE R
    IGHT LANE."
120 PRINT
130 PRINT"FIRST TO COMPLETE 100 LAPS I
    S THE WINNER."
140 PRINT
150 PRINT"PRESS ENTER TO SEE YOUR CARS
    COMMANDS";:INPUT X:CLS
160 PRINT:PRINT
170 PRINT"THE RACE WILL BE MOVING FROM
    BOTTOM TO TOP OF VIDEO."
180 PRINTCHR$(91);TAB(5);"THIS WILL BE
    THE ACCELERATOR (GAS PEDAL)."
190 PRINTCHR$(93);TAB(5);"TO MOVE CAR
    LEFT."
200 PRINTCHR$(94);TAB(5);"TO MOVE CAR
    RIGHT."
210 PRINT"USE THE <CLEAR> KEY TO STOP
    CAR."
220 PRINT
225 PRINT"IF YOU WANT TO CHANGE LANES,
    LET OFF THE GAS PEDAL !!"
230 PRINT"YOU MUST REMEMBER ALL THE AB
    OVE IF YOU PLAN TO WIN."
240 PRINT"PRESS ENTER TO START THE RAC
    E";:INPUT X:CLS
250 REM DRAW THE TRACK AND CARS
255 LL=30:RR=90:N=162:R=170:A=979:B=98
    9:C=999:N$="        "
256 YL=0:BL=0:CL=0:YF=500:BF=YF:CF=YF
260 FOR X=0TO47:SET(LL,X):NEXT
270 FOR XX=0TO47:SET(RR,XX):NEXT
280 A$=STRING$(4,N):B$=STRING$(2,R)
285 RANDOM
```

```
290 IF YF<=0 THEN300:ELSE PRINT@A,A$;:
    PRINT@A+1,B$;
300 IF BF<=0 THEN310:ELSE PRINT@B,A$;:
    PRINT@B+1,B$;
```

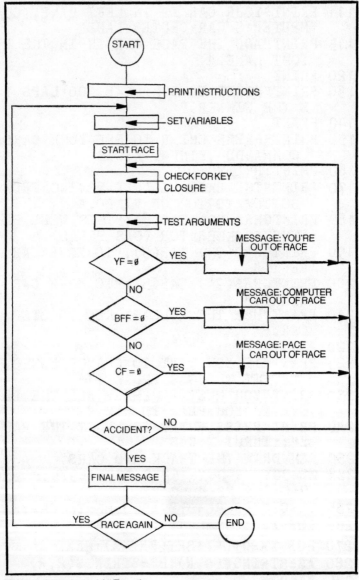

Fig. 3-8. Flowchart of All Together.

```
310 IF CF<=0 THEN320:ELSE PRINT@C,A$;:
    PRINT@C+1,B$;
320 PRINT@A,N$;:PRINT@B,N$;:PRINT@C,N$
    ;
325 IF B>=15 AND B<=45 THEN B=B+900+60
    :IF BF<=0 BF=0:BL=BL:ELSE BL=BL+1
    :BF=BF-5:REM TOP BOUNDRIES
330 IF C>=15 AND C<=45 THEN C=999:IF C
    F<=0 CF=0:CL=CL:ELSE CL=CL+1:CF=C
    F-5:REM TOP BOUNDRIES
335 IF B>=207 THEN B=B-BS:ELSE B=B-64
340 IF C>=207 THEN C=C-CS:ELSE C=C-64
345 K=PEEK(15350)
350 IF K=64 THEN A=A+4:H=1
360 IF K=32 THEN A=A-4:H=2
365 IF K=0 H=0
370 IF A>=15 AND A<=45 THEN A=A+900+60
    :IF YF<=0 YF=0:YL=YL:ELSE YL=YL+1
    :YF=YF-5
400 IF B>=0 AND B<=14 THEN800
410 IF B>=46 AND B<=63 THEN800
420 IF C>=0 AND C<=14 THEN800
430 IF C>=46 AND C<=63 THEN800
440 IF A>=0 AND A<=14 THEN800
450 IF A>=46 AND A<=63 THEN800
460 BB=RND(3):IF BB=1 THEN BS=128:ELSE
    IF BB=3 THEN BS=192:ELSE BS=64
465 IF H=1 THEN BS=2:ELSE IF H=2 THEN
    BS=-4:ELSE BS=BS
470 CC=RND(3):IF CC=2 THEN CS=128:ELSE
    IF CC=1 THEN CS=192:ELSE CS=64
480 IF A>=207 AND K=8 THEN A=A-128:BE=
    RND(30)
485 IF BE=7 AND YL>50 PRINT@320,"YOU'V
    E BLOWN";:PRINT@384,"YOUR ENGINE"
    ;:GOTO850
490 PRINT@111,"YOUR LAPS:";YL;
500 PRINT@175."COMP LAPS:";BL;
510 PRINT@239,"PACE LAPS:";CL;
520 PRINT@64,"YOUR FUEL:";YF;
530 PRINT@128,"COMP FUEL:";BF;
```

```
540 PRINT@192,"PACE FUEL:";CF;
550 IF K=2 THEN A=A:GOTO290
560 IF A=B OR A=C THEN800
570 IF B=A OR B=C THEN800
580 IF C=A OR A=B THEN800
590 IF YF<=0 THEN1100
600 IF BF<=0 THEN1120
610 IF CF<=0 THEN1140
620 IF YL>=100 THEN1200
630 IF BL>=100 THEN1220
640 IF CL>=100 THEN1240
650 IF YF<=0 PRINT@A,N$;
660 IF BF<=0 PRINT@B,N$;
670 IF CF<=0 PRINT@C,N$;
680 A=A-64:GOTO290
800 FOR ZZ=1TO1000:NEXT:CLS:PRINTCHR$(
810 PRINT"SORRY........"
820 FOR ZZ=1TO500:NEXT
830 PRINT"THERE HAS BEEN"
840 PRINT"AN ACCIDENT..."
850 FOR ZZ=1TO1200:NEXT
860 PRINT"SHALL WE START"
870 PRINT"THE RACE AGAIN";
880 INPUT X$
890 IF X$="YES"THEN CLS:GOTO250
900 PRINT:PRINT"CHICKEN.........."
910 PRINT"AREN'T YOU ?????"
920 END
1100 PRINT@A,N$;:PRINT@320,"YOU ARE OU
     T";:PRINT@384,"OF FUEL !!";
1110 GOTO680
1120 PRINT@B,N$;:PRINT@320,"COMP CAR H
     AS";:PRINT@384,"RAN OUT OF";
1130 PRINT@448,"FUEL !!";:GOTO680
1140 PRINT@C,N$;:PRINT@320,"PACE CAR H
     AS";:PRINT@384,"USED ALL FUEL";
1150 GOTO680
1160 FOR ZZ=1TO1200:NEXT:CLS:PRINTCHR$
     (23):RETURN
1200 GOSUB1160
1210 PRINT"THAT'S THE RACE !! YOU'VE W
     ON !!":GOTO850
```

```
1220 GOSUB1160
1225 PRINT"THAT IS THE RACE....THE COM
     PUTER CAR HAS WON !"
1230 GOTO850
1240 GOSUB1160
1250 PRINT"WOULD YOU BELIEVE ???"
1260 PRINT"THE PACE CAR HAS WON THIS R
     ACE !!!"
1270 GOTO850
```

ANCHORS AWAY

No, this isn't a ship builder's course. But it is away-out-in-space. The game provides computer simulation of travelling through space fighting aliens. You'll have a destination, a certain amount of fuel and oxygen.

The computer will let you know if you are on RED ALERT by flashing it next to the ALERT CODE. Below this will be printed ENCOUNTER, where the computer will try to identify a UFO by printing either ALIEN or UNKNOWN.

Down below your panel will be a square, inside this square will be two plus signs. When you are on RED ALERT these plus signs will move closer together, when superimposed, and you see only one, fire your laser cannon by pressing the space bar. All this will happen within 3 seconds, so if your ENCOUNTER is UNKNOWN you must decide fast whether or not to fire, as you could end up destroying one of the allied spaceships (Fig. 3-9). See Fig. 3-10 for the flowchart.

So, in general, the idea is to reach your destination MILES=0, in one piece. Of course, you'll be in for some other surprises...

Program Notes

Line 280 sets most of the counters.

Line 390 is the area for the plus signs.

Lines 500-580 set miles, fuel and oxygen.

Lines 630-690 are print statements for the control panel.

Line 720 is a random function that sets up most of the attacks you'll encounter, also determines fuel and oxygen used.

Lines 780-820 print @ statement for RED ALERT.

Line 830 determines if it's alien or unknown.

Lines 850-890 move the plus signs inward, and check for key closure (laser fired).

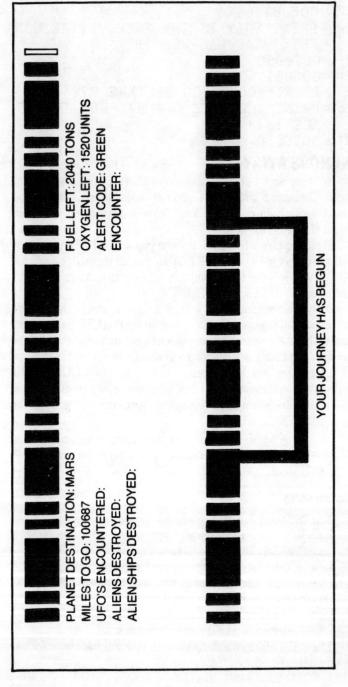

PLANET DESTINATION: MARS
MILES TO GO: 100687
UFO'S ENCOUNTERED:
ALIENS DESTROYED:
ALIEN SHIPS DESTROYED:

FUEL LEFT: 2040 TONS
OXYGEN LEFT: 1520 UNITS
ALERT CODE: GREEN
ENCOUNTER:

YOUR JOURNEY HAS BEGUN

Fig. 3-9. Sample run of Anchors Away.

Lines 910-990 are generally print statements and counters.
Lines 1000-1005 check for ship destroyed or a hit to your ship.
The remaining lines are self-explanatory.

Program Listing

```
10 REM PROGRAM TITLE: ANCHORS AWAY
20 CLS:PRINTTAB(10),"** ANCHORS AWAY *
   *"
30 RANDOM:PRINT
40 PRINT"IF YOU WERE EXPECTING SOME SH
   IP-BUILDING"
50 PRINT"INSTRUCTIONS YOU'RE OUTTA-LUCK.
    YES, THIS"
60 PRINT"PROGRAM IS CALLED ANCHORS AWA
   Y, BUT YOUR"
70 PRINT"ANCHORS ARE GOING TO BE AWAY-
   OUT-IN-SPACE !!"
80 PRINT"YOUR SHIP? IT'S GOING TO BE A
    BATTLE STAR CRUISER."
90 PRINT"IN A SENSE YOU'LL BE RUN THRO
   UGH A TEST."
95 PRINT"HOW ?"
100 PRINT"YOU'LL BE GIVEN A DESTINATIO
    N AND AMOUNT OF MILES"
110 PRINT"YOU HAVE TO GET THERE. BUT N
    ATURALLY IT DOESN'T"
120 PRINT"END THERE, AT ANY RANDOM MOM
    ENT YOU WILL"
130 PRINT:GOSUB140:GOTO150
140 PRINT"PRESS ENTER";:INPUT Y:CLS:PR
    INT:RETURN
150 PRINT"GO ON RED ALERT (ALL OF THIS
     INFORMATION WILL BE"
160 PRINT"PRINTED ON YOUR PANEL) THE C
    OMPUTER WILL EITHER"
170 PRINT"LIST THE UFO AS ALIEN OR UNK
    NOWN. IN THE SQUARE"
180 PRINT"BELOW YOUR PANEL WILL BE TO
    + SIGNS, WHEN THESE SIGNS"
185 PRINT"ARE EQUAL (AS ONE) FIRE YOUR
     LASER BY PRESSING THE"
```

```
190 PRINT"'SPACE BAR'."
195 PRINT"THE OBJECT OF THE SIMULATION
        IS TO REACH YOUR"
200 PRINT"DESTINATION (MILES = 0). IF
        YOU DESTROY 10 ALLIED"
210 PRINT"SHIPS YOU'LL BE BANNED FROM
        THE JOURNEY AND ASKED"
```

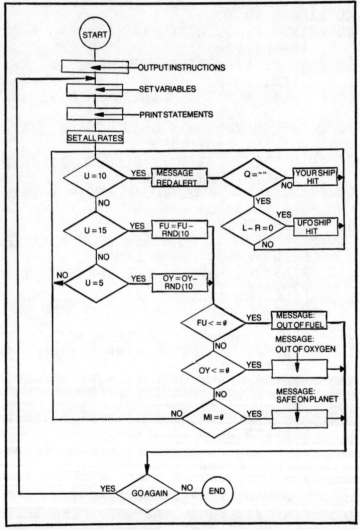

Fig. 3-10. Flowchart of Anchors Away.

```
220  PRINT"IF YOU WANT TO TRY ANOTHER.
     YOU'LL ALSO HAVE TO"
230  PRINT"WORRY ABOUT FUEL AND OXYGEN
     SUPPLY."
240  PRINT:GOSUB140:N=0:M=63:GOTO280
250  REM DRAW INSIDE FRONT PANEL OF
260  REM BATTLE CRUISER
270  FOR T=NTOMSTEP2:PRINT@T,CHR$(191):
     NEXT
275  FOR T=NTOMSTEP2.5:PRINT@T,CHR$(191
     ):NEXT:RETURN
280  GOSUB270:A=64:B=128:C=192:D=23:E=6
     64:UE=0:UD=0:WT=0:YH=0
285  MS=0
290  PRINT@A,"PLANET DESTINATION:";
300  PRINT@B,"MILES TO GO:";
310  PRINT@C,"UFO'S ENCOUNTERED:";
320  PRINT@C+A,"ALIENS DESTROYED:";
330  PRINT@C+B,"ALLIED SHIPS DESTROYED:
     ";
340  PRINT@B-D,"FUEL LEFT:";
350  PRINT@C-D,"OXYGEN LEFT:";
360  PRINT@(C-D)+A,"ALERT CODE:";:REM G
     REEN FOR CLEAR
370  PRINT@(C-D)+B,"ENCOUNTER:";
380  N=384:M=447:GOSUB270
385  FOR Y=21TO27:SET(36,Y):SET(37,Y):S
     ET(88,Y):SET(89,Y):NEXT
388  FOR X=37TO87:SET(X,27):NEXT
390  L=532:R=554:T$=CHR$(43)
500  REM SET VITAL INFORMATION
510  FOR I=1TO5:READ P$(I):NEXT
520  DATA EARTH,MARS,VENUS,OPOETO,ZERIS
530  REM MILES
540  MI=RND(1000)+1E+05:I=RND(5):PL$=P$
     (I)
550  REM FUEL
560  FU=(RND(2000)*3):IF FU<=2000 THEN5
     60
570  REM OXYGEN
580  OY=(RND(500)*4):IF OY<1000 THEN580
```

```
590 REM ALERT CODE
600 R$="RED":G$="GREEN"
610 REM ENCOUNTER
620 U$="UNKNOWN":AL$="ALIEN"
630 REM PRINT SOME INFORMATION ON PANE
    L
640 PRINT@(A+20),PL$;
650 PRINT@(A+76),MI;
660 PRINT@(D*5),FU;"TONS";
670 PRINT@(C-11),OY;"UNITS";
680 PRINT@(C+A)-11,G$;
690 PRINT@E-4,"YOUR JOURNEY HAS BEGUN"
    ;
700 FOR ZZ=1TO2000:NEXT
710 PRINT@E-4,"                        "
    ;
720 U=RND(40):IF MI<=50 THEN740
730 IF U=10 THEN780
740 MI=MI-1:PRINT@(A+76),MI;
745 IF MI<=0 MI=0:GOTO1250
750 IF U=15 THEN FU=FU-RND(10):PRINT@(
    D*5),FU;:ELSE FU=FU
755 IF FU<=0 FU=0:GOTO1280
760 IF U=5 THEN OY=OY-RND(10):PRINT@(C
    -11),OY;:ELSE OY=OY
765 IF OY<=0 OY=0:GOTO1320
770 IF RR=1 THEN840:ELSE GOTO720
780 V=0:PRINT@(C+A)-11,"        ";
790 PRINT@(C+A)-11,R$;:FOR VV=1TO100:N
    EXT
800 PRINT@(C+A)-11,"        ";:FOR VV=1TO
    50:NEXT
810 V=V+1:IF V<>10 THEN790
820 PRINT@(C+A)-11,R$;
830 K=RND(2):IF K=1 PRINT@(B+C)-11,U$;
    :TT=2:ELSE PRINT@(B+C)-11,AL$;:TT
    =1
835 IF TT=2 THEN TV=RND(3)
840 PRINT@L,T$;:PRINT@R,T$;:PRINT@E,"T
    ARGET SEQUENCE";
850 Q$=INKEY$:IF Q$=" "THEN1000
```

58

```
870 PRINT@L," ";:PRINT@R," ";
880 L=L+1:R=R-1
890 IF L>(R+4) THEN910
900 RR=1:GOTO740
910 IF TV=2 THEN1100:ELSE PRINT@E," MI
    SSED UFO      ";
915 MS=MS+1
920 RR=0
940 PRINT@(B+C)-11,"          ";
950 FOR ZZ=1TO1500:NEXT:PRINT@E-3,"
                                    ";
960 PRINT@(C+A)-11,G$;
970 UE=UE+1:PRINT@210,UE;
980 PRINT@L," ";:PRINT@R," ";
985 IF MS>=10 THEN1410
990 L=532:R=554:Q$="":GOTO720
1000 IF ABS(L-R)<>0 AND TV=2 THEN1100
1005 IF ABS(L-R)>0 THEN910
1010 IF TT=2 THEN SS=RND(2):IF SS=1 TH
     EN1040
1020 PRINT@E-3,AL$;" SHIP DESTROYED !!
     ";:UD=UD+1
1030 PRINT@273,UD;:GOTO1080
1040 PRINT@E-3,"THAT WAS AN ALLIED SHI
     P !!";
1050 WT=WT+1:PRINT@343,WT;:MI=MI+100
1060 GOSUB1140:IF WT>=10 THEN1370
1070 TT=0:GOTO1090
1080 GOSUB1140
1090 GOTO920
1100 PRINT@E-2,"YOU'VE BEEN HIT !!";
1110 YH=YH+1:IF YH>=10 THEN1130:ELSE 1
     090
1120 GOSUB1140
1130 GOSUB1140:GOTO1150
1135 FOR ZZ=1TO2100:NEXT:PRINT@E-10,;:
     RETURN
1140 FOR ZZ=1TO2000:NEXT:RETURN
1145 FOR ZZ=1TO2200:NEXT:PRINT@E-8,;:R
     ETURN
1150 PRINT@E-3,"YOU'VE BEEN HIT A  ":G
     OSUB1140
```

```
1160  PRINT@E-3,"TOTAL OF";YH;"TIMES   "
      :GOSUB1140
1170  PRINT@E-3,"YOUR BATTLE CRUISER IS"
      :GOSUB1140
1180  PRINT@E-3,"BURNING RAPIDLY......"
      :GOSUB1135
1190  GOSUB1135:PRINT"  YOU WANT TO TR
      Y ANOTHER JOURNEY";
1200  INPUT J$
1210  IF J$="YES" THEN RESTORE:GOTO2240
1220  PRINT@E+54,"COULDN'T DECIDE ON TH
      E UNKNOWNS ?????"
1230  END
1250  GOSUB1135:PRINT"YOU'RE HOME SAFE, O
      N THE PLANET ";PL$
1260  GOSUB1140
1270  GOTO1190
1280  GOSUB1135:PRINT"YOU'RE COMPLETELY O
      UT OF FUEL !!!"
1285  GOSUB1135
1290  PRINT"YOU'RE GOING TO DRIFT IN SPAC
      E.....UNLESS   "
1300  GOSUB1140
1310  GOTO1190
1320  GOSUB1135:PRINT"GASP !! GASP !!
      YOU'RE OUT OF OXYGEN !!"
1330  GOSUB1135
1340  PRINT"YOU'LL NEVER SEE THE PLANET
      ";PL$;"...UNLESS"
1350  GOSUB1140
1360  GOTO1190
1370  GOSUB1135:PRINT"YOU HAVE DESTROYE
      D";WT;"OF THE ALLIED"
1375  GOSUB1135
1380  PRINT"STAR SHIPS, YOU'RE BANNED FRO
      M THIS JOURNEY."
1390  GOSUB1140
1400  GOTO1190
1410  GOSUB1145:PRINT"BECAUSE OF THE FA
      CT YOU WERE SLEEPING."
1415  GOSUB1145
```

```
1420 PRINT"YOU HAVE MISSED";MS;"UFO'S.
     ACTION "
1425 GOSUB1145
1430 PRINT"HAS BEEN TAKEN FOR YOUR MIS
     TAKES. "
1435 GOSUB1145
1440 PRINT"A HUNDRED MILES HAS BEEN AD
     DED TO "
1445 GOSUB1145
1450 PRINT"YOUR TOTAL JOURNEY.........
     ......"
1460 MI=MI+100:MS=0:GOSUB1145
1470 PRINT"
              "
1480 GOTO900
```

Chapter 4
Risk and War

TIME BOMB

This program constructs a time bomb before your eyes, adding the dynamite, the clock, and finally, seven connecting wires. You'll have to decide which two wires to disconnect (wires will be disconnected using the INKEY$ function, so wait for the first wire to break before you input the second wire). After the computer receives your two choices it will connect them together (Fig. 4-1). If you were only one wire off (you picked one wire correctly), you'll get a chance to select another, if both were incorrect..... Goodbye!!!

Naturally, if both wires were correct, the clock will stop. All this will have to take place in a matter of seconds. The clock will only stop for a short while for print statements. See Fig. 4-2 for the flowchart.

Program Notes

Lines 260-500 draw the complete time bomb.

Line 625 sets one correct wire.

Line 630 adds the tick, while line 670 adds the tock.

Line 650 checks for expired time.

Lines 690-760 break the user selected wires.

Line 770 sets the two wires the user has entered and counts the wires.

Line 790 contains the second correct wire, placed after you have entered both of your wire choices. There is no possible way to cheat, unless of course you alter the program.

Lines 835-860 contain the arguments for processed wires, completely connected wires are at line 840.

Lines 880-1040 are suitable print statements for disconnected wires and expired time.

Lines 1050-1150 contain the display for the grand explosion?

Lines 1160-1230 are self-explanatory.

Program Listing

```
10 REM PROGRAM TITLE: TIME BOMB !!
15 CLS
20 PRINT@15,"** TIME BOMB !! **"
30 PRINT
40 PRINT"A TIME BOMB WILL BE CONSTRUCT
     ED BEFORE YOUR"
50 PRINT"EYES, CONSTRUCTION WILL BEGIN
      WITH THE DYNAMITE,"
```

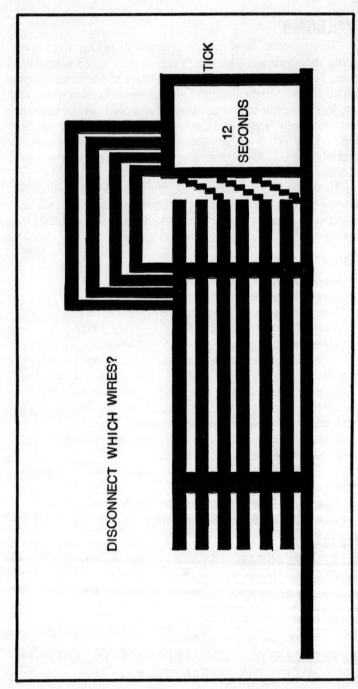

Fig. 4-1. Sample bomb of Time Bomb.

```
60 PRINT"MOVING TO THE CLOCK, THEN FIN
     ALLY THE WIRES."
70 PRINT"ALL WIRES WILL BE READ FROM T
     OP TO BOTTOM (1-7)."
80 PRINT"THIS PROGRAM USES THE INKEY$
     FUNCTION, MEANING"
90 PRINT"WHEN YOU INPUT A WIRE NUMBER
     - DON'T PRESS ENTER !!"
100 PRINT"FROM THESE 7 WIRES YOU'LL SE
     LECT 2 OF THEM TO"
110 PRINT"DISCONNECT, WAIT FOR THE FIR
     ST WIRE TO 'BREAK'"
120 PRINT"BEFORE YOU INPUT THE SECOND
     WIRE."
130 PRINT
140 PRINT"PRESS A KEY......"
150 A$=INKEY$:IF A$=""THEN150
160 CLS:PRINT
170 PRINT"AFTER YOUR 2 WIRES ARE RECEI
     VED BY THE COMPUTER THE"
175 PRINT"CLOCK WILL STOP, THE COMPUTE
     R WILL CONNECT THESE"
180 PRINT"WIRES. ONE OF THREE THINGS W
     ILL HAPPEN: 1. YOU'LL BE BLOWN"
185 PRINT"ALL OVER SEVERAL DIFFERENT C
     OUNTRIES. 2. YOU'LL HAVE"
190 PRINT"ONE WIRE CORRECT AND GET A C
     HANCE TO DISCONNECT"
200 PRINT"ANOTHER. 3. YOU'LL BECOME PA
     RT OF THE COMPUTER"
210 PRINT"BOMB-SQUAD BECAUSE YOU'VE DI
     SARMED THE BOMB !!"
220 PRINT
230 PRINT"PRESS A KEY......"
240 A$=INKEY$:IF A$=""THEN240
250 CLS:TT=470:W3=0:WW=0:MV=0:RANDOM
260 REM CONSTRUCT THE TIME BOMB
270 Y=35
280 FOR X=24TO87:SET(X,Y):NEXT
285 PRINT@TT,"THE DYNAMITE......."
290 Y=Y+2
```

65

```
300 IF Y<=46 THEN280
310 FOR X=0T0127:SET(X,Y-1):NEXT
320 FOR Y=36T045STEP2:SET(34,Y):SET(35
    ,Y):SET(36,Y):SET(37,Y)
330 SET(74,Y):SET(75,Y):SET(76,Y):SET(
    77,Y):NEXT

335 GOSUB600:PRINT@TT,"THE CLOCK......
    "
340 REM THE CLOCK
350 FOR Y=34T045:SET(93,Y):SET(94,Y):S
    ET(114,Y):SET(115,Y):NEXT
355 FOR X=95T0113:SET(X,34):NEXT:T=818
360 TI=RND(25):IF TI<=15 THEN360
365 PRINT@T,TI;:PRINT@T+63,"SECONDS";
370 GOSUB600:PRINT@TT,"THE WIRES......
    ..."
375 REM THE WIRES (7 TOTAL)
380 U=34:Y=34:X=77:J=2
390 FOR W=UTOY-JSTEP-1:SET(X,W):NEXT
400 Y=Y-2:X=X-2:IF X>=71 THEN390
410 J=34
420 FOR W=X+2TOX+J:SET(W,Y):NEXT
430 X=X+2:J=J-4:Y=Y+2
440 IF X<>77 THEN420
450 J=32:M=97
460 FOR W=JTOU:SET(M,W):NEXT
470 J=J-2:M=M+2:IF M<>105 THEN460
490 X=93
500 FOR Y=35T040:SET(X,Y-1):SET(X,Y+2)
    :SET(X,Y+6):X=X-1:NEXT
505 GOSUB600
510 PRINT@TT,"                        ";
520 IF TV=1 THEN GOSUB530:GOTO580:ELSE
    GOSUB530:GOTO540
530 PRINT@64,"
                              ";
535 PRINT@64,;:RETURN
540 PRINT"ALL WIRES WILL BE READ FROM
    TOP TO BOTTOM."
550 GOSUB600:GOSUB530
560 PRINT"READ 1, 2, 3, 4, 5, ETC."
```

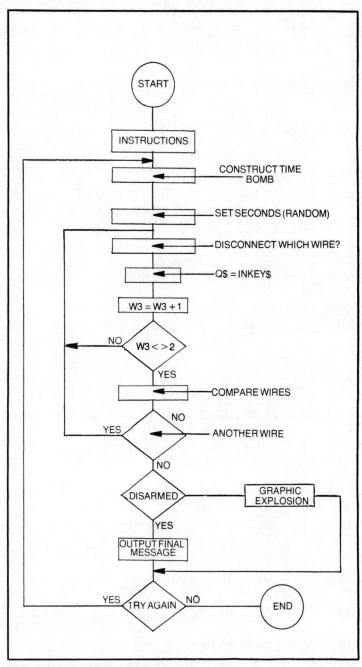

Fig. 4-2. Flowchart of Time Bomb.

```
570 GOSUB600:GOSUB530
580 PRINT"GET READY, THE CLOCK IS ABOU
    T TO TICK !!"
590 GOSUB600:GOSUB530:GOTO610
600 FOR ZZ=1TO2000:NEXT:RETURN
610 IF MM=1 PRINT"DISCONNECT WHICH WIR
    E ?":ELSE PRINT"DISCONNECT WHICH
    WIRES ?"
620 Q$=INKEY$:IF MM=1 PRINT@88,Q$;:ELS
    E PRINT@89,Q$;
625 W1=RND(7)
630 PRINT@T+9,"TICK";:IF TI<=9 PRINT@T
    +1,TI;:ELSE PRINT@T,TI;
640 FOR I=1TO250:NEXT
650 IF TI<=0 TI=0:GOTO1030
660 TI=TI-1
670 PRINT@T+9,"TOCK";:FOR I=1TO250:NEX
    T
675 IF WW=1 THEN630:REM MISSED WIRES
680 IF VAL(Q$)=0 THEN620
690 ON VAL(Q$) GOTO 700,710,720,730,74
    0,750,760
700 RESET(71,U):GOTO770
710 RESET(73,U):GOTO770
720 RESET(75,U):GOTO770
730 RESET(77,U):GOTO770
740 RESET(92,U+1):GOTO770
750 RESET(92,U+4):GOTO770
760 RESET(92,U+8)
770 W(W3)=VAL(Q$):W3=W3+1
780 IF W3<>2 THEN620
785 REM SECOND WIRE PLACED HERE TO VOI
    D ALL CHEATERS
790 W2=RND(7)
800 IF W2=W1 THEN790
810 GOSUB530
820 PRINT"CONNECTING YOUR TWO WIRES...
    .."
825 FOR XX=1TO1000:NEXT
830 IF MM=1 THEN W(0)=W1
```

```
835 IF W(0)=W1 AND W(1)=W2 THEN960:REM
    ONE ON ONE
840 IF (W(0)+W(1))=(W1+W2) THEN960:REM
    A COMBINATION OF WIRES
845 IF MM=1 THEN MV=MV+1:IF MV=1 THEN
    GOSUB530:GOTO885
850 IF W(0)=W1 OR W(0)=W2 THEN920
860 IF W(1)=W1 OR W(1)=W2 THEN920
870 WW=1:GOSUB530
880 PRINT"SORRY.....BOTH YOUR WIRES WE
    RE INCORRECT.":GOTO890
885 PRINT"THAT'S THE WIRE THAT KEEPS T
    HE CLOCK RUNNING !!"
890 GOSUB600:GOSUB530
900 PRINT"YOU MIGHT HAVE ENOUGH TIME T
    O RUN !!"
910 GOSUB600:GOSUB530:GOTO630:REM KEEP
    CLOCK RUNNING
920 GOSUB530
930 PRINT" ONE OF YOUR WIRES WAS CORRE
    CT, TRY ONE OTHER !"
940 GOSUB600:GOSUB530
950 MM=1:W3=1:GOTO610
960 GOSUB530
970 PRINT"YOU SHOULD JOIN THE COMPUTER
    BOMB SQUAD !!!"
980 GOSUB600:GOSUB530
990 PRINT"YOU'VE DISARMED THE BOMB....
    ......."
1000 GOSUB600:GOSUB530
1010 PRINT"AND STILL HAD";TI+1;"SECOND
     S TO SPARE !!!"
1020 GOTO1160:REM GOTO PLAY AGAIN
1030 REM SO-LONG
1040 PRINT@TT,"G O O D B Y E !!!!!";
1050 REM THE GRAND EXPLOSION ????
1060 FOR I=1TO10:READ A(I):NEXT
1070 DATA 649,654,659,664,669,674,679,
     684,689,694
1080 FOR I=1TO10:PRINT@A(I),"*";:NEXT
1090 JJ=RND(959):IF JJ<768 THEN1090
```

```
1095 PRINT@JJ,"                    ";
1100 FOR I=1TO5:A(I)=A(I)-66:NEXT
1110 FOR I=6TO10:A(I)=A(I)-62:NEXT
1120 IF A(1)<=0 THEN1130:ELSE 1080
1130 Y=0
1135 X=RND(959)
1140 PRINT@X,"*";
1150 Y=Y+1:IF Y<>100 THEN1135
1160 GOSUB600:CLS:PRINT
1170 PRINT"ARE YOU IN THE MOOD FOR ANO
     THER BOMB";
1180 INPUT A$
1190 IF LEFT$(A$,1)="N" THEN1220
1200 RESTORE:CLS
1210 TV=1:GOTO220
1220 PRINT"HOW MANY TIMES WERE YOU BLO
     WN AWAY ???"
1230 END
```

UP PERISCOPE!

Get ready to launch the torpedos!! This graphics submarine game does just about everything a submarine does, including raising up the periscope!

Your submarine can't be destroyed, but you must destroy the enemy ships that pass before your eyes. The periscope will be equipped with cross hairs, you will launch torpedos (up to 20) one at a time by using the keys numbered 1, 2, 3 and 4.

Torpedos 1 and 2 will fire off to the right, while 3 and 4 will fire toward the left. The choice is yours; fire whichever ones seem appropriate. The ship must be hit in a vital area (computer determined) exactly; if not you'll only be wasting your torpedos.

All information will be printed at the top, bottom, right and left sides of the periscope (Fig. 4-3). The printout will tell you whether you've hit or missed the ship, how many ships you've destroyed and the number of torpedos remaining on board. See Fig. 4-4 for the flowchart.

Program Notes

A few things that could be added to this program are: varying the range between you and ship. This could be added so that the torpedo would not only have to be fired at the right moment but at the right range.

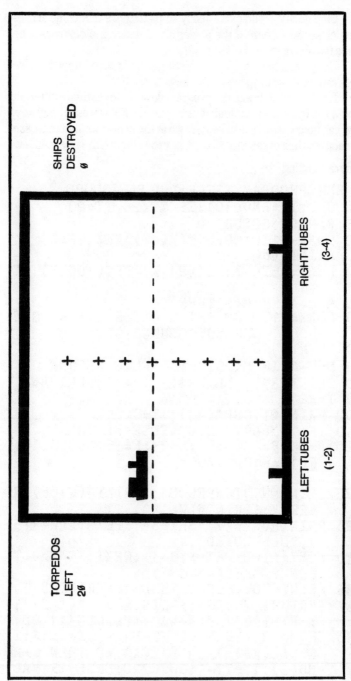

Fig. 4-3. Sample run of Up Periscope.

Ship decoys: Add extra decoy ships to those that come across the periscope screen. If the player hits a decoy and destroys it he loses two extra torpedos for it.

Have certain ships fire back: Ships could be equipped to fire back randomly or drop depth charges.

If you want to break the program down to investigate different lines, run it and step through it using the SHIFT key and the @ key. You can hold both of these keys down at the same moment to freeze the action, then press the BREAK key to establish the line number.

Program Listing

```
5 REM PROGRAM TITLE: UP PERISCOPE
10 CLS:TT=RND(30):IF TT<20 TT=20
15 RANDOM:GOSUB700
20 FORX=21TO100:SET(X,47):NEXT:M=0
30 PRINT@960,
40 FORX=45TO47:SET(21,X):SET(100,X):NE
      XT
50 M=M+1:IF M<>9THEN30
55 FORX=21TO100:SET(X,47):NEXT:M=0:GOS
      UB60:GOSUB80:GOSUB90:GOTO120
60 PRINT@960,
70 M=M+1:IF M<>5THEN60 ELSE RETURN
80 PRINT@395,STRING$(39,"-");:RETURN
90 T=221
100 PRINT@T,CHR$(43);:T=T+64
110 IF T<>669THEN100 ELSE RETURN
120 A=24:B=27:C=33:E=23:F=35:M=0:G=15:
      F(1)=F:G(1)=G
121 W=129
125 PRINT@W,"TORPEDOS";:PRINT@(W+66),"
      LEFT";:PRINT@(W+130),TT;
126 PRINT@(W+53),"SHIPS";:PRINT@(W+115
      ),"DESTROYED";
130 FORX=ATOB:SET(X,G+1):NEXT:IF M>0 T
      HEN RESET(A-1,G+1)
135 PRINT@781,"LEFT TUBES";:PRINT@805,
      "RIGHT TUBES";:PRINT@847,"(1-2)";
      :PRINT@872,"(3-4)";:PRINT@311,DD;
136 IF M>=2 AND M<=46 THEN A$=INKEY$:I
      F VAL(A$)=1 OR VAL(A$)=2 THEN Q=R
      ND(2):TT=TT-1:GOTO220:ELSE IF VAL
```

72

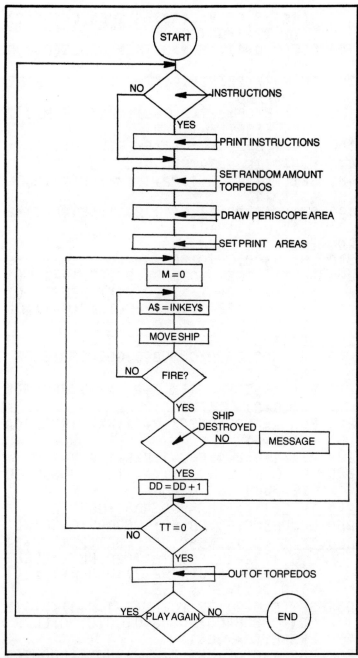

Fig. 4-4. Flowchart of Up Periscope.

```
      (A$)=3 OR VAL(A$)=4 THEN Q=RND(2)
      :TT=TT-1:GOTO260
140 SET(C,G+1):IF M>0 THEN RESET(C-1,G
    +1)
145 IF M=47 PRINT@19,"TOO LATE TO FIRE
     TORPEDO";
150 FORX=ETOF:SET(X,G+2):NEXT:IF M>0 T
    HEN RESET(E-1,G+2)
160 A=A+1:B=B+1:C=C+1:E=E+1:F=F+1
170 M=M+1:IF M=39THEN GOSUB90
180 SET(F(1)+1,G(1)*2+1):SET(F(1)+2,G(
    1)*2+1)
190 SET(F(1)*2+13,G(1)*2+1):SET(F(1)*2
    +14,G(1)*2+1)
200 IF M<>64 THEN 130
210 GOSUB300:GOTO120
220 IF TT<0THEN550:ELSE SET(F(1)+1,G(1
    )*2+1):FOR I=1TO20:NEXT:RESET(F(1
    )+1,G(1)*2+1):F(1)=F(1)+Q:G(1)=G(
    1)-.5
221 SET(C,G+1):IF POINT(C-1,G+1)<>-1TH
    EN GOSUB400:GOSUB90:GOTO120:ELSE
    RESET(C-1,G+1)
222 FOR X=ETOF:SET(X,G+2):NEXT:RESET(E
    -1,G+2)
223 FOR X=ATOB:SET(X,G+1):NEXT:RESET(A
    -1,G+1)
224 A=A+1:B=B+1:C=C+1:E=E+1:F=F+1
225 IF POINT(C-1,G+1)<>-1THEN GOSUB400
    :GOSUB90:GOTO120
240 IF G(1)<>6THEN GOSUB80:GOTO220
250 GOSUB300:GOSUB350:GOSUB90:GOTO120
260 IF TT<0 THEN550:ELSE SET(F(1)*2+14
    ,G(1)*2+1):FOR I=1TO20:NEXT:RESET
    (F(1)*2+14,G(1)*2+1):Q=2:F(1)=F(1
    )-Q:G(1)=G(1)-1.5
261 SET(C,G+1):IF POINT(C-1,G+1)<>-1TH
    EN GOSUB400:GOSUB90:GOTO120:ELSE
    RESET(C-1,G+1)
262 FOR X=ETOF:SET(X,G+2):NEXT:RESET(E
    -1,G+2)
```

74

```
263 FOR X=ATOB:SET(X,G+1):NEXT:RESET(A
    -1,G+1)
264 A=A+1:B=B+1:C=C+1:E=E+1:F=F+1
265 IF POINT(C-1,G+1)<>-1THEN GOSUB400
    :GOSUB90:GOTO120
280 IF G(1)<>6 THEN GOSUB80:GOTO260
290 GOSUB300:GOSUB350:GOSUB90:GOTO120
300 REM RESET SHIP RIGHT SIDE
310 FOR X=FTOF-13STEP-1:RESET(X,G+1):R
    ESET(X,G+2):NEXT:PRINT@19,"
                            ";
320 RETURN
350 K=1
360 PRINT@920,"MISSED SHIP";:FOR I=1TO
    100:NEXT
370 PRINT@920,"              ";:FOR J=1T
    O25:NEXT
380 K=K+1:IF K<>10THEN360
390 RETURN
400 GOSUB300:GOSUB450:K=1:DD=DD+1
410 PRINT@919,"SHIP DESTROYED";:FOR I=
    1TO100:NEXT
420 PRINT@919,"              ";:FOR J
    =1TO25:NEXT
430 K=K+1:IF K<>10THEN410
440 RETURN
450 QQ=1
460 SET(X-1,G+2):FOR I=1TO25:NEXT:RESE
    T(X-1,G+2):SET(X+2,G+2):FOR I=1TO
    10:NEXT:RESET(X+2,G+2)
470 SET(X,G+2):FOR I=1TO10:NEXT:RESET(
    X,G+2):SET(X+3,G+2):FOR I=1TO15:N
    EXT:RESET(X+3,G+2)
475 SET(X+4,G+2):FOR I=1TO25:NEXT:RESE
    T(X+4,G+2)
476 SET(X+6,G+2):FOR I=1TO15:NEXT:RESE
    T(X+6,G+2)
477 SET(X+7,G+2):FOR I=1TO10:NEXT:RESE
    T(X+7,G+2)
480 QQ=QQ+1
490 IF QQ<>10 THEN460
```

75

```
500 RETURN
550 GOSUB300:GOSUB90:S=1
560 PRINT@19,"YOU ARE OUT OF TORPEDOS"
    ;:FOR I=1TO100:NEXT
570 PRINT@19,"
    ";:FOR I=1TO50:NEXT
580 S=S+1:IF S<>20 THEN560
590 PRINT@19,"READY TO HIT SOMEMORE";
600 INPUT Q$
610 IF Q$="YES"THEN DD=0:GOTO10
620 PRINT@19,"CHICKEN, ARE YOU ???
    ";
630 FOR I=1TO 1500:NEXT
640 CLS
650 END
700 PRINTCHR$(23)
710 PRINT
720 PRINT"INSTRUCTIONS";
730 INPUT Q$:IF Q$<>"YES"THEN HH=1:GOT
    0870
740 PRINT"UP PERISCOPE!!"
750 PRINT"YOU ARE IN A SUB"
760 PRINT"A SUB THAT NO SHIPS CAN"
770 PRINT"DESTROY. BUT YOU MUST"
780 PRINT"DESTROY THE ENEMY SHIPS."
790 PRINT
800 PRINT"USING KEYS 1-4 YOU WILL"
810 PRINT"LAUNCH THE TORPEDOS, THE"
820 PRINT"SHIPS MUST BE HIT IN A VITAL
    "
830 PRINT"AREA OR THEY WILL NOT BE"
840 PRINT"DESTROYED !!"
850 PRINT"PRESS A KEY....."
860 Q$=INKEY$:IF Q$=""THEN860
870 CLS:PRINT@404,"UP PERISCOPE!!"
880 FOR I=1TO1000:NEXT:RETURN
890 REM IF YOU CAN'T DESTROY A SHIP
900 REM LOOK AT LINES 200-300 NOTICE T
    HE POINT
910 REM STATEMENTS. ALSO IF YOU WONDER
    WHY
```

```
920 REM THE TORPEDOS GO IN THE DIRECTI
      ON THEY
930 REM DO, THE COMPUTER LAUNCHES THEM
      RANDOMLY
940 REM TO DIFFERENT ANGLES PER TUBE.
950 REM IF YOU HAD TO READ ALL THIS TO
      HIT
960 REM A SHIP, DON'T JOIN THE NAVY !!!
```

FIND THE SPOT (MINE SWEEP)

Actually there will be no problem in finding the spot at all. What you will be doing is controlling a mine sweeper through a field of mines (Fig. 4-5). To pick up a mine all you have to do is hit it straight on (movement through the field is left to right). If the mines are close together and, while picking up one mine your ship hits another, that will count as a hit to your ship, (hits, meaning to top or bottom of ship) and you'll have to start at the beginning position again. Five hits to your ship will destroy it.

Movement of the ship through the field will be rather slow (as a real ship, in a real mine field). You'll control the ship using only the arrow keys (up, down, left or right). Something else that should be pointed out now is that, while all of this is going on, you'll only have a certain amount of time to pickup all the mines. After all mines are picked up, you hit the frame on the right side of the video to stop the clock. The computer will determine if all mines were collected. The computer will print you a "mission completed" statement if they were all collected. See Fig. 4-6 for the flowchart.

Don't try to cheat by heading straight for the right wall and pass up all the mines. That won't work. The computer will keep tabs on all the mines you missed or collected. The highest amount of mines you might face is 35; you'll have to pick up at least 21.

Program Notes

Some program changes you might want to consider are:

• More or less total time to collect the mines. Line 115, you could change the random number (2) to a higher number for more time or a smaller number for less time.

• If you feel that five hits to the ship (before it's destroyed) is either too much or not enough, you can change the argument in line 770 to a higher or lower number.

• Let your imagination go. There are countless changes that could be made to this program to suit your own needs. If you want

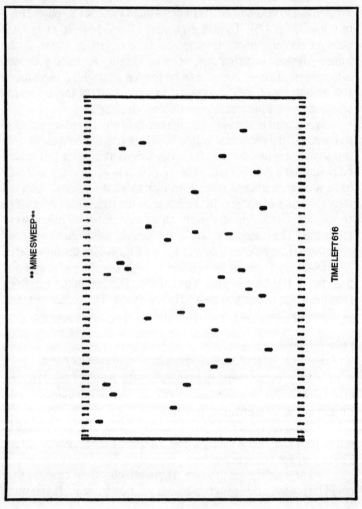

Fig. 4-5. Sample run of Minesweep.

** MINE SWEEP **

TIME LEFT 616

the ship to move faster, all that's needed is to change the numerals in lines 350 - 380. But be sure to change the RESET function to the same number or the ship will leave traces.

Program Listing

```
50 REM PROGRAM TITLE: FIND THE SPOT (M
      INE SWEEP)
100 CLS:RANDOM:DIM X(127),Y(127):GOSUB
      3000
105 N=RND(35):IF N<20 N=30:REM AMOUNT
      OF MINES
110 V=144:R=129:S=149
115 TL=(N*(RND(2)+20)):REM AMOUNT OF T
      IME
120 FOR X=15616 TO 16192STEP64:POKE X,
      S:NEXT
130 FOR X=15679 TO 16255STEP64:POKE X,
      S:NEXT
140 FOR X=15552 TO 15615:POKE X,V:NEXT
150 FOR X=16256 TO 16319:POKE X,R:NEXT
200 M=0:L=0:HT=0:TS=0:TP=0:PT=0
205 REM SET MINES
210 X=RND(120):IF X <10 THEN210
220 Y=RND(39):IF Y<14 THEN220
230 SET(X,Y):X(M)=X:Y(L)=Y
240 M=M+1:L=L+1
250 IF M<>N THEN210
260 X=7:Y=13:K=0
265 PRINT@146,"TOTAL MINES TO PICKUP =
      ";M;:FOR TU=1TO1200:NEXT
268 PRINT@146,"
              ";
269 PRINT@23,"* * MINE  SWEEP * *";
270 RESET(X,Y):IF TS>=1 PRINT@985,"TIM
      E LEFT";TL;:TL=TL-1:IF TL<=0 TL=0
      :GOTO600:ELSE GOTO280
275 PRINT@985,"TIME LEFT";TL;:IF X>7 T
      HEN TL=TL-1:IF TL<=0 TL=0:GOTO600
280 SET(X,Y):IF X+3 >=126 THEN500
283 IF TL>=25 AND TL<=75PRINT@128,"CHE
      CK REMAINING TIME";:ELSE PRINT@12
      8,"                        ";
```

79

```
285 IF (POINT(X+1,Y))THEN PRINT@156,"P
    ICKUP !!";:X(HT)=0:Y(HT)=0:HT=HT+
    1:RESET(X,Y):X=X+2:Y=Y:RESET(X-1,
    Y):SET(X,Y):ELSE PRINT@156,"
        ";
288 IF(POINT(X,Y-1)) OR (POINT(X,Y+1))
    THEN700
290 Q=PEEK(14400):REM HIGH END OF KEYB
    OARD MEMORY FOR YOUR SHIP
295 IF X>=125 GOTO500
300 IF Q=8 THEN350
310 IF Q=16 THEN360
320 IF Q=32 THEN370
330 IF Q=64 THEN380
340 IF Q=0THEN X=X:Y=Y:GOTO270
350 Y=Y-1:RESET(X,Y+1):GOTO390
360 Y=Y+1:RESET(X,Y-1):GOTO390
370 X=X-1:RESET(X+1,Y):GOTO390
380 X=X+1:RESET(X-1,Y)
390 PRINT@985,"TIME LEFT";TL;:SET(X,Y)
    :RESET(X-1,Y-1)
400 IF X<=2 PRINT@156,"OUT OF RANGE...
    ..";:FOR LL=1TO150:NEXT:PRINT@156
    ,"                ";:RESET(X,Y)
    :X=2:ELSE IF Y<=12 OR Y>=41 PRINT
    @156,"OUT OF RANGE.....";:FOR LL=
    1TO150:NEXT:RESET(X,Y):PRINT@156,
    "                ";:IF Y<=12 Y=1
    3:ELSE IF Y>=41 Y=40
410 GOTO270
500 REM END OF MINE FIELD
505 X=X:Y=Y
510 RESET(X,Y)
520 PRINT@136,"END OF FIELD
            ";
530 PRINT@165,"TOTAL PICKUPS =";HT;
540 GOTO900
600 Z=1
610 PRINT@985,"OUT OF TIME.....";:FOR
    TU=1TO100:NEXT
```

```
620 PRINT@985,"                    ";::FOR
    TU=1TO50:NEXT
630 Z=Z+1
640 IF Z<>15 THEN 610
650 GOTO500
```

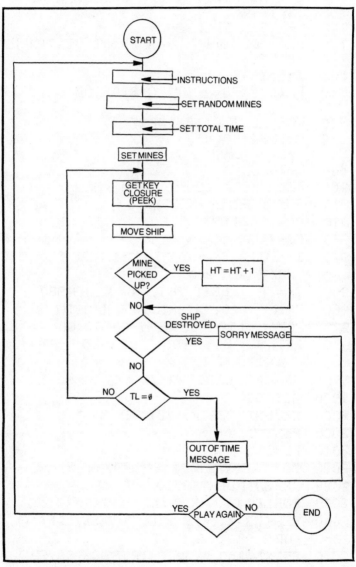

Fig. 4-6. Flowchart of Minesweep.

```
700    REM START OVER
710    REM MINE HIT WITH SIDE
720    REM OF SHIP = INVALID MOVE
730    REM IF HIT WITH SIDE OF SHIP
740    REM 5 TIMES, SHIP WILL
750    REM BE DESTROYED - END OF GAME
760    TS=TS+1
770    IF TS=5 THEN2000
780    REM HOLD TIME FOR PRINT STATEMENT
790    RESET(X,Y)
800    X=7:Y=13
810    PRINT@150,"HIT TO SIDE OF SHIP !!"
       ;
820    FOR LL=1TO1000:NEXT
830    PRINT@150,"                          "
       ;
840    GOTO285
900    REM CHECK COUNT OF MINES
910    REM TO SEE IF ANY STRAYS
920    REM WERE LEFT
930    FOR I=0 TO M
940    IF X(I)< >0 AND Y(I)< >0 THEN PT=PT+1:
       NEXT:GOTO 980
950    TP=TP+1:NEXT:IF TP-1 < M THEN 980
960    PRINT @ 20,"MISSION COMPLETED ! !";
970    FOR LL=1 TO 1200:NEXT:GOTO 2100
980    PRINT @ 20,"YOU   MISSED";PT;
       "MINES    ";
990    REM ANOTHER FIELD ? ? ?
1000   GOTO 970
2000   REM SHIP DESTROYED BY MINE
2005   RESET(X,Y)
2010   KL=0
2020   SET(X-1,Y):SET(X,Y):SET(X+1,Y)
2025   REM SHIP DESTROYED
2030   FOR LL=1 TO 100:NEXT
2040   RESET(X-1,Y):RESET(X,Y):RESET(X+1,Y)
2050   FOR LL=1 TO 50:NEXT
2060   PRINT@150,"YOUR SHIP IS DESTROYED!!";
2070   KL=KL+1
```

```
2080   IF KL< >15 THEN 2020
2090   CLS
2100   REM INPUT FOR ANOTHER ROUND
2110   PRINT@268,"ARE YOU READY TO TRY
          ANOTHER FIELD";
2120   PRINT @304,;
2125   INPUT D$
2130   IF D$="YES" THEN 2160
2135   IF D$="NO" THEN 2170
2140   REM WHAT WAS THAT ??
2150   PRINT @268,"TRY A LOGICAL ANSWER.
          ";:FOR LL=1 TO 1200:NEXT:GOTO
          2100
2160   CLS:GOTO 105
2170   PRINT @332,"TRY A REAL MINE FIELD,
          CHICKEN ! ! ! ";
2180   GOTO 2180
3000   PRINT@ 20," ** MINE SWEEP ** ";
3010   PRINT:PRINT
3020   PRINT"YOUR MISSION—TO PICK UP AS MANY"
3030   PRINT"OF THE MINES AS YOU CAN IN A
          CERTAIN AMOUNT"
3040   PRINT"OF TIME. ALL MINES WILL BE THE
          SET BLOCKS,"
3050   PRINT"YOUR MINE SWEEPER WILL BE THE
          FLASHING"
3060   PRINT"BLOCK. YOU WILL WORK FROM LEFT
          TO RIGHT"
3070   PRINT"AND PICK UP THE MINES BY HITTING
          THEM STRAIGHT"
3080   PRINT"ON. IF YOU HIT A MINE WITH THE TOP
          END OR BOTTOM"
3090   PRINT"END OF YOUR SHIP THIS WILL BE
          AN ERROR AND"
3100   PRINT"YOU'LL HAVE TO START AT THE
          BEGINNING OF THE"
3110   PRINT"FIELD, FIVE HITS WILL DESTROY
          YOUR SHIP."
```

```
3120    PRINT
3130    PRINT"PRESS A KEY . . . . . "
3140    X$=INKEY$: IF X$="" THEN 3140
3150    CLS: PRINT: PRINT
3160    PRINT"SHIP COMMANDS ARE AS FOLLOWS: "
3170    PRINT CHR$(91)TAB(5); "TO MOVE SHIP UP. "
3180    PRINT CHR$(92)TAB(5);" TO MOVE SHIP DOWN ."
3190    PRINT CHR$(93)TAB(5);"TO MOVE SHIP LEFT ."
3200    PRINT CHR$(94)TAB(5);"TO MOVE SHIP RIGHT."
3210    PRINT
3220    PRINT"WHEN AND IF YOU COLLECT ALL MINES"
3230    PRINT"RAM YOUR SHIP INTO THE RIGHT
           WALL OF "
3240    PRINT"THE DISPLAY, TIME WILL STOP AND "
3250    PRINT"TOTAL SCORE WILL BE PRINTED. "
3255    PRINT
3260    PRINT"PRESS A KEY TO BEGIN SWEEP ."
3270    X$=INKEY$: IF X$="" THEN 3270
3280    CLS: RETURN
```

Chapter 5
Words and Crosswords

TEACH YOUR CHILDREN

This program is designed to help your child recognize and learn the 26 different letters of the alphabet, while they have fun with your computer!

The first part of the program will print each letter of the alphabet on a blackboard. As each letter is printed, help your child say it. A time delay is included between the printing of each letter. After all 26 letters are printed, let your child study them as long as they wish, before pressing ENTER to continue (Fig. 5-1).

The next part of the program will select a random letter and blank it off of the blackboard. Your child will then press the missing letter on the keyboard (this uses the INKEY$ function, so *don't* press ENTER). This process continues until all 26 letters have been randomly drawn. The computer will print the alphabet again, and print a message to your child about his/her score.

The final part of the program will help your child recognize simple words. The computer will read a list of 10 words (these words can be changed to whatever you like). All words will be simple.

After the computer prints the words each word will be broken apart and each letter of the word will flash on the blackboard in order. Your child will then be asked to spell the word and press ENTER. If correct he/she will receive a CORRECT message, if not, the computer will ask your child to try again. The same word will then flash on the blackboard.

After all 10 words have been correctly entered the computer will come up with one more name, your child's. Each letter to your childs first name will flash on the blackboard as did the other words. Then your child will be asked to spell the word. Hopefully, they'll recognize their name. See Fig. 5-2 for the flowchart.

Program Notes

Lines 200-250 contain all necessary data for the alphabet. Variable T sets the location for the letters of the alphabet to be placed.

Line 310 randomly selects a letter that hasn't been used already. The argument IF L>=17 is used so the letters Q-Z will be blanked out at their appropriate place.

The ASC function in lines 325 and 385 is used for letter location.

Lines 490-520 flash the letters selected; variable Q determines their location.

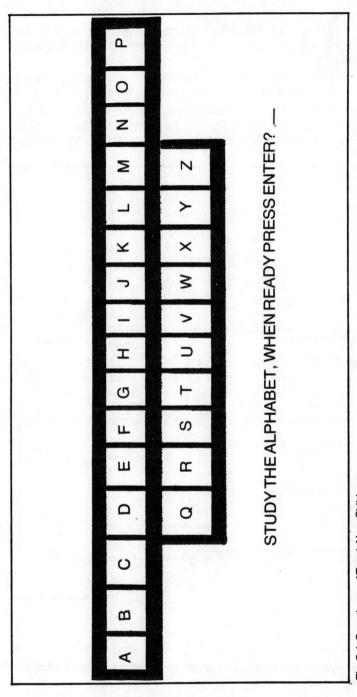

A	B	C	D	E	F	G	H	I	J	K	L	M	N	O	P
			Q	R	S	T	U	V	W	X	Y	Z			

STUDY THE ALPHABET, WHEN READY PRESS ENTER? __

Fig. 5-1. Sample run of Teach Your Children.

Lines 715-735 select the letters, one at a time, to be flashed for the word portion of the program, while line 740 steps each letter.

If you decide to add more words to the last part of the program, be sure to change the DIM statement for W$ line 110. (10 words were selected as after that amount most pre-schoolers will lose interest.) Be sure to change the instructions for that part of the program, amount of words, and change the READ/DATA state-

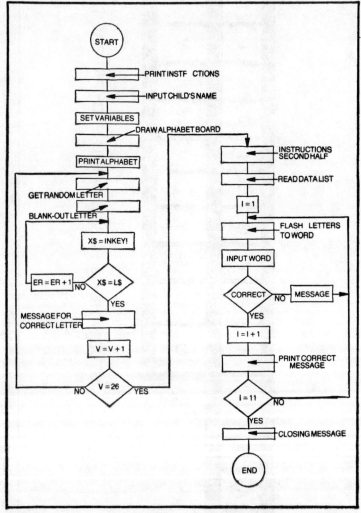

Fig. 5-2. Flowchart of Teach Your Children.

ment line 690. You will also have to change line 750 so that the extra words will be used.

Also, if you feel the time-loop interval is too short or too long, you can change variable R, line 105, to fit your child's learning ability.

Program Listing

```
10 REM PROGRAM TITLE: TEACH YOUR CHILD
      REN
20 CLS:PRINT@15,"TEACH YOUR CHILDREN"
30 PRINT
35 PRINT"THIS PROGRAM IS DESIGNED TO H
      ELP YOUR YOUNG-ONE"
40 PRINT"RECOGNIZE THE 26 DIFFERENT LET
      TERS OF THE ALPHABET."
45 PRINT"MOREOVER, IT WILL TEACH THEM
      TO RECOGNIZE 10"
50 PRINT"SIMPLE, EVERYDAY WORDS. THESE
      WORDS CAN BE CHANGED"
55 PRINT"TO ANYTHING YOU DESIRE TO HEL
      P YOUR CHILD LEARN"
60 PRINT"MORE ABOUT THE ALPHABET AND P
      UTTING WORDS TOGETHER."
65 PRINT
70 INPUT"PLEASE ENTER YOUR CHILDS FIRS
      T NAME";NA$
75 REM ALL 26 LETTERS WILL BE RANDOMLY
      SELECTED
80 REM FOR THE FIRST PART OF THE PROGR
      AM
85 REM YOU MIGHT FIND THE COMPUTER WIL
      L TAKE A
90 REM LITTLE LONGER TO 'WEED' OUT THE
      LAST FEW
95 REM LETTERS OF THE ALPHABET
100 CLS
105 PRINT:PRINT"HELP YOUR CHILD PRONOU
      NCE THE LETTERS AS THEY'RE PRINTED.
      ":R=1000:GOSUB300:CLS
110 DIM A$(26),K$(26),W$(12)
120 RANDOM:V=0:REM SET ALPHABET BOARD
```

89

```
130 FOR X=0TO127:SET(X,1):SET(X,6):NEX
    T
140 X=1:Y=5:M=0
150 FOR Z=XTOY:SET(M,Z):NEXT
155 IF M=24 THEN FOR Z=X+5TOY:SET(M-1,
    Z):NEXT:ELSE IF M=104 THEN FOR Z=
    X+5TOY:SET(M+1,Z):NEXT
160 M=M+8:IF M>=24 AND M<=104 THEN Y=1
    2:ELSE Y=6
170 IF M<>128 THEN 150
180 FOR X=1TO5:SET(127,X):NEXT
190 FOR X=24TO104:SET(X,12):NEXT:IF V=
    26 THEN215
195 GOSUB300:PRINT@345,"THE ALPHABET";
    :ER=0

200 FOR I=1TO16:READ A$(I):NEXT
210 DATA A,B,C,D,E,F,G,H,I,J,K,L,M,N,O
    ,P,Q,R,S,T,U,V,W,X,Y,Z
215 REM PRINT THE ALPHABET PER RIGHT S
    QUARE
220 T=66

230 FOR I=1TO16:PRINT@T,A$(I);:GOSUB30
    0
240 T=T+4:NEXT:IF V=26 THEN260
250 FOR I=17TO26:READ A$(I):NEXT
260 T=206
270 FOR I=17TO26:PRINT@T,A$(I);:GOSUB3
    00
280 T=T+4:NEXT
285 IF V=26 THEN575
290 GOSUB430:PRINT"STUDY THE ALPHABET,
    WHEN READY PRESS ENTER";:INPUT Z
    :GOTO310

300 FOR ZZ=1TOR:NEXT:RETURN:REM R CAN
    BE LONGER/SHORTER INTERVALLOOP FO
    R PRINT STATEMENTS
310 L=RND(26):L$=A$(L):FOR W=1TOV:IF K
    $(W)=L$THEN310:ELSE NEXT
315 N$=" ":T=66:S=206:IF L>=17THEN385
320 REM BLANK OUT RANDOM LETTER
```

```
325 ON ASC(L$)-64 GOTO330,331,332,333,
    334,335,336,337,338,339,340,341,3
    42,343,344,345
330 T=T:GOTO380
331 T=T+4:GOTO380
332 T=T+8:GOTO380
333 T=T+12:GOTO380
334 T=T+16:GOTO380
335 T=T+20:GOTO380
336 T=T+24:GOTO380
337 T=T+28:GOTO380
338 T=T+32:GOTO380
339 T=T+36:GOTO380
340 T=T+40:GOTO380
341 T=T+44:GOTO380
342 T=T+48:GOTO380
343 T=T+52:GOTO380
344 T=T+56:GOTO380
345 T=T+60
380 PRINT@T,N$;:Q=T:GOSUB430:IF MN=1 T
    HEN490:ELSE 440
385 ON ASC(L$)-80 GOTO 386,387,388,389
    ,390,391,392,393,394,395
386 S=S:GOTO420
387 S=S+4:GOTO420
388 S=S+8:GOTO420
389 S=S+12:GOTO420
390 S=S+16:GOTO420
391 S=S+20:GOTO420
392 S=S+24:GOTO420
393 S=S+28:GOTO420
394 S=S+32:GOTO420
395 S=S+36
420 PRINT@S,N$;:Q=S:GOSUB430:IF MN=1 T
    HEN490:ELSE440
430 PRINT@332,"
                            ":PRINT@332
    ,;:RETURN
432 PRINT@384,"
                                    ":
    PRINT@384,;:RETURN
434 PRINT@453,"
```

```
                                             ":PR
     INT@453,;:RETURN
435 REM INKEY$ SO ENTER DOESN'T NEED T
     O BE PRESSED
440 PRINT"PRESS THE MISSING LETTER (ON
     THE KEYBOARD)"
450 X$=INKEY$:IF X$=""THEN450
460 IF X$<>L$THEN GOSUB430:PRINT"  THE
     LETTER YOU ENTERED IS INCORRECT"
     :ER=ER+1:GOSUB300:GOSUB430:GOTO44
     0
470 GOSUB430
480 PRINT"VERY GOOD !!            THE
     LETTER WAS ";L$
490 X=0
500 PRINT@Q,L$;:FOR K=1TO200:NEXT
510 PRINT@Q,N$;:FOR J=1TO150:NEXT
520 X=X+1:IF X<>10THEN500:ELSE PRINT@Q
     ,L$;
525 IF MN=1 THEN740
530 V=V+1:IF V=26 THEN570:ELSE GOSUB43
     0
540 PRINT"          LET'S TRY ANOTHER LE
     TTER."
550 K$(V)=L$
560 GOSUB300:GOTO310
570 GOSUB300:CLS:GOTO130
575 GOSUB432:PRINT"THAT IS ALL";V;"LET
     TERS OF THE ALPHABET."
580 IF ER<>0 THEN600
590 PRINT"AND YOU'VE LEARNED IT VERY W
     ELL, YOUR SCORE IS 100 !!":GOSUB6
     10:GOTO630
600 PRINT"I'M SORRY, BUT YOU DID MISS"
     ;ER;"OF THE LETTERS."
605 PRINT"PRACTICE MAKES PERFECT, RIGH
     T ?":GOSUB1000:GOSUB432:GOTO630
610 PRINT"PRESS ENTER";
620 INPUT X$:GOSUB432:RETURN
630 PRINT"NOW WE WILL TRY SOME SIMPLE
     WORDS.       "
```

```
640 PRINT"EACH LETTER, ONE AT A TIME W
    ILL FLASH,":GOSUB650:GOTO660
650 FOR ZZ=1TO2500:NEXT:GOSUB432:RETUR
    N
660 PRINT"IN THE ORDER THE WORD IS SPE
    LLED.    "
670 PRINT"YOU MUST THEN ENTER THE WORD
     THAT WAS PUT TOGETHER"
675 PRINT"BY THE FLASHING LETTERS."
680 GOSUB610:GOSUB1000
690 FOR I=1TO10:READ W$(I):NEXT
700 DATA DOG,CAT,COW,MOM,DAD,TOYS,TRAI
    N,HOUSE,LOVE,YOU
710 I=1:LI=1:MN=1
715 REM SET AMOUNT OF LETTERS IN WORD
720 WW=LEN(W$(I))
725 REM LEFT LETTER FIRST
730 L$=MID$(W$(I),LI,1):L=ASC(L$)-64
735 GOTO315:REM TO FLASH LETTER IN WOR
    D
740 LI=LI+1
750 IF LI<WW+1 THEN730
760 GOSUB432
770 PRINT"NOW ENTER (SPELL) THE WORD"
780 PRINT"THAT WAS JUST PRINTED WITH T
    HE"
790 PRINT"FLASHING LETTERS";
800 INPUT FL$
810 IF FL$<>W$(I) THEN860
820 PRINT"THAT IS CORRECT !!"
822 IF II=12 THEN910
825 IF I=10 THEN900
830 PRINT"WE STILL HAVE";10-I;"WORDS T
    O GO."
840 PRINT"ARE YOU READY";
850 INPUT X$:GOTO880
860 PRINT"I'M SORRY, THAT WAS NOT THE
    WORD."
870 PRINT"TRY AGAIN, PLEASE.....":LI=1
    :GOSUB300:GOSUB1000:GOTO730
880 I=I+1:LI=1
890 IF I<>11 THEN GOSUB1000:GOTO720
```

```
900 GOSUB300:GOSUB1000:GOSUB432:PRINT"
      LET'S TRY ONE MORE WORD, YOU SHOU
      LD KNOW IT.":GOSUB610:GOSUB1000
905 W$(I)=NA$:LI=1:II=12:GOTO720
910 GOSUB432
920 PRINT"THAT WAS YOUR NAME YOU JUST
      SPELLED !!"
930 PRINT"DID YOU RECOGNIZE IT, I HOPE
      SO !!"
940 PRINT"THAT'S THE END OF THE PROGRA
      M, I NOW"
950 PRINT"RETURN YOU TO YOUR T.V. SET.
      ...."
960 PRINT"GOODBYE FOR NOW."
970 END
1000 PRINT@384,"
                 "
1010 PRINT@448,"
                 "
1020 PRINT@512,"
                 "
1030 PRINT@576,"
                 "
1040 PRINT@640,"
                 "
1050 PRINT@704,"
                 "
1060 REM KEEP THE CHALKBOARD CLEAN
1070 RETURN
```

EDUCATION WAVES (COMPUTER CROSSWORD)

This program will draw a crossword puzzle and give you 18 different definitions to find words for. All letters to your answers will be input via the INKEY$ function. ENTER will not be used. See Fig. 5-3.

After you have input all the letters to your answer press 0 (zero) and the computer will advance to the next definition (all meanings to the words will be printed about the lower center of the video). If you want to skip a question, press 0.

You cannot backspace at any time. Once the letter is pressed and printed, that's that. So be sure of the letter before pressing it. Also, when working down, you might have part or all of a word

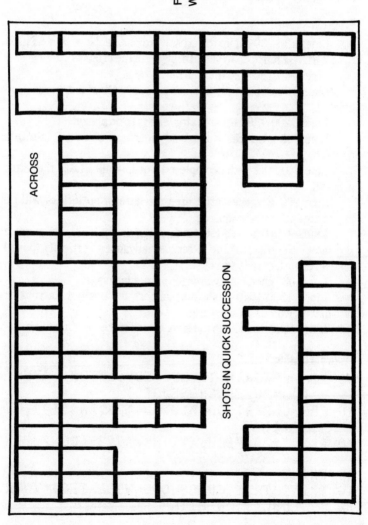

Fig. 5-3. Sample run of Education Waves.

ACROSS

SHOTS IN QUICK SUCCESSION

95

already printed from going across. Press these letters again anyway or the computer will not receive a down word for that one location.

After you tire of the same meanings and words it's very simple to change them. Lines 750-770 contain the data for the words, these can be changed to suit your needs. Just keep the same number of letters, unless you decide to change the entire crossword. Lines 1400-1490 contain the data for the meanings of the words. These can be changed to fit the data in lines 750-770. See Fig. 5-4 for the flowchart.

Program Notes

Lines 180-730 set up the crossword puzzle. Note that A$ uses the STRING$ function to speed drawing of the crossword.

Lines 760-780 read the data list.

Lines 790-800 set the area for the meanings of the words to be printed.

Lines 1200-1390 set areas for letters to be placed.

Line 855 advances words and meanings when a 0 (zero) is pressed.

Line 880 AN$ is the completed word, while LL$ is the letter pressed.

Line 900 advances print area for letters, so letters will be printed in appropriate squares.

Lines 915-1010 are for words going down. This works much the same as across but the letters are advanced vertically (down) instead of horizontally (across).

Line 1020 checks all words for proper message.

Lines 1500-1540 flash the numbers for position (across or down) with which you are working.

Lines 1550-1560 keep the slate clean for the next meaning.

Program Listing

```
10 REM PROGRAM TITLE: EDUCATION WAVES
      (COMPUTER CROSSWORD)
20 CLS:CLEAR1000:DIM A$(19),AN$(19),QU
      $(19)
30 PRINT@20,"EDUCATION WAVES (COMPUTER
      CROSSWORD)"
40 PRINT
50 PRINT"THIS CROSSWORD WILL TEST YOUR
      EDUCATION WITH"
```

```
60 PRINT"DIFFERENT MEANINGS TO DIFFERE
      NT WORDS."
70 PRINT"GETTING STARTED WILL BE THE O
      NLY TIME YOU'LL"
80 PRINT"USE THE 'ENTER' KEY. ALL WORD
      S WILL BE INPUT"
90 PRINT"USING THE INKEY$ FUNCTION."
100 PRINT"ALL MEANINGS WILL BE PRINTED
      ABOUT THE LOWER"
```

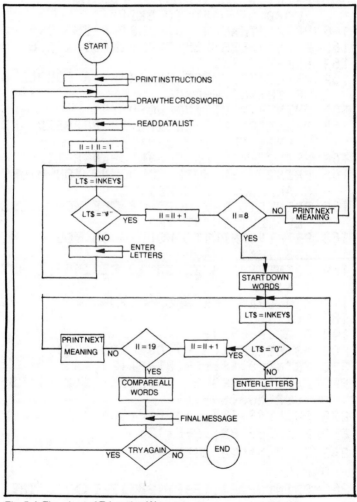

Fig. 5-4. Flowchart of Education Waves.

```
110 PRINT"CENTER OF THE VIDEO. BEFORE
     A MEANING IS PRINTED"
120 PRINT"THE COMPUTER WILL TELL YOU W
     HICH ONE YOU'LL BE"
130 PRINT"WORKING ON, 1 ACROSS, 2 ACRO
     SS, 1 DOWN, ETC."
140 PRINT"THAT NUMBER WILL APPEAR ABOV
     E OR NEXT TO THAT"
150 PRINT"COLUMN OR ROW."
155 PRINT"AFTER YOU HAVE INPUT THE
     WORD OR WANT TO SKIP"
156 PRINT"THAT WORD, JUST PRESS 0."
160 PRINT"PRESS ENTER";:INPUT X:CLS
161 PRINT:PRINT
162 PRINT"YOU MUST REMEMBER A COUPLE O
     F THINGS WHEN"
163 PRINT"INPUTTING WORDS:"
164 PRINT"ONCE A LETTER IS PRESSED AND
      PRINTED, YOU CAN'T"
165 PRINT"BACKSPACE AND CHANGE IT."
166 PRINT"WHEN WORKING DOWN, YOU MIGHT
      ALREADY HAVE LETTERS"
167 PRINT"TO THE WORD OR THE WORD ITSE
     LF, BUT INPUT THE"
168 PRINT"COMPLETE WORD - OR YOU'LL MI
     SS THAT ONE."
169 PRINT"PRESS ENTER TO BEGIN";:INPUT
      X:CLS
170 REM DRAW THE CROSSWORD
180 L=131:G=0
190 S=27:P=68:N=3
200 A$=STRING$(S,L):D$=CHR$(149)
210 PRINT@P,A$;:PRINT@P+128,A$;
220 P=P+128:S=S-24:B$=STRING$(S,L):C$=
     STRING$(S+3,L)
225 PRINT@P+128,C$;:P=P+128
230 PRINT@P,B$;:P=P+128
240 IF P<>1092 THEN230
250 P=98
260 PRINT@P,B$;:P=P+128:IF P<>738 THEN
     260
```

```
280 P=339:PP=P-6
290 PRINT@P,B$;:PRINT@PP,B$;:P=P+128:P
    P=PP+128:IF P<>723 THEN290
310 P=714:PP=P+15
320 PRINT@P,B$;:PRINT@PP,B$;
330 P=P+128:PP=PP+128:IF P<>842 THEN32
    0
335 PRINT@839,A$;:PRINT@967,A$;
340 P=116:PP=125
350 PRINT@P,B$;:PRINT@PP,B$;
360 P=P+128:PP=PP+128:IF P<>500 THEN35
    0
370 PRINT@PP,B$;
380 PP=PP+128:IF PP<>1021 THEN370
390 Y=8
400 FOR X=3TO45:SET(Y,X):SET(Y+5,X):SE
    T(121,X):SET(127,X):NEXT
405 SET(120,21):SET(120,27):FOR X=121T
    O126:SET(X,45):NEXT
410 Y=Y+11
420 FOR X=40TO44:SET(Y,X):NEXT
430 Y=Y+6:IF Y<>73 THEN420
440 FOR X=3TO27:SET(Y-6,X):SET(Y,X):NE
    XT
460 Y=19:FOR X=4TO14:SET(Y,X):NEXT
480 Y=Y+6:FOR X=4TO8:SET(Y,X):NEXT
490 IF Y<>67 THEN480
500 X=37
510 FOR Y=10TO27:SET(X-12,Y):SET(X-6,Y
    ):SET(X,Y):NEXT:X=X+6
520 IF X<>49 THEN510
525 C=(LEN(A$)-12):GOSUB600:PRINT@747,
    A$;:PRINT@875,A$;
530 X=19:M=31
540 FOR Y=33TO39:SET(X,Y):NEXT:X=X+6
550 IF X<>M THEN540
555 IF M=61 THEN580:ELSE IF M=121 THEN
    590
570 X=X+18:M=61:GOTO540
580 X=X+24:M=121:GOTO540
590 C=C-4:GOSUB600:GOTO610
```

```
600 A$=STRING$(C,L):RETURN
610 PRINT@342,A$;:PRINT@470,A$;
620 C=C+12:GOSUB600
630 PRINT@485,A$;:PRINT@613,A$;:REM:SE
    T(73,21):SET(73,27)
640 C=C-11:GOSUB600
650 PRINT@229,A$;:PRINT@357,A$;:SET(66
    ,15):SET(66,21)
660 X=49:J=16:K=20:M=67
670 FOR Y=JTOK:SET(X,Y):NEXT:X=X+6
680 IF X<>M THEN670
685 IF M=103 THEN700:ELSE IF M=121 THE
    N710
690 X=X+12:J=J-6:K=K-6:M=103:GOTO670
700 X=79:J=J+12:K=K+12:M=121:GOTO670
710 X=103:FOR Y=3TO20:SET(X,Y):SET(X+6
    ,Y):NEXT
720 FOR Y=28TO32:SET(X+6,Y):SET(X+12,Y
    ):NEXT
730 X=85:FOR Y=16TO20:SET(X,Y):SET(X+6
    ,Y):NEXT
740 REM READ DATA LIST FOR WORDS ACROS
    S & DOWN
750 FOR I=1TO18:READ A$(I):NEXT
760 DATA RAPIDFIRE,ED,AFTER,MODERN,DIS
    CIPLINE,CHILL,RIPPLEMARK
770 DATA RECOVER,AD,IDEA,FAME,SAND,ETC
    ,SOIL,ILL,BENEFIT,AP,DA
775 REM GET MEANING OF WORDS
780 GOSUB1400:Q=I
785 REM SET AREA FOR MEANING OF WORDS
790 AR=655:AC$="ACROSS":DN$="DOWN":GOT
    O810
800 PRINT@AR,;:RETURN
810 REM SET AREA FOR LETTERS TO BE PLA
    CED PER QUESTION
820 II=I:II=1:GOSUB1200
825 PRINT@0,AC$;:GOSUB1500
830 GOSUB800:PRINTQU$(II);
840 GOSUB800:AN$=""
850 LT$=INKEY$:IF LT$=""THEN850
```

```
855 IF LT$="0"THEN AN$(II)=AN$:II=II+1
    :IF II=8 THEN 920:ELSE GOSUB1200:
    GOSUB1550:GOSUB1500:GOTO830
870 REM WORDS + LETTER
880 AN$=AN$+LT$:LL$=LT$
890 PRINT@LT,LL$;
900 LT=LT+3
910 GOTO850
915 REM DOWN
920 GOSUB1550:PRINT@0,DN$ ;:GOSUB1200
930 GOSUB1500
940 GOSUB800:AN$="":PRINTQU$(II);
950 LT$=INKEY$:IF LT$=""THEN950
960 IF LT$="0" THEN AN$(II)=AN$:II=II+
    1:IF II=19 THEN 1020:ELSE GOSUB12
    00:GOSUB1550:GOSUB1500:GOTO940
970 REM WORDS (DOWN) + LETTERS
980 AN$=AN$+LT$:LL$=LT$:LT=LT+128
985 IF II>=17 PRINT@LT+2,LL$;:GOTO1000
990 PRINT@LT+1,LL$;
1000 REM GET MORE LETTERS ?
1010 GOTO950
1020 FOR I=1TO18:IF AN$(I)<>A$(I) THEN
     G=G+1:NEXT:ELSE NEXT
1030 GOSUB800
1040 IF G=0 THEN1060
1050 PRINT"YOU MISSED";G;"OF THE WORDS
     , SORRY !!":GOTO1070
1060 PRINT"THAT IS GREAT, ALL WORDS CO
     RRECT !!";
1070 FOR KL=1TO2000:NEXT:GOSUB1550:GOS
     UB800
1080 PRINT"ARE YOU READY TO TRY AGAIN"
     ;
1090 INPUT QQ$
1100 IF QQ$="YES" THEN FOR I=1TO18:AN$
     ="":NEXT:RESTORE:CLS:GOTO170
1110 GOSUB1550:GOSUB800
1120 PRINT"STUDY THE DICTIONARY !!!!";
1130 END
1200 REM FOR LETTER POSITIONS
```

```
1210 ON II GOTO 1220,1230,1240,1250,12
     60,1270,1280,1290,1300,1310,1320,
     1330,1340,1350,1360,1370,1380,139
     0
1220 LT=133:RETURN
1230 LT=261:RETURN
1240 LT=291:RETURN
1250 LT=405:RETURN
1260 LT=547:RETURN
1270 LT=812:RETURN
1280 LT=901:RETURN
1290 LT=4:RETURN
1300 LT=7:RETURN
1310 LT=13:RETURN
1320 LT=19:RETURN
1330 LT=34:RETURN
1340 LT=171:RETURN
1350 LT=52:RETURN
1360 LT=439:RETURN
1370 LT=61:RETURN
1380 LT=649:RETURN
1390 LT=664:RETURN
1400 REM SET MEANINGS TO WORDS
1410 FOR Q=1TO18:READ QU$(Q):NEXT
1420 DATA SHOTS IN QUICK SUCCESSION,ED
     ITOR - ABBR.
1430 DATA FOLLOWING IN TIME OR PLACE,C
     ONTEMPORARY
1440 DATA TRAINING THAT CORRECTS,TO BE
     COME COLD
1450 DATA ONE OF A SERIES OF SMALL RID
     GES,REGAIN
1460 DATA ADVERTISEMENT - ABBR.,A PLAN
      FOR ACTION,RENOWN
1470 DATA A LOOSE GRANULAR MATERIAL, ODD
     S AND ENDS,EARTH,UNFAVORABLE
1480 DATA ADVANTAGE,ASSOCIATED PRESS -
      ABBR.
1490 DATA DISTRICT ATTORNEY - ABBR.
1495 RETURN
1500 REM FLASH NUMBER AT POSITION
```

```
1505 E=0
1510 IF II>=8 PRINT@LT,II-7;:ELSE PRIN
     T@LT-5,II;
1515 FOR FL=1TO100:NEXT
1520 IF II>=8 PRINT@LT,"    ";:ELSE PRI
     NT@LT-5,"    ";
1525 FOR FL=1TO50:NEXT
1530 E=E+1:IF E<>10 THEN1510
1535 IF II=4 THEN FOR Y=16TO20:SET(37,
     Y):NEXT:LT=404
1540 LT$="":RETURN
1550 PRINT@AR,"
              ";
1560 RETURN
```

SOMETHING ON MY SCREEN

This is a word game. The computer will print up to 192 letters on the video screen. You will select a number of words (up to 25) out of these letters. All words will be read across. Some words might start on one line and continue to the one below or the one above (Fig. 5-5).

If you are unable to locate and enter all words, press ENTER for a word, and the counter (to input words) will continue. After you have entered all words, the computer compares your word list with the list in memory, and prints a correct/incorrect amount. See Fig. 5-6 for the flowchart.

Program Notes

Line 170 reads the data list of 50 words. You can change these words to anything you desire, but try and keep the letter length of the word to 15 letters.

Lines 250-370 select random words and deletes them from the list so they're only selected once. Variable J in lines 280 & 320 is used to print letters at a certain location. While variable LT is the letter amount on the screen, read at line 365 to keep the screen from over-filling with letters.

Lines 390-460 alphabetize the computer list of words. This must be done so the computer can compare the words in a minimum length of time.

Lines 510-570 are for entering your words.

Lines 590-655 alphabetize your list for the same reason given above.

```
NEETNACEELDDAPHC
ORPPAREHTONALRIG
SEFERETSLOHEGARU
OCNEETAREGAUGNAL
ENILDAEHEMANKCIN
EIFTREGNILEEIDTA
FMODEERFNNAEVIHE
EBSRACYASLLIHSOV
SMILSSEFEKOOHSKO
OTLEEQRAIRFMIALC
EREGAVLAS

WORD NUMBER 1?
```

Fig. 5-5. Sample run of Something On My Screen.

Lines 800-860 step through each of your words and the computer's. If the words are not equal, the computer will delete that one word from your list. After variable K (your words) reaches total words, variable M, the computer returns to lines 690-715 where the computer gives you a final message.

With slight modifications you can change variable J so the letters would be printed in an up/down fashion.

Program Listing

```
10 REM PROGRAM TITLE: SOMETHING ON MY
   SCREEN
20 CLS:PRINT:CLEAR500:DIM A(50),M(50),
   W$(50),Y$(50),C$(50),V$(50)
30 PRINT"THIS IS A WORD GAME WHERE YOU
   'LL SELECT WORDS"
40 PRINT"OUT OF A SET OF LETTERS (192
   OR LESS)."
50 PRINT"ALL WORDS WILL BE READ ACROSS
   . YOU WILL ENTER UP"
60 PRINT"TO 25 WORDS, IF YOU CAN'T LOC
   ATE ALL WORDS, THEN PRESS"
70 PRINT"'ENTER' FOR A WORD. AFTER ALL
    WORDS ARE ENTERED"
80 PRINT"THE COMPUTER WILL COMPARE BOT
   H LISTS AND GIVE YOU"
85 PRINT"A CLOSING MESSAGE (TOTAL CORR
   ECT - OR MISSED)."
90 PRINT
150 PRINT"PRESS ENTER TO BEGIN";:INPUT
    X:CLS:PRINTCHR$(23)
160 REM READ DATA LIST OF WORDS
170 FOR I=1TO50:READ W$(I):NEXT
180 DATA ETERNITY,SEFE,HEADLINE,EIFT,S
    ALVAGE,SPACE,GRANT
190 DATA GIRL,EEID,SAY,ANN,SEF,SINGER,
    FREEDOM,CARTOON,CARS
200 DATA AMAAM,TOOK,SHOOK,LEEQ,BEEHIVE
    ,PADDLE,MIMICS,NICKNAME
210 DATA FRIAR.SWETCEQARS,SHORT,TAMMO,
    SLIM,FAT,ENCOURAGE
220 DATA HILL,AFFIRMATIVE,APPROACH,RAT
    E,RAT,ANOTHER,LANGUAGE
```

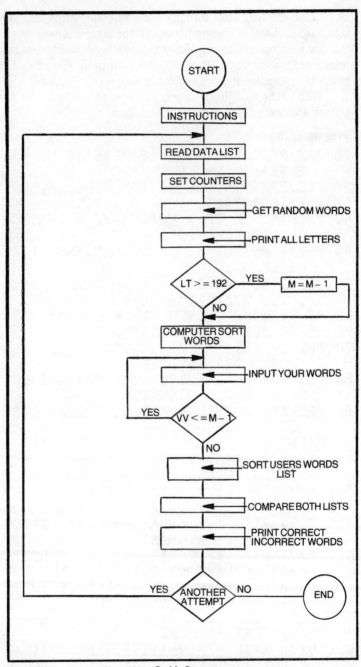

Fig. 5-6. Flowchart of Something On My Screen.

```
230 DATA MOVING,SOVS,EAR,WQW,MATCH,REC
    ENT,RECLAIM,FORMER
240 DATA CANTEEN,TUMBLER,HOLSTER,DECAN
    TER
245 FOR I=1TO50:M(I)=I:NEXT:M=1:J=0:CC
    =0:LT=0
250 I=RND(50):IF M(I)=0 THEN250
255 IF I=2 OR I=4 OR I=9 OR I=12 OR I=
    17 OR I=20 OR I=26
    OR I=28 OR I=4
    0 OR I=42 THEN Y$(I)=W$(I):GOTO26
    0:ELSE GOTO300
260 FOR LL=1TOLEN(Y$(I))
270 PRINT@J,MID$(Y$(I),LL,1);
280 J=J+4:LT=LT+1:NEXT
290 GOTO250
300 FOR WW=LEN(W$(I))TO1STEP-1
310 PRINT@J,MID$(W$(I),WW,1);
320 J=J+4:LT=LT+1:NEXT
350 REM DELETE THE USED WORDS
360 A(M)=M(I):M(I)=0:M=M+1
365 IF LT>=192 THEN M=M-1:GOTO380
370 IF M<=25 THEN250
380 REM ALPHABETIZE THE LIST
385 GOSUB530:PRINT"SORTING OUT WORDS..
    .."
390 T=0:U=1
400 IF W$(A(U))<=W$(A(U+1))THEN450
410 Q$=W$(A(U+1))
420 W$(A(U+1))=W$(A(U))
430 W$(A(U))=Q$
440 T=1
450 U=U+1:IF U<=M-1 THEN400
460 IF T=1 THEN390
510 REM ENTER THE WORDS
520 V=1:VV=1:GOTO535
530 PRINT@896,,:RETURN
535 GOSUB530:PRINT"THEIR ARE";M-1;"WOR
    DS.        ":FOR ZZ=1TO1500:NEXT
538 GOSUB530
540 PRINT"WORD NUMBER";VV;
```

```
550 INPUT V$(V)
560 PRINT@924,"                    ";:V=V
    +1:VV=VV+1:GOSUB530
570 IF VV<=M-1 THEN540
580 PRINT"PROCESSING BOTH WORD LISTS."
    ;
585 REM ALPHABETIZE USERS LIST
590 T=0:U=1
600 IF V$(U)<=V$(U+1)THEN650
610 Z$=V$(U+1)
620 V$(U+1)=V$(U)
630 V$(U)=Z$
640 T=1
650 IF V$(U)=V$(U+1) THEN V$(U+1)=""
652 U=U+1:IF U<=M-1 THEN600
655 IF T=1 THEN590
660 GOTO800:REM COMPARE THE TWO LISTS
670 REM LINE 800 - 860 WAS USED TO DEL
    ETE NON WORDS
680 REM WAS USED TO DELETE 'NON' WORDS
690 GOSUB530
700 IF CC<=0 PRINT"ALL CORRECT !! ALL"
    ;M-1;"WORDS !!":GOTO720
710 PRINT"YOU MISSED A GRAND TOTAL   "
715 PRINT"OF";CC;"WORDS......";
720 FOR ZZ=1TO2500:NEXT
730 GOSUB530
740 PRINT"ARE YOU READY TO CHALLANGE
    "
745 PRINT"ANOTHER SET OF LETTERS";
750 INPUT X$
760 IF X$="NO" THEN770
765 FOR I=2TOM:V$(I)="":NEXT:RESTORE:C
    LS:PRINTCHR$(23):GOTO160
770 GOSUB530
780 PRINT"DID YOU ACQUIRE ..........."
785 PRINT"A SELF-INDUCED HEADACHE ??"
790 FOR LA=1TO1200:NEXT:END
800 K=2:J=2
810 IF V$(K)<>W$(A(J))THEN830
820 V$(K)=W$(A(J)):GOTO850
```

```
830 J=J+1
840 IF J<=M THEN810:ELSE V$(K)="":J=2:
    K=K+1:CC=CC+1:GOTO860
850 J=J:K=K+1
860 IF K<=M THEN810
870 GOTO690
```

Chapter 6
Beginner's and Learner's Graphics

WHOSE CHART?

Using graphics you can make a handy graph bar chart for whatever purpose you choose.

It is set up to span a ten year period, but with several modifications it can be set up for a monthly chart, by following the REM statements (Fig. 6-1).

After you have created the chart and studied it, you then press any key, this will clear the screen and return you to the list of commands. You can then save the current chart on tape, load a chart from tape, make another chart, or terminate the program. See Fig. 6-2 for the flowchart.

Program Notes

Lines 65 and 70 input the years 'from - to', while the arguments in lines 70 and 72 make sure that 'from' isn't larger than 'to'.

Lines 600-780 get the percentages and set the boundaries for the graphic bars.

Lines 85-300 draw the chart and all bars to their proper percentages.

Line 275 can be used for a delay loop, between drawing of each bar.

Program Listing

```
10 REM PROGRAM TITLE: WHOSE CHART
15 GOTO910
20 REM THIS PROGRAM WILL DRAW A CHART
30 REM YOU WILL INPUT THE NEEDED INFOR
     MATION SO
40 REM THE COMPUTER CAN SET UP THE CHA
     RT AREA
50 REM CHART WILL PRINT A 10 YEAR SPAN
55 GOTO320:REM GET FUNCTION
60 CLS:PRINT:PRINT"WHOSE CHART";:INPUT
     C$
65 INPUT"ENTER YEARS, FROM";F
70 INPUT"TO";Y:IF Y<=F THEN PRINT:PRIN
     T"THAT WAS FROM / TO !!":PRINT:GO
     TO65
72 IF ABS(Y-F)>10 THEN PRINT:PRINT"ONL
     Y A SPAN OF 10 YEARS.....":PRINT:
     GOTO65
```

111

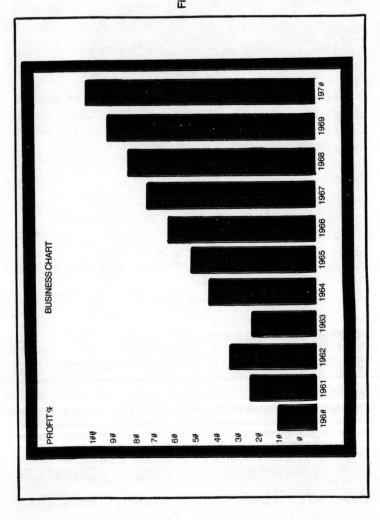

Fig. 6-1. Sample run of Whose Chart?.

```
75 FF=F:FY=F:GOTO600:REM GET PERCENTAG
   E PER YEAR
80 CLS:F=FY:REM SET BOUNDARIES
85 FOR X=0TO127:SET(X,0):SET(X,1):SET(
   X,46):SET(X,47):NEXT
90 FOR Z=0TO047:SET(0,Z):SET(1,Z):SET(1
   26,Z):SET(127,Z):NEXT
100 REM SET AREA FOR YEARS
110 A=900
120 PRINT@A,F;
130 A=A+5:F=F+1
140 IF F<Y+1 THEN120
150 REM SET AREA FOR PERCENT
160 P=100:Q=65:PP=133
170 PRINT@Q,"PROFIT %";:PRINT@Q+22,C$;
    "  CHART";:PRINT@Q+128,P;
180 Q=Q+128
190 P=P-10:Q=Q+64
200 PRINT@Q,P;
210 IF P<>0 THEN190
230 REM GET AMOUNT FOR YEAR
240 B=41:L=10:R=18:I=0
250 REM YP(I) WILL DETERMINE HEIGHT OF
    BLOCK (PERCENTAGE)
255 IF YP(I)=0 THEN290
260 FOR X=LTOR:SET(X,B):NEXT
270 B=B-1
275 REM:FOR TT=1TO150:NEXT:REM TIME LO
    OP
280 IF B<>YP(I) THEN260
290 L=L+10:R=R+10:B=41:I=I+1
300 IF R<>128 THEN250
310 A$=INKEY$:IF A$=""THEN310
320 CLS:PRINT
330 PRINT"TO MAKE A CHART, ENTER 1"
340 PRINT"TO SAVE CURRENT CHART ON TAP
    E, ENTER 2"
350 PRINT"TO LOAD A CHART FROM TAPE, E
    NTER 3"
355 PRINT"TO SEE CURRENT CHART, ENTER
    4
360 PRINT"TO END PROGRAM, ENTER 5"
```

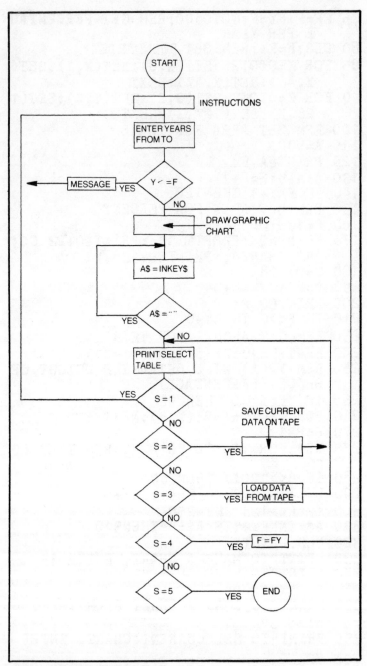

Fig. 6-2. Flowchart of Whose Chart?.

```
370 INPUT S
380 ON S GOTO 60,400,470,80,550
400 PRINT"READY TAPE PLAYER, NOTE LOCA
    TION OF COUNTER"
410 PRINT"AND PRESS ENTER";
420 INPUT X$
430 PRINT"LOADING FILE ON TAPE....."
440 PRINT #-1,FY,Y,C$
450 FOR I=0TO10:PRINT #-1,YP(I):NEXT
460 PRINT"COMPLETE.....":FOR ZP=1TO120
    0:NEXT:GOTO320
470 PRINT"WHEN TAPE IS READY, PRESS EN
    TER";:INPUT X$
480 PRINT"INPUTTING FILE FROM TAPE....
    ."
490 INPUT #-1,FY,Y,C$
500 FOR I=0TO10:INPUT #-1,YP(I):NEXT
510 PRINT"NOW IN COMPUTER MEMORY, PRES
    S ENTER";:INPUT X$:GOTO320
550 CLS:PRINT
560 PRINT"END OF *** WHOSE CHART ***"
570 END
600 PRINT@64,"NOW YOU WILL ENTER THE P
    ROFIT PERCENTAGES"
610 PRINT"FOR EACH YEAR (IF LESS THAN
    10% - ENTER 0)"
620 FOR I=0TO(Y-F)
630 PRINT@192,"ENTER PERCENTAGE FOR ";
    FF;
640 INPUT YP(I):PRINT@218,"          "
645 IF YP(I)>100 PRINT@192,"ONLY UP TO
    AND INCLUDING 100%":FOR ZX=1TO12
    00:NEXT:GOTO630
650 IF YP(I)<10 YP(I)=0
660 FF=FF+1:NEXT
670 I=0
680 IF YP(I)=10 YP(I)=36:GOTO780
690 IF YP(I)>=11 AND YP(I)<=20 YP(I)=3
    3:GOTO780
700 IF YP(I)>=21 AND YP(I)<=30 YP(I)=3
    0:GOTO780
```

115

```
710 IF YP(I)>=31 AND YP(I)<=40 YP(I)=2
    7:GOTO780
720 IF YP(I)>=41 AND YP(I)<=50 YP(I)=2
    4:GOTO780
730 IF YP(I)>=51 AND YP(I)<=60 YP(I)=2
    1:GOTO780
740 IF YP(I)>=61 AND YP(I)<=70 YP(I)=1
    8:GOTO780
750 IF YP(I)>=71 AND YP(I)<=80 YP(I)=1
    5:GOTO780
760 IF YP(I)>=81 AND YP(I)<=90 YP(I)=1
    2:GOTO780
770 IF YP(I)>91 YP(I)=9
780 I=I+1:IF I<>11 THEN680
790 PRINT

800 PRINT"AFTER YOU ARE THROUGH LOOKIN
    G AT THE CHART"
810 PRINT"PRESS A KEY."
820 FOR ZP=1TO1200:NEXT
830 PRINT:PRINT"THANK YOU....."
840 FOR ZP=1TO1000:NEXT:GOTO80
850 REM SOME SIMPLE CHANGES AND YOU CO
    ULD
860 REM MAKE THIS A MONTHLY CHART
870 REM BUT DON'T EXCEED A 10 MONTH SP
    AN
880 REM UNLESS YOU MAKE SUITABLE CHANG
    ES
890 REM IN SET STATEMENTS ALONG WITH T
    HE

900 REM PRINT @ STATEMENTS
905 REM SEE FURTHER REM STATEMENTS LIN
    ES 1020-1060
910 CLS
920 PRINT@20,"** WHOSE CHART **"
930 PRINT
940 PRINT"THIS PROGRAM LET'S YOU CREAT
    E A GRAPH CHART"
950 PRINT"FOR ANY APPPLICATION YOU WIS
    H. IT WILL SHOW"
```

```
960 PRINT"YOU RISE OR DECLINE OF PROFI
      TS FOR A PERIOD OF"
970 PRINT"10 YEARS. ALL YOU DO IS ANSW
      ER THE NEEDED"
980 PRINT"INFORMATION AND THE COMPUTER
      WILL DO THE REST."
990 PRINT"YOU CAN FOLLOW THE INSTRUCTI
      ONS TO SAVE THAT"
1000 PRINT"CHART ON TAPE, LOAD A CHART
      FROM TAPE OR CREATE"
1010 PRINT"ANOTHER CHART."
1020 REM YOU CAN MAKE THIS A MONTHLY C
      HART BY CHANGING
1030 REM THE INPUT STATEMENTS AND FIXI
      NG LINES 120-210
1040 REM TO OUTPUT A STRING. ALSO, YOU
      WOULD HAVE TO CHANGE
1050 REM THE STATEMENTS THAT FEED INFO
      RMATION TO AND FROM
1060 REM THE RECORDER
1070 PRINT"PRESS ENTER TO SEE A LIST C
      OMMANDS.";:INPUT X
1080 CLS:GOTO55
```

ARCHITECT

This program will let you draw to your heart's content, using the video display as your drawing board.

Using 18 different key closures, singly and in combination, you can draw anything within the range of your computer. You can even experiment with some different keys and come up with other drawing combinations.

The key closures for drawing are picked up by the PEEK statement, line 550. Each time a key is closed (assuming it's in the argument) variable A will be changed to that PEEK number. Then the computer will seek out the argument for that particular closure. When no key is closed, variable A will equal 0 (zero) and the block will flash. See Fig. 6-3 for the flowchart.

Program Notes

All REM statements are contained within the program, so you'll know what is going on with each key closure. These REM statements can be deleted if you are short of memory space. You can also follow the REM statements and add a few functions of your own.

It's very simple...so start drawing!!

Program Listing

```
100 REM PROGRAM TITLE: ARCHITECT
105 CLS:PRINT
110 PRINTTAB(5),"A R C H I T E C T"
120 PRINT
130 PRINT"YOU ARE IN TOTAL CONTROL OF
    THE COMPUTER"
140 PRINT"WITH THIS PROGRAM. YOU CAN D
    RAW JUST ABOUT"
150 PRINT"ANYTHING (WITHIN THE RANGE O
    F THE COMPUTER)."
160 PRINT"ALL YOU HAVE TO DO IS PRESS
    THE RIGHT KEYS."
170 PRINT"THESE KEYS ARE AS FOLLOWS:"
180 PRINTTAB(2);"(";CHR$(91);") TO DRA
    W STRAIGHT UP."
190 PRINTTAB(2);"(";CHR$(92);") TO DRA
    W STRAIGHT DOWN."
200 PRINTTAB(2);"(";CHR$(93);") TO DRA
    W STRAIGHT LEFT."
210 PRINTTAB(2);"(";CHR$(94);") TO DRA
    W STRAIGHT RIGHT."
220 PRINT
230 PRINT"PRESS ENTER";:INPUT X
240 CLS:PRINT
250 PRINT"TO USE OTHER DRAWING EFFECTS
    , COMBINATION"
260 PRINT"KEYS WILL BE USED."
270 PRINTTAB(2);"("CHR$(91);" + ";CHR$
    (94);") TO MOVE UP, RIGHT, ON AN
    ANGLE."
280 PRINTTAB(2);"(";CHR$(92);" + ";CHR
    $(94);") TO MOVE DOWN, RIGHT, ON
    AN ANGLE."
290 PRINTTAB(2);"(";CHR$(91);" + ";CHR
    $(93);") TO MOVE UP, LEFT, ON AN
    ANGLE."
```

118

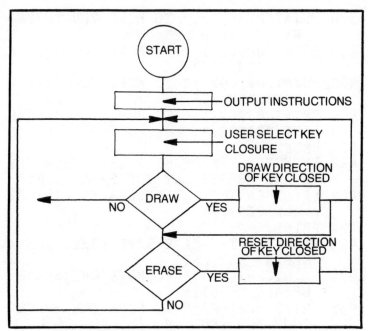

Fig. 6-3. Flowchart of Architect.

```
300 PRINTTAB(2);"(";CHR$(92);" + ";CHR
    $(93);") TO MOVE DOWN, LEFT, ON A
    N ANGLE."
310 PRINT
320 PRINT"ONLY USE THE ARROW KEYS, NOT
     THE + SIGN."
330 PRINT
335 PRINT"THE NEXT 8 FUNCTIONS WILL MO
    VE THE FLASHING BLOCK"
336 PRINT"AND NOT DRAW ANY LINES (SO Y
    OU CAN GET TO A CERTAIN"
337 PRINT"AREA ON THE VIDEO BEFORE DRA
    WING. ALSO THEY CAN"
338 PRINT"BE USED TO ERASE LINES ALREA
    DY DRAWN)."
340 PRINT"PRESS ENTER";::INPUT X
350 CLS
360 PRINT
370 PRINT"AT THE SAME TIME PRESS THE <
    SPACE BAR> AND"
```

119

```
380 PRINTCHR$(94);" TO MOVE TWO SPACES
       RIGHT AND RESET."
390 PRINTCHR$(91);" TO MOVE TO UPPER R
       IGHT CORNER."
400 PRINTCHR$(92);" TO MOVE TO LOWER R
       IGHT CORNER."
410 PRINTCHR$(93);" TO MOVE TO LOWER L
       EFT CORNER."
420 PRINT
422 PRINT"(NOTE: BE SURE THE BELOW KEY
       S ARE PRESSED AT THE SAME TIME"
423 PRINT"OR THE ENTIRE SCREEN WILL BE
       CLEARED)."
424 PRINT
425 PRINT"AT THE SAME TIME PRESS THE <
       CLEAR> KEY AND"
430 PRINTCHR$(91);" TO MOVE ONE SPACE
       UP AND RESET."
435 PRINTCHR$(92);" TO MOVE ONE SPACE
       DOWN AND RESET."
440 PRINTCHR$(93);" TO MOVE ONE SPACE
       LEFT AND RESET."
445 PRINTCHR$(94);" TO MOVE ONE SPACE
       RIGHT AND RESET."
450 PRINT"PRESS ENTER";:INPUT X
455 CLS:PRINT
460 PRINT"PRESS THE <CLEAR> KEY TO CLE
       AR SCREEN COMPLETELY"
465 PRINT"AND RETURN FLASHING BLOCK TO
       STARTING POINT."
470 PRINT
475 PRINT"PRESS <ENTER> TO RETURN FLAS
       HING BLOCK TO STARTING"
480 PRINT"POSITION AND NOT CLEAR WHAT'
       S ON THE SCREEN."
485 PRINT
490 PRINT"DON'T JUST SIT THERE, PRESS
       ENTER AND GET STARTED";
495 INPUT X
500 CLS
510 REM SET STARTING POINT
520 X=0:Y=0
```

```
530 SET(X,Y)
540 REM PEEK INTO HIGH END OF KEYBOARD
        MEMORY
550 A=PEEK(15340)
560 REM NO OPERATION - FLASH BLOCK
570 IF A=0 THEN 1020
580 REM RESTART AT (0,0) BY PRESSING E
        NTER DOES NOT CLEAR SCREEN
590 IF A=1 THEN510
600 REM SET AND MOVE UP
610 IF A=8 THEN Y=Y-1
620 REM MOVE ONE SPACE UP AND RESET
630 IF A=10 THEN Y=Y-1:RESET(X,Y+1)
640 REM SET AND MOVE DOWN
650 IF A=16 THEN Y=Y+1
660 REM MOVE ONE SPACE DOWN AND RESET
670 IF A=18 THEN Y=Y+1:RESET(X,Y-1)
680 REM MOVE TO UPPER RIGHT CORNER OF
        DISPLAY
690 IF A=136 THEN RESET(X,Y):Y=0:X=127
700 REM MOVE TO LOWER RIGHT CORNER OF
        DISPLAY
710 IF A=144 THEN RESET(X,Y):Y=47:X=12
        7
720 REM SET AND MOVE ONE SPACE RIGHT
730 IF A=32 THEN X=X-1
740 REM MOVE ONE SPACE LEFT AND RESET
750 IF A=34 THEN X=X-1:RESET(X+1,Y)
760 REM MOVE TO LOWER LEFT CORNER OF D
        ISPLAY
770 IF A=160 THEN RESET(X,Y):X=0:Y=47
780 REM MOVE ONE SPACE RIGHT AND SET
790 IF A=64 THEN X=X+1
800 REM MOVE ONE SPACE RIGHT AND RESET
810 IF A=66 THEN X=X+1:RESET(X-1,Y)
820 REM MOVE TWO SPACES RIGHT AND RESE
        T
830 IF A=192 THEN X=X+2:RESET(X-2,Y)
840 REM SET AND MOVE DOWN RIGHT
850 IF A=80 THEN X=X+1:Y=Y+1
860 REM SET AND MOVE UP RIGHT
```

```
870 IF A=72 THEN X=X+1:Y=Y-1
880 REM SET AND MOVE DOWN LEFT
890 IF A=48 THEN X=X-1:Y=Y+1
900 REM SET AND MOVE UP LEFT
910 IF A=40 THEN X=X-1:Y=Y-1
920 REM CLEAR SCREEN AND START OVER
930 IF A=2 THEN 500
940 REM CHECK POSITIONS BEFORE SETTING
        OR RESETTING
950 REM TO OVER RIDE ERROR
960 IF X<=0 X=0
970 IF X>=127 X=127
980 IF Y<=0 Y=0
990 IF Y>=47 Y=47
1000 REM NOW SET AND CONTINUE
1010 SET(X,Y):GOTO540
1020 REM FLASH BLOCK AND CONTINUE AT S
        AME POINT
1030 RESET(X,Y)
1040 FOR Q=1TO150:NEXT
1050 SET(X,Y)
1060 GOTO540
```

FILL YOUR GLASS

Everyone can fill a glass, right? But, have you tried to fill a computer glass lately? The computer's full graphics will help you throughout this program (Fig. 6-4).

The INKEY$ function lets you enter a fill amount. The fill amount you input can range from 001 to 999 (be sure to input leading zeros where necessary). The computer receives your input, doubles it, adds a random amount and begins to fill the glass slowly.

As your glass is filling, the fill amount (yours), elapsed time (seconds), the computer's total fill amount and total minutes elapsed will be printed. The best time to fill glass, believe it or not, is 5 minutes. If the contents reach the top rim of the glass and you must add another fill amount, you'll have to guess at where the contents are When the contents are at this point, it won't be long before they run over (maybe); if this happens, a spill-over will even be simulated.

As soon as the computer has finished with all the graphics the timing will start, so it might be wise to have a fill amount in your

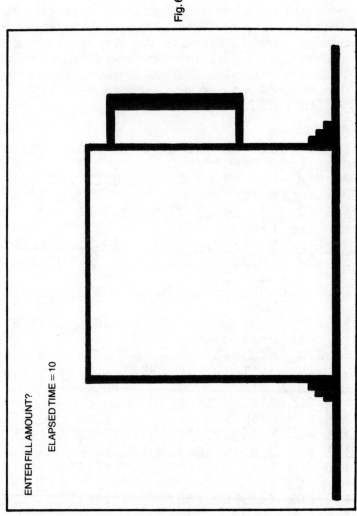

ENTER FILL AMOUNT?

ELAPSED TIME = 10

Fig. 6-4. Sample run of Fill Your Glass.

head before you start. Also, each time you are asked to enter a fill amount, the word enter will appear before fill amount and below enter will be an up-arrow, think fast and enter your amount. See Fig. 6-5 for the flowchart.

Program Notes

Unless you change half the program listing, there's no way you can cheat. The timing doesn't stop unless the computer is satisfied the glass is full. Study the program listing, you might find something you want to change. Add or delete a few lines of your choosing. If you decide to break-out a stopwatch to check the timing rate and discover some slight flaw, the timing rate is controlled at lines 232, 233 and 234. Also change the + amount at line 260. Timing is kept at line 260 for when the glass is filling. Timing is kept at lines 232, 233 and 234 for when the user is sitting there staring at the video, deciding on a fill amount.

DON'T RUN IT OVER!!!

Program Listing

```
10 REM THIS IS THE GAME OF FILL YOUR G
      LASS (MUG)
20 REM FULL GRAPHICS ARE USED AND BY F
      OLLOWING
30 REM THE REM STATEMENTS THROUGHOUT T
      HE PROGRAM
40 REM IT CAN BE CHANGED TO YOUR NEEDS
50 REM TIMING IN THIS GAME IS NOT PRES
      ICE BUT IT'S
60 REM CLOSE. FILLING OF THE GLASS WIL
      L SLOW DOWN
70 REM NEARING THE TOP BECAUSE OF THE
      ARGUMENTS
80 REM INVOLVED
90 REM DON'T TRY TO CHEAT - IT WON'T W
      ORK !!
100 CLS:RANDOM:GOSUB1000
105 REM DRAW BASE
110 FOR X=16320TO16383:POKE X,140:NEXT
115 REM NOW THE GLASS (MUG)
120 FOR Y=15TO45:SET(30,Y):SET(90,Y):N
      EXT
130 FOR X=30TO90:SET(X,15):NEXT
```

```
140 X=29:XX=91:XM=28:XN=92
150 FOR Y=43TO45:SET(X,Y):X=X-1:SET(XX
    ,Y):XX=XX+1
155 SET(XM,Y):XM=XM-1:SET(XN,Y):XN=XN+
    1:NEXT
160 FOR X=28TO29:SET(X,45):NEXT
170 FOR X=91TO93:SET(X,45):NEXT
180 SET(29,44):SET(91,44)
190 FOR Y=91TO99:SET(Y,17):SET(Y,33):N
    EXT
200 FOR Y=17TO33:SET(100,Y):SET(101,Y)
    :SET(102,Y):SET(103,Y):NEXT
210 REM NOW ENTER AMOUNTS
220 REM START AT BOTTOM - WORK TO TOP
225 XY=30:YY=90:M=45:ZX=0:T=0
230 PRINT@0,"ENTER FILL AMOUNT ?";
231 PRINT@66,CHR$(91);
232 A$=INKEY$:IF A$=""THEN PRINT@70,"E
    LAPSED TIME =";INT(T);:T=T+.1:GOT
    O232:ELSE V=VAL(A$):V=V*100
233 B$=INKEY$:IF B$=""THEN PRINT@70,"E
    LAPSED TIME =";INT(T);:T=T+.1:GOT
    O233:ELSE U=VAL(B$):U=U*10
234 C$=INKEY$:IF C$=""THEN PRINT@70,"E
    LAPSED TIME =";INT(T);:T=T+.1:GOT
    O234:ELSE W=VAL(C$)
235 A=W+U+V:REM A = USER FILL AMOUNT
236 PRINT@0,"       ";:PRINT@18,A;
240 REM R FOR COMPUTER TO DOUBLE A + R
    ANDOM AMOUNT
245 GOSUB600
250 R=((A+A)+CF):RX=R
255 ZX=0:REM START FILL LEFT SIDE
260 SET(XY,M):T=T+.2
265 PRINT@70,"ELAPSED TIME =";INT(T);:
    IF INT(T/60)>=1 THEN MN=INT(T/60)
    :PRINT@198,"TOTAL MINUTES =";MN;
268 REM XY FOR FILL MOVEMENT RIGHT
270 SET(XY+1,M):XY=XY+1
271 IF RX=1 RX=0:PRINT@66,CHR$(91);:EL
    SE PRINT@66,"  ";
```

```
272 PRINT@134,"COMPUTER'S TOTAL FILL A
    MOUNT =";RX;
274 REM KEEP CONTENTS OF GLASS WITHIN
    GLASS AREA
275 IF XY=YY THEN M=M-1:XY=30:GOTO260
278 REM ZX FOR TOTAL FILL PER INPUT +
    R
```

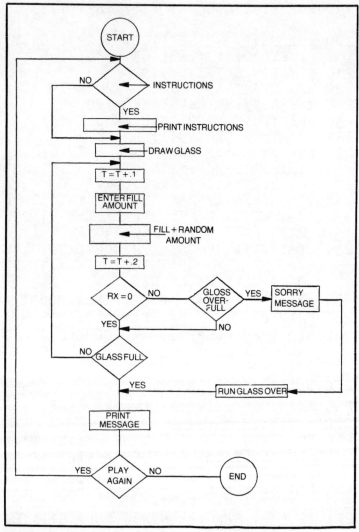

Fig. 6-5. Flowchart of Fill Your Glass.

```
280 ZX=ZX+1:RX=RX-1:IF ZX<>R AND M>=22
    THEN260
285 IF M=14THEN400:ELSE IF M=21 PRINT@
    275,"BETTER THAN HALF FULL !!";:E
    LSE IF M=>19 AND M<=20 PRINT@275,
    "ADJUST VIDEO BRIGHTNESS ";:ELSE
    PRINT@275,"
        ";
290 IF ZX<>R THEN260:ELSE IF M>=18 THE
    N300
295 IF POINT(89,17) AND XY=30 OR XY=89
    THEN500
300 PRINT@18,"      ";:GOTO230
400 PRINT@272,"YOU'VE RUN IT OVER, DUM
    MY !!!";
410 X=60:XS=45:XR=61:XL=60:XV=59
420 FOR Y=15TOXS:SET(X,Y):SET(XL,Y):XL
    =XL+1:X=X-1:NEXT
430 XR=XR-1:X=XR-1:XV=XV+1:XL=XV+1
440 IF XR<>37 THEN420
450 GOTO700
500 PRINT@277,"THAT'S EXCELLENT !!!";
510 IF MN>5 PRINT@0,"BUT YOU TOOK TO L
    ONG !!!";:GOTO530
515 IF MN=5 PRINT@0,"AND IN";MN;"MINUT
    ES !!";:GOTO530
520 IF MN<5 PRINT@0,"AND IN LESS THAN
    5 MINUTES !!!";
530 GOTO700
600 CA=RND(5)
610 ON CA GOTO 620,630,640,650,660
620 CF=RND(5):GOTO670
630 CF=RND(10):GOTO670
640 CF=RND(20):GOTO670
650 CF=RND(30):GOTO670
660 CF=RND(40)
670 RETURN
700 FOR I=1TO2000:NEXT
710 CLS
720 PRINTCHR$(23)
730 PRINT:PRINT:PRINT
740 PRINT"ARE YOU READY TO TRY"
```

127

```
750 PRINT"ANOTHER GLASS";
760 INPUT X$
770 IF X$="YES" THEN100
780 IF X$="NO" THEN800
790 PRINT"TRY ANOTHER ANSWER.....":GOT
    O700
800 PRINT
810 PRINT"FINGERS GOT TIRED, DID THEY
    ???"
820 FOR I=1TO1200:NEXT
830 CLS
840 PRINTCHR$(23)
850 PRINT:PRINT:PRINT
860 PRINT"* E N D   O F   P R O G R A M
    *"
870 GOTO870
1000 PRINTCHR$(23)
1010 PRINT"DO YOU REQUEST INSTRUCTIONS
     ";
1020 INPUT X$
1030 IF X$="NO" THEN CLS:RETURN
1040 CLS:PRINTCHR$(23)
1050 PRINT
1060 PRINT"THIS IS THE GAME OF"
1070 PRINT"FILL YOUR GLASS (MUG)."
1080 PRINT"SOUNDS SIMPLE, EVERYONE"
1090 PRINT"CAN FILL A GLASS. BUT HAVE"
1100 PRINT"YOU TIRED A COMPUTER'S GLAS
     S ?"
1110 PRINT
1120 PRINT"PRESS ENTER.....";
1130 INPUT X$:CLS
1140 PRINTCHR$(23)
1150 PRINT
1160 PRINT"THIS GLASS (MUG) WILL BE"
1170 PRINT"FILLED FROM BOTTOM TO TOP"
1180 PRINT"YOU WILL ENTER A FILL AMOUN
     T"
1190 PRINT"RANGING FROM 001 TO 999. BE
     "
1200 PRINT"SURE TO ENTER LEADING ZERO'
     S"
```

```
1210 PRINT"WHEN NECESSARY. THE COMPUTE
     R"
1220 PRINT"WILL TAKE YOUR AMOUNT"
1225 PRINT"AND DOUBLE IT THEN ADD"
1230 PRINT"A RANDOM AMOUNT, HENCE"
1240 PRINT"THE GLASS WILL BEGIN TO FIL
     L."
1250 PRINT
1260 PRINT"PRESS ENTER....."; 
1270 INPUT X$:CLS
1280 PRINTCHR$(23)
1290 PRINT
1300 PRINT"TOTAL TIME WILL BE KEPT, TH
     E"
1310 PRINT"BEST TIME FOR FILLING IS 5"
1320 PRINT"MINUTES. EVERYTIME YOU ARE"
1330 PRINT"ASKED TO <ENTER> A ";CHR$(9
     1)
1340 PRINT"WILL APPEAR BELOW THE WORD"
1350 PRINT"ENTER, THEN YOU WILL INPUT"
1360 PRINT"YOUR AMOUNT. THE GAME IS"
1370 PRINT"COMPLETE WHEN THE GLASS IS"
1375 PRINT"FULL OR IT RUNS OVER....."
1380 PRINT
1390 PRINT"PRESS ENTER TO BEGIN......"
     ;
1400 INPUT X$
1410 CLS:RETURN
```

VIEWER

This program was written and designed specifically with the beginner in mind. It will increase your understanding of the SET, PRINT@, STRING$ and POKE functions.

The first part of the program draws squares using the SET/RESET statements. POKEing the squares is next, to illustrate the difference in execution speed between the two techniques. Then the squares are drawn at top speed (in my opinion) using PRINT@, STRING$ and POKE.

Finally the conclusion of the program lets the computer print its garbage all over the video screen. To end the garbage (and program) hold down the space bar. See Fig. 6-6 for the flowchart.

Program Notes

After you become familiar with the different statements you can experiment with the foundation of the program and create designs of your choosing. Be very careful to enter the POKE statements as they should be; it only takes one mis-keyed number to wreck an entire program.

Program Listing

```
100 REM PROGRAM TITLE: VIEWER
110 REM OR 'SIT BACK AND WATCH'. IT WI
    LL
120 REM SHOW YOU DIFFERENT PATTERNS YO
    UR
130 REM TRS-80 CAN MAKE. YOU CAN IN FA
    CT
140 REM EXPERIMENT WITH THE DIFFERENT
    LINES
150 REM A COME UP WITH A FEW OF YOUR O
    WN
160 REM THIS PROGRAM IS JUST LAYING TH
    E
170 REM FOUNDATION
180 GOSUB1750:REM INSTRUCTIONS
240 REM SET SOME VARIABLES
250 X=0:Y=0:P=47:Q=127:GM=526:RANDOM
260 REM NOW SOME GRAPHICS
270 CLS:A=1
280 PRINT@GM,"GRAPHIC DISPLAY USING TH
    E SET STATEMENT"
285 GOSUB290:GOTO300
290 FOR JJ=1TO1500:NEXT:RETURN
300 CLS
340 REM SET AREA WILL BE LARGE SQUARES
350 FOR XX=XTOP:SET(X,XX):SET(Q,XX):NE
    XT
360 FOR YY=YTOQ:SET(YY,Y):SET(YY,P):NE
    XT
370 X=X+2:Y=Y+2:P=P-2:Q=Q-2
380 IF Y<>P-3 THEN350
390 A$="NOW FOR A REVERSE"
400 REM COMPUTER WILL PRINT A$ ONE
```

```
410 REM LETTER A A TIME
420 B=GM+10:L=1
440 PRINT@B,MID$(A$,L,1);
450 B=B+1:L=L+1
460 IF L<>LEN(A$)+1THEN FOR LL=1TO150:
    NEXT:GOTO440
465 GOSUB290:CLS:REM REVERSE THE SQUAR
    ES
470 FOR XX=PTOXSTEP-1:SET(X,XX):SET(Q,
    XX):NEXT
480 FOR YY=QTOYSTEP-1:SET(YY,Y):SET(YY
    ,P):NEXT
490 X=X-2:Y=Y-2:P=P+2:Q=Q+2
500 IF X<>0 THEN470
510 GOSUB290
520 CLS:PRINT
530 PRINT"YOU COULD DO ALMOST THE SAME
     THING BUT 'POKE IT'"
540 PRINT"WHICH WOULD SPEED THE GRAPHI
    CS BY A FACTOR"
550 PRINT"OF 6, LET'S TRY IT."
560 GOSUB570:GOTO580
570 FOR JJ=1TO2500:NEXT:CLS:RETURN
580 REM POKE THE SQUARES
590 A=15361:B=15422
600 C=15360:D=16256
610 E=15423:F=16319
620 G=16320:H=16383
630 I=131:J=191
640 FOR X=ATOB:POKE X,I:NEXT
650 FOR X=GTOH:POKE X,I:NEXT
660 FOR X=CTODSTEP64:POKE X,J:NEXT
670 FOR X=ETOFSTEP64:POKE X,J:NEXT
680 IF H=15921 THEN710
690 C=C+66:D=D-62:E=E+62:F=F-64:A=A+66
    :B=B+62:G=G-62:H=H-66
700 GOTO640
710 REM NOW REVERSE THE SQUARES
720 GOSUB570
730 PRINT@GM+10,A$;
740 GOSUB570:F=15857:E=F
```

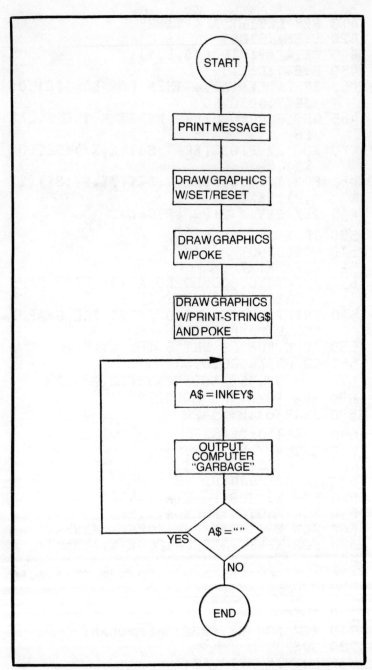

Fig. 6-6. Flowchart of Viewer.

```
750 FOR X=DTOCSTEP-64:POKE X,J:NEXT
760 FOR X=FTOESTEP-64:POKE X,J:NEXT
770 FOR X=BTOASTEP-1:POKE X,I:NEXT
780 FOR X=HTOGSTEP-1:POKE X,I:NEXT
790 IF G=16320 THEN820
800 C=C-66:D=D+62:E=E-62:F=F+66:A=A-66
    :B=B-62:G=G+62:H=H+66
810 GOTO750
820 GOSUB570
830 PRINT:PRINT
840 PRINT"AND IF THAT WASN'T FAST ENOU
    GH, YOU CAN USE"
850 PRINT"THE PRINT ` STATEMENT AND TH
    E STRINGS STATEMENT,"
855 PRINT"ALONG WITH THE POKE STATEMEN
    T."
860 PRINT"YOU WILL HAVE TOP SPEED OF E
    XECUTION."
870 PRINT"THE HORZONTAL BARS WILL USE
    PRINT @ AND STRINGS,"
880 PRINT"WHERE AS THE VERTICAL BARS W
    ILL BE POKED."
900 PRINT
910 PRINT"PRESS ENTER.....";
915 CLEAR 1000:I=131:J=191
920 INPUT X$:CLS
930 Y=63:H$=STRING$(Y,I):V$=STRING$(Y,
    I)
940 A=0:B=66:C=132:D=198:E=264:F=330:G
    =396:H=462:K=526:AA=960:BB=898:CC
    =836:DD=774:EE=712:FF=650:GG=588:
    AB=15360:AC=16256:AD=15422:AE=163
    18
945 REM GOSUB2100 IS THE POKE STATEMEN
    T
950 PRINT@A,H$;:PRINT@AA,V$;:GOSUB2100
    :GOSUB2000
960 PRINT@B,H$;:PRINT@BB,V$;:GOSUB2100
    :GOSUB2000
970 PRINT@C,H$;:PRINT@CC,V$;:GOSUB2100
    :GOSUB2000
```

133

```
980  PRINT@D,H$;:PRINT@DD,V$;:GOSUB2100
     :GOSUB2000
990  PRINT@E,H$;:PRINT@EE,V$;:GOSUB2100
     :GOSUB2000
1000 PRINT@F,H$;:PRINT@FF,V$;:GOSUB210
     0:GOSUB2000
1010 PRINT@G,H$;:PRINT@GG,V$;:GOSUB210
     0:GOSUB2000
1020 PRINT@H,H$;
1030 PRINT@K,H$;:GOSUB2000
1040 PRINT@462,CHR$(J);:PRINT@496,CHR$
     (J);
1045 IF POINT(0,0)=0 THEN FOR JJ=1TO10
     0:NEXT:CLS:GOTO1190
1050 GOSUB570
1060 PRINT:PRINT
1070 PRINT"WAS THAT FAST ENOUGH ?"
1080 PRINT"IF NOT YOU'LL HAVE TO REVER
     T TO MACHINE LANGUAGE,"
1090 PRINT"AND THAT IS NOT COVERED HER
     E."
1100 PRINT
1110 PRINT"NOW, WE'LL ADD A LITTLE ANI
     MATION TO THE SAME PROGRAM"
1120 PRINT"WITH JUST ONE ADDITION TO I
     T, INSERTING A 'CLS' STATEMENT"
1130 PRINT"BETWEEN THE DRAWING OF THE
     SQUARES."
1140 PRINT
1150 PRINT"PRESS ENTER";
1160 INPUT X$
1170 R=1
1180 CLS:GOTO930
1190 GOSUB570
1200 PRINT:PRINT
1210 PRINT"BY USING 'POKE' TO SET UP Y
     OUR GRAPHICS YOU CAN"
1220 PRINT"OBTAIN JUST ABOUT ANY DISPL
     AY DESIRED. USING THE"
1230 PRINT"ALPHABET OR NUMBERS OR BLOC
     K AREAS OR A COMBINATION"
1240 PRINT"OF ALL THREE."
```

```
1245 PRINT"(NOTE: 'POKE' MEANING TO PO
     KE AT LOCATIONS IN THE"
1246 PRINT"VIDEO MEMORY, WHERE THE ACT
     UAL PRINTING WILL USE"
1247 PRINT"THE CHR$ STATEMENT)."
1250 PRINT
1260 PRINT"SELECT ONE:"
1270 PRINT"(A) CHARACTERS/LETTERS/NUMB
     ERS"
1280 PRINT"(B) GRAPHIC BLOCKS"
1290 INPUT X$:CLS
1300 IF X$="A" THEN C=33:CC=94:GOTO133
     0
1310 IF X$="B" THEN C=129:CC=191:GOTO1
     330
1320 PRINT:PRINT"TRY TO ANSWER WITH WH
     AT WAS ASKED OF YOU !!!":PRINT:GO
     TO1250
1330 AB=15360:AC=16256:AD=15422:AE=163
     18:IF R=1 THEN1350
1340 CLS
1350 FOR X=ABTOACSTEP64:POKE X,C:NEXT
1360 FOR X=ADTOAESTEP64:POKE X,C+1:NEX
     T
1370 GOSUB2020
1380 C=C+1
1390 IF AB=15888 THEN R=1:GOSUB570:GOT
     O1330
1400 IF C<>CC THEN1350
1420 GOSUB570
1430 PRINT:PRINT
1440 PRINT"THIS IS ONLY A PART OF WHAT
     YOUR COMPUTER"
1450 PRINT"IS CAPABLE OF DOING. WITH A
     LITTLE PRACTICE"
1460 PRINT"YOU CAN INVENT  NUMEROUS GR
     APHIC DISPLAYS THAT"
1470 PRINT"WILL JOG THE MIND."
1480 PRINT
1490 PRINT"SO WITH CLOSING OF THIS PRO
     GRAM YOUR COMPUTER"
```

135

```
1500 PRINT"WILL DO THE PRINTING. ANYTI
     ME YOU WANT TO STOP"
1510 PRINT"JUST HOLD DOWN THE <SPACE B
     AR>."
1520 PRINT
1530 PRINT"PRESS ENTER";
1540 INPUT X$:CLS
1550 A$=INKEY$
1560 IF A$=" "THEN1670
1570 A=RND(94):IF A<=31 THEN 1570:ELSE
      IF A=32 THEN CLS
1575 AA=RND(40)
1580 P=RND(960)
1590 FOR X=15360TO16383 STEPAA
1595 A=RND(94):IF A<=32 THEN1595

1600 PRINT@P,CHR$(A+1);
1610 POKE X,A:NEXT:CLS
1615 A=RND(94):IF A<=32 THEN1615
1620 FOR X=16383TO15360STEP-AA
1625 AA=RND(25)
1630 P=RND(960)
1640 PRINT@P,CHR$(A+3);:FOR J=1TO10:NE
     XT J:PRINTCHR$(23)
1645 A=RND(94):IF A<=32 THEN1645
1650 POKE X,A:NEXT
1655 IF AA<=10 AND AA>=20 THEN CLS
1660 GOTO1550
1670 REM END PROGRAM
1680 CLS:PRINT:PRINT
1690 PRINT"SO LONG FOR NOW....."

1700 END
1750 CLS:PRINT:PRINT
1760 PRINT"THIS PROGRAM IS CALLED VIEW
     ER BECAUSE OF THE"
1770 PRINT""FACT THAT ALL YOU HAVE TO
      DO IS WATCH THE"
1780 PRINT"VIDEO. IT WILL HELP YOU BET
     TER UNDERSTAND THE"
1790 PRINT"DIFFERENCE BETWEEN SET, PRI
     NT@, AND POKE. YOU CAN"
```

136

```
1800 PRINT"EXPERIMENT WITH THE PROGRAM
        TO MAKE DESIGNS OF"
1810 PRINT"YOUR OWN. JUST KEEP IN MIND
        THE POKE STATEMENTS."
1820 PRINT"BE COMPLETELY SURE YOU KNOW
        WHERE YOU'RE POKING"
1830 PRINT"IF YOUR NOT ADD <STOP> STAT
        EMENTS WITHIN YOUR"
1840 PRINT"PROGRAM, AS IT WILL BE FAR
        EASIER TO DELETE A"
1850 PRINT"<STOP> STATEMENT THAN HAVE
        TO 'POWER UP' AGAIN"
1860 PRINT"AND TRY TO FIGURE WHERE YOU
        WERE AT WHEN THE"
1870 PRINT"COMPUTER WENT BERSERK."
1880 PRINT
1890 INPUT"PRESS ENTER";X$
1900 CLS:RETURN
2000 HH=LEN(H$):HH=HH-4
2010 H$=STRING$(HH,I):V$=STRING$(HH,I)
2020 AB=AB+66:AC=AC-62:AD=AD+62:AE=AE-
        64
2030 RETURN
2100 FOR X=ABTOACSTEP64:POKE X,J:NEXT
2150 FOR X=ADTOAESTEP64:POKE X,J:NEXT
2200 IF R=1 THEN FOR JJ=1TO100:NEXT:CL
        S:RETURN
2250 RETURN
```

PLACE THE BOX

This program will give you the feel of computer animation. You will be moving a box around the video screen, guiding it to a section marked 1 or 2 (Fig. 6-7). The box can be placed in either section as long as it's centered and it matches the computer's choice.

Anytime you hit an obstacle going through the course, ERROR will flash on the screen, and you'll have to try it over again.

Keys that will be used are:

↓ to move the box down.

< to move the box left.

> to move the box right.

And pressing the space bar stops movement of the box. Be sure to use the SHIFT key when pressing the < > keys.

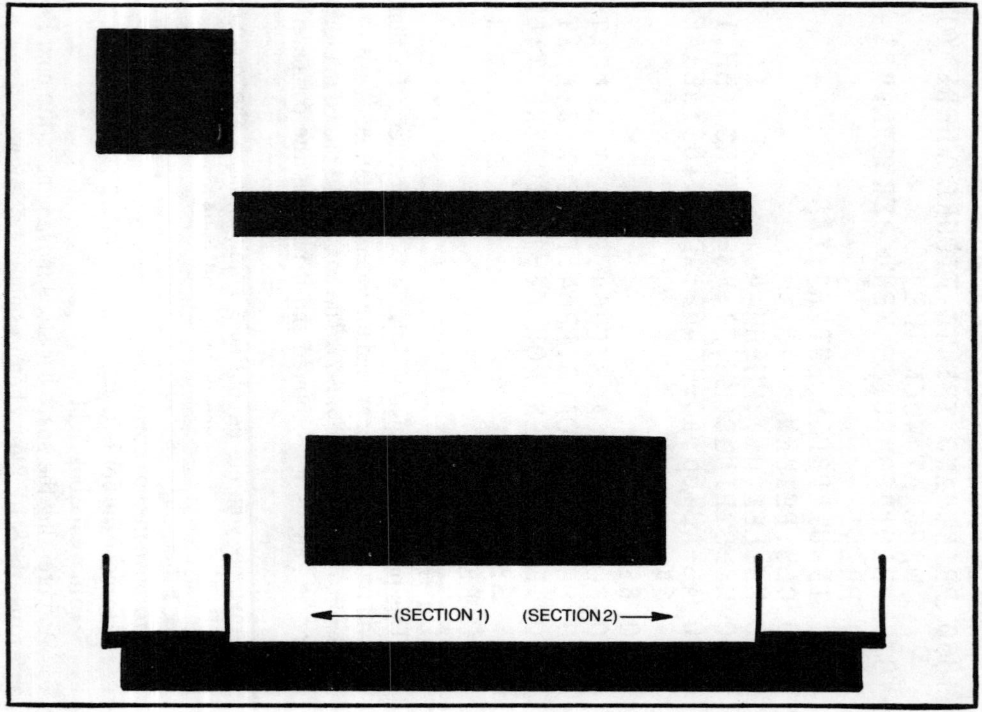

Fig. 6-7. Sample run of Place the Box.

(SECTION 1)

(SECTION 2)

If you lose control of the box at any point (running off the video) the computer will stop it and give you another ERROR.

So remember, the object of the game is to guide the box around all the obstacles and place it in section 1 or 2. The box must be guided exactly between the two vertical bars, into section 1 or 2. See Fig. 6-8 for the flowchart.

Program Notes

You can add some more spice to this game by adding more obstacles. For example every time the player encounters an ERROR another obstacle could be added to the course. The bar at the bottom center of the video screen could be deleted and 2 more sections could be added, making it more difficult for the user to decide on a section to choose.

Be very careful when entering the POKE addresses contained within this program. One number out of place will send the computer into a world of its own.

Program Listing

```
50 REM PROGRAM TITLE: PLACE THE BOX
90 GOSUB2100
100 CLS:ER=0:PL=0:RANDOM
105 A=RND(2)
110 L$=CHR$(191):U=16020:UU=16045:VU=1
    6084:UV=16109:VF=16148:FV=16173:U
    X=916:XU=930:DM=200
112 CLS:FOR X=0TO9:PRINT@X,L$;:NEXT:N=
    143:J=191
120 FOR X=64TO73:PRINT@X,L$;:NEXT
125 FOR X=128TO137:PRINT@X,L$;:NEXT
130 FOR X=15626TO15668:POKE X,N:NEXT
135 FOR X=16321TO16381:POKE X,N:NEXT
138 GOSUB800
140 X=0:Y=64:Z=128:XX=X+10:YY=Y+10:ZZ=
    Z+10
145 A$=INKEY$
146 IF A$=CHR$(62)THEN150
147 IF A$=CHR$(60)THEN300
148 IF PEEK(15359)=16THEN400
149 GOTO145
150 PRINT@XX,L$;:PRINT@X," ";
155 PRINT@YY,L$;:PRINT@Y," ";
```

```
160 PRINT@ZZ,L$;:PRINT@Z," ";
164 IF PEEK(U)+PEEK(VU)+PEEK(VF)<>573
    THEN GOSUB700:GOTO112:ELSE IF PEE
    K(UU)+PEEK(UV)<>382 THEN GOSUB700
```

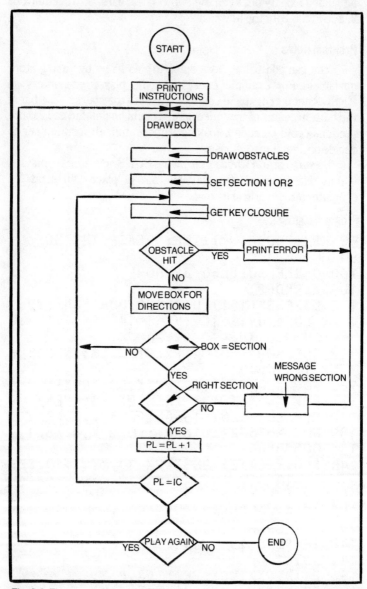

Fig. 6-8. Flowchart of Place the Box.

```
      :GOTO112:REM THESE PEEK ADDRESSES
       CONTAIN THE CODE 191 FOR ALL BIT
       S ON
165   X=X+1:XX=XX+1
170   Y=Y+1:YY=YY+1
180   Z=Z+1:ZZ=ZZ+1
185   IF XX>=65 AND XX<=70 THEN GOSUB700
       :GOTO112
190   A=RND(2):A$=INKEY$
200   IF A$<>" "THEN150:ELSE 145
300   REM LEFT MOVEMENT
305   IF X<=0 OR XX<=0 THEN145
310   PRINT@X,L$;:PRINT@XX," ";
320   PRINT@Y,L$;:PRINT@YY," ";
330   PRINT@Z,L$;:PRINT@ZZ," ";
335   IF PEEK(UU)+PEEK(UV)+PEEK(FV)<>573
       THEN GOSUB700:GOTO112:ELSE IF PE
       EK(UU)+PEEK(UV)<>382 THEN GOSUB70
       0:GOTO112:REM THESE PEEK ADDRESSE
       S CONTAIN THE CODE 191 FOR ALL BI
       TS ON
340   X=X-1:XX=XX-1
350   Y=Y-1:YY=YY-1
360   Z=Z-1:ZZ=ZZ-1
370   A=RND(2):A$=INKEY$
380   IF A$<>" "THEN305:ELSE 145
400   REM BOX MOVEMENT - DOWN
405   IF X>=768 AND X<=959 THEN GOSUB600
       :GOSUB610:GOSUB620:GOSUB950:GOTO1
       12
410   GOSUB600:X=X+192:XX=X+10
415   FOR D=XTOXX-1:PRINT@D,L$;:NEXT
420   GOSUB610:Y=X+64:YY=Y+10
425   FOR D=YTOYY-1:PRINT@D,L$;:NEXT:IF
       Y>=256 AND Y<=309 THEN GOSUB700:G
       OTO112
430   GOSUB620:Z=Y+64:ZZ=Z+10
435   FOR D=ZTOZZ-1:PRINT@D,L$;:NEXT
440   IF A=1 AND POINT(1,G)+POINT(19,G)=
       -2 THEN 2000:ELSE IF POINT(1,G)+P
       OINT(19,G)=-2 AND A<>1 THEN GOSUB
       900:GOTO112
```

141

```
450 IF A=2 AND POINT(107,G)+POINT(125,
    G)=-2 THEN 2000:ELSE IF POINT(107
    ,G)+POINT(125,G)=-2 AND A<>2 THEN
    GOSUB900:GOTO112
500 IF DM=1 THEN505:ELSE FOR JK=1TODM:
    NEXT
505 A=RND(2):A$=INKEY$
510 IF A$<>" "THEN405:ELSE 145
600 FOR D=XTOXX-1:PRINT@D," ";:NEXT:R
    ETURN
610 FOR D=YTOYY-1:PRINT@D," ";:NEXT:R
    ETURN
620 FOR D=ZTOZZ-1:PRINT@D," ";:NEXT:R
    ETURN
700 K=0
710 PRINT@280," E R R O R ";:FOR CV=1T
    O100:NEXT
720 PRINT@280,"              ";:FOR CV=1T
    O50:NEXT
730 K=K+1:FOR CV=1TO150:NEXT
740 IF K<>5 THEN710
750 U=U-2:UU=UU+2:VU=VU-2:UV=UV+2:VF=V
    F-2:FV=FV+2:UX=UX-2:XU=XU+2
760 IF DM<=0 DM=1:ELSE DM=DM-50
780 ER=ER+1:RETURN
790 REM LINE 750 TO DECREASE OPEN SPAC
    E - LINE 760 TO INCREASE DOWN MOV
    EMENT
800 REM THIS GOSUB INCREASES THE SIZE
    OF THE BLOCK AREA
801 REM BOTTOM - MIDDLE OF VIDEO - TO
    INCREASE LEVEL OF
802 REM DIFFICULTY FOR EACH ERROR MADE
804 REM BLOCK AREA REMAINS WHEN UU=160
    51 (TO LEAVE ROOM FOR BOX PLACEME
    NT)
805 IF UX<=908 THEN UX=907:XU=936
810 IF UU>=16051 THEN UU=16052:U=16010
815 FOR X=UTOUU:POKE X,J:NEXT
816 IF UV>=16115 THEN UV=16116:VU=1607
    4
```

142

```
818 FOR X=VUTOUV:POKE X,J:NEXT
819 IF FV>=16179 THEN FV=16180:VF=1613
    8
820 FOR X=VFTOFV:POKE X,J:NEXT
825 FOR BN=16256TO16265:POKE BN,176:NE
    XT
826 FOR BN=16309TO16318:POKE BN,176:NE
    XT
827 FOR G=39TO44:SET(0,G):SET(20,G):SE
    T(106,G):SET(126,G):NEXT
830 PRINT@UX,CHR$(93);"(SECTION 1)";
840 PRINT@XU,"(SECTION 2)";CHR$(94);
850 G=G-2
860 RETURN
900 GOSUB700:PRINT@275," W R O N G  S
     E C T I O N ";
905 REM MESSAGE FOR PLACING BOX IN WRO
    NG SECTION
910 FOR JK=1TO1000:NEXT
920 REM ERROR VALID THIS MOVE
930 CLS
940 RETURN
950 REM BOX NOT CENTERED IN SECTION CO
    RRECTLY
960 REM ERROR NOT VALID FOR THIS MOVE
970 PRINT@272," B O X  N O T  C E N T
     E R E D ":
980 FOR JK=1TO1000:NEXT
990 CLS
1000 RETURN
2000 PRINT@334," C O N G R A T U L A T
      I O N S ! ! ";
2010 PRINT@398,;
2020 IF ER<=5 THEN2040
2030 PRINT" BUT YOU DID MAKE";ER;"ERRO
     RS.....";:GOTO2050
2040 PRINT" WITH ONLY";ER;"ERRORS, THA
     T'S GREAT !!";
2045 PL=PL+1:IF PL<>11THEN PRINT@463,"
     THAT'S PLACEMENT #";PL;:FOR JK=1T
     O1500:NEXT:GOTO0112
2050 PRINT@463,;
```

143

```
2060 INPUT"READY TO TRY AGAIN";A$
2070 IF A$="YES"THEN100
2080 PRINT@527,"END OF PROGRAM....."
2090 END
2100 CLS
2110 PRINT
2120 PRINTTAB(5)," P L A C E   T H E   B
       O X"
2130 PRINT
2140 PRINT"THIS GAME USES VIDEO ANIMAT
       ION MOVING A BOX."
2150 PRINT"THE KEYS YOU WILL BE USING
       ARE:"
2160 PRINTCHR$(92);" TO MOVE THE BOX D
       OWNWARD."
2170 PRINTCHR$(60);" TO MOVE THE BOX L
       EFT."
2180 PRINTCHR$(62);" TO MOVE THE BOX R
       IGHT."
2190 PRINT"AND THE SPACE BAR TO STOP M
       OVEMENT OF THE BOX."
2200 PRINT"(NOTE: BE SURE TO USE THE '
       SHIFT' KEY WHEN"
2210 PRINT"PRESSING THE ";CHR$(60) ;"
       "; CHR$(62);" KEYS)."
2220 PRINT
2230 PRINT"PRESS A KEY....."
2240 A$=INKEY$:IF A$=""THEN2240
2250 CLS:PRINT
2260 PRINT"TRYING NOT TO HIT ANYTHING
       YOU WILL MOVE THIS"
2270 PRINT"BOX DOWN (STARTING POSITION
        IS UPPER LEFT CORNER)"
2280 PRINT"AND PLACE IT IN EITHER SECT
       ION 1 OR SECTION 2, THE"
2290 PRINT"CHOICE IS YOURS, BUT YOU MU
       ST MATCH THE COMPUTER"
2300 PRINT"IF YOU DON'T YOU'LL HAVE TO
        TRY AGAIN."
2310 PRINT"REMEMBER, THE BOX MUST FIT
       PERFECTLY WITHIN THE"
```

```
2320 PRINT"TWO VERTICAL BARS AT SECTIO
     N 1 OR SECTION 2."
2330 PRINT"(NOTE: THE HORIZONTAL BARS
     AT THE TOP AND BOTTOM"
2340 PRINT"OF THE VIDEO ARE OBSTACALS
     YOU MUST GO AROUND,"
2345 PRINT"TOTAL GAME IS 10 BOXES BEIN
     G PLACED IN THE RACKS)."
2350 PRINT
2360 PRINT"PRESS A KEY TO BEGIN....."
2370 A$=INKEY$:IF A$=""THEN2370
2380 RETURN
```

Chapter 7
Thought and Mind Provoking

LOGIC DEDUCTION

A number game pits you against the computer logic. The suprising part is, the lowest score wins. You'll use a total of 54 numbers that range from only 1 through 9. The object is for you to get the computer to draw over 9 (block positions added together). The computer will also be trying to get you to do the same thing. Each time you or the computer go over 9 (blocks selected) that amount goes on your total score (Fig. 7-1).

The game ends when all 54 numbers have been used. Each number comes from a set containing 6 of each number between one and nine. See Fig. 7-2 for the flowchart.

Program Notes

Lines 100-190 provide the graphics for the numbers.

Lines 200-245 set print@ areas for numbers.

Lines 260 set N(I) for 54 numbers while variable Q divides the total by 6 (for 6 sets of 1 through 9).

Lines 270-320 draw a random number, then delete it.

Lines 500-595 draw the first eight numbers.

Lines 635-650 select who will go first - you or the computer.

Lines 660-745 are your turn, if the computer has played (total 9) PI=2 will branch user's input to correct lines.

Lines 800-848 are arguments for the computer to use in determining which number(s) if any, will total 9.

Lines 850-900 blank the computer's numbers and set variable R, so that the drawn numbers will be located at the right squares.

Lines 1100-1145 blank your numbers and draw another amount of numbers equal to those used.

Lines 1150-1205 draw numbers for computer and place them at right PRINT@ areas.

Line 1208 changes variable PI to 2 so that you will have to use the same positions the computer used.

Lines 1250-1320 add the amount of computer numbers that had to be used (up to 9).

Lines 1325-1405 notify you if you don't use the same locations that the computer used (total 9).

Lines 1425-1460 draw two numbers if neither you nor the computer can play. Variable BB will equal two.

Lines 1500-1540 use variable R and variables D1 through D4 to use against your input (if computer had a total of 9).

Lines 1550-1815 are closing messages and instructions.

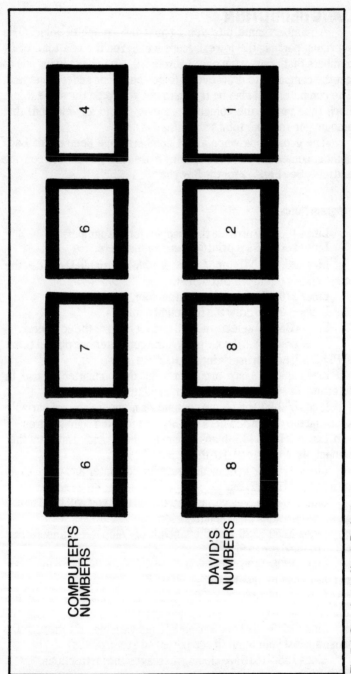

COMPUTER'S
NUMBERS

| 6 | 7 | 6 | 4 |

DAVID'S
NUMBERS

| 8 | 8 | 2 | 1 |

Fig. 7-1. Sample run of Logic Deduction.

Program Listing

```
10 REM PROGRAM TITLE: LOGIC DEDUCTION
20 CLS:DEFINT S,W:DIM N(55)
30 RANDOM:GOSUB1620:GOTO350
100 REM SET SQUARE AREAS FOR NUMBERS
110 X=22:XX=105:V=40
120 FOR M=XTOXX:SET(M,0):SET(M,7):SET(
    M,12):SET(M,19)
130 IF M=V THEN M=M+4:V=V+22
140 NEXT
150 X=22:XX=40:I=1
160 FOR M=0TO7:SET(X,M):SET(XX,M):NEXT
170 FOR N=12TO19:SET(X,N):SET(XX,N):NE
    XT
180 X=XX+4:XX=XX+22:I=I+1
190 IF I<>5 THEN160
200 REM NUMBER LOCATIONS (PRINT @)
210 A=78:Z=334:J=1
220 A(J)=A:Z(J)=Z
230 A=A+11:Z=Z+11:J=J+1
240 IF J<>5 THEN220
245 A(J)=64:Z(J)=320:A(J+1)=523:RETURN
250 REM NUMBERS -- SIX SETS -- 1 THROU
    GH 9
260 FOR I=1TO54:N(I)=I:NEXT:Q=(I-1)/6:
    G=6:RETURN
270 U=RND(54)
280 IF N(U)=0 THEN 270:REM DRAW NUMBER
    ONLY ONCE
290 S=(N(U)-1)/Q
300 W=N(U)-S*Q
310 N(U)=0
320 RETURN
350 CLS
360 PRINT"ENTER YOUR FIRST NAME (IF GR
    EATER THAN 8 LETTERS"
370 PRINT""JUST ENTER YOUR FIRST AND LA:
    ST INITIALS";
380 INPUT N$
390 C$="COMPUTER":NU$="NUMBERS":T$="
    TURN ":CLS:GOSUB100
```

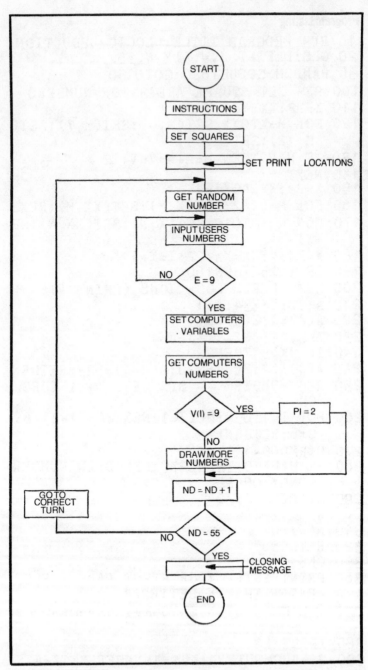

Fig. 7-2. Flowchart of Logic Deduction.

150

```
400 PRINT@0,C$;"'S";:PRINT@A(5),NU$;:P
    RINT@256,N$;"'S";:PRINT@Z(5),NU$;
410 GOSUB260
500 REM SELECT 8 RANDOM NUMBERS
510 I=1
520 GOSUB270
530 PRINT@A(I),W;:V(I)=W
540 I=I+1:IF I<>5 THEN520
545 ND=I+ND
550 REM NUMBERS FOR USER
560 I=1
570 GOSUB270
580 PRINT@Z(I),W;:X(I)=W
590 I=I+1:IF I<>5 THEN570
595 ND=I+(ND-2)
600 REM FIRST PLAYER
610 GOSUB1000
620 PRINT"HIGHEST NUMBER IN FIRST POSI
    TION GOES FIRST."
630 GOSUB1050
635 I=1
640 IF ABS(V(I)-X(I))=0 THEN I=I+1:GOT
    O640
645 IF V(I)>X(I) PRINT@A(G-1),T$;:GOSU
    B1000:GOSUB1050:GOTO655
650 IF V(I)<X(I) PRINT@Z(G-1),T$;:GOSU
    B1000:GOSUB1050:GOTO660
655 GOTO800:REM GOTO COMPUTER PLAY
660 REM USERS TURN
665 GOSUB1000:IF PI=2 THEN I=1:E=0:GOT
    O690:ELSE IF ND>12 THEN I=1:E=0:G
    OTO690
670 PRINT"SUM OF YOUR NUMBERS SHOULD N
    OT EXCEED 9."
675 GOSUB1050:GOSUB1000:I=1:E=0
680 PRINT"TO EXECUTE YOUR PLAY, ENTER
    0 FOR A NUMBER.":GOSUB1050.
682 GOSUB1000:PRINT"IF UNABLE TO PLAY,
    ENTER 99.":GOSUB1050
685 GOSUB1000
690 PRINT""ENTER THE NUMBER BY ITS PLA
    CEMENT 1-4" ;
```

151

```
691 IF PI=2 GOSUB1050
692 IF PI=2 GOSUB1000:PRINT"YOUR INPUT
     MUST MATCH THE COMPUTER'S";:GOTO
     1325
695 INPUT Y:IF Y=0 THEN 715 ELSE IF Y=
     99 PI=0:BB=BB+1:IF BB=2 BB=0:GOSU
     B1425:GOTO800:ELSE GOTO800
700 ZZ(I)=X(Y):MN(I)=Y
705 I=I+1:IF PI=2 THEN692:ELSE GOTO685
715 FOR J=1TOI:E=ZZ(J)+E:NEXT
718 IF PI=2 GOTO1410
720 IF E<>9 THEN730
725 GOSUB1000:PRINT"                EXC
     ELLENT !!!":BB=0:PI=1:XI=I:GOSUB1
     050:GOTO1100
730 GOSUB1000
735 PRINT"WE'RE LOOKING FOR A TOTAL OF
      9...REMEMBER ??"
740 GOSUB1050
745 FOR I=1TO4:ZZ(I)=0:NEXT:E=0:GOTO68
     5
800 REM COMPUTER PLAY
805 PRINT@A(G-1),T$;:PRINT@Z(G-1),NU$;
     :GOSUB1000:IF PI=1 THEN1250
808 D1=0:D2=0:D3=0:D4=0
815 I=1:IJ=1:IK=1:R=0:RR=0:IF PI<>1 YU
     =0
816 IF I=1 AND IJ=2 AND V(I)+V(IJ)+V(I
     +2)+V(IJ+2)+YU=9 THEN850
820 IF I-1>0 AND I-1<>IJ AND V(I-1)+V(
     IJ)+YU=9 THEN870
821 IF I-1>0 AND V(I)+V(I-1)+YU=9 THEN
     875
822 IF I=3 AND IJ=1 AND V(I)+V(IJ)+V(I
     -1)+YU=9 THEN880
823 IF I=3 AND IJ=4 AND V(I)+V(IJ)+V(1
     )+YU=9 THEN885
824 IF I<>IJ AND V(I)+V(IJ)+YU=9 THEN8
     90
825 IF I=4 AND IJ=1 AND V(I)+V(IJ)+V(I
     -1)+YU=9 THEN880
```

```
826 IF I=4 AND IJ=2 AND V(I)+V(IJ)+V(I
    -1)+YU=9 THEN880
828 IF I=3 AND IJ=4 AND V(I)+V(IJ)+YU=
    9 THEN890
829 IF IJ=4 AND I=1 AND V(I)+V(I+1)+V(
    IJ)+YU=9 THEN900
830 R=10:GOTO834
831 FOR I=1TO4:IF V(I)+YU=9 RR=I:GOTO8
    45:ELSE NEXT
832 FOR I=1TO4:IF V(IJ)+YU=9 RR=I:GOTO
    845:ELSE NEXT
833 IF R=10 THEN845
834 IJ=IJ+1
835 IF IJ=5 IJ=IK:I=I+1
840 IF I<>4 THEN 816
842 IF R=10 THEN831
845 IF RR>0 PI=2:GOTO1150
846 PI=0:BB=BB+1:IF BB=2 BB=0:GOSUB142
    5:GOTO1210
848 GOTO1210
850 PRINT@A(IJ)," ";:PRINT@A(I+2),"
       ";:PRINT@A(IJ+2)," ";:R=5:
    GOTO1150
870 PRINT@A(I-1)," ";:PRINT@A(IJ),"
      ";:R=6:GOTO1190
875 PRINT@A(I-1)," ";:R=4:GOTO1150
880 PRINT@A(IJ)," ";:PRINT@A(I-1),"
      ";:R=2:GOTO1150
885 PRINT@A(IJ+1)," ";:R=8:GOTO1150
890 PRINT@A(IJ)," ";:R=1:GOTO1150
900 PRINT@A(I+1)," ";:PRINT@A(IJ),"
      ";:R=9:GOTO1150
1000 PRINT@A(G),"
                                    "
1010 PRINT@A(G),;
1020 RETURN
1050 FOR P=1TO1500:NEXT
1060 RETURN
1100 REM BLANK USED NUMBERS
1105 II=1
1110 PRINT@Z(MN(II))," ";:GOSUB1130
1115 II=II+1
```

```
1120 IF II<>I THEN1110
1125 FOR I=1TO4:ZZ(I)=0:NEXT:GOTO800
1130 ND=ND+1:IF ND=55 GOTO1550
1135 GOSUB270
1140 PRINT@Z(MN(II)),W;:X(MN(II))=W
1145 RETURN
1150 GOTO1165:REM DRAW NUMBER FOR COMP
     UTER
1155 ND=ND+1:IF ND=55 GOTO1550
1160 GOSUB270:RETURN
1165 PRINT@A(I),"    ";:GOSUB1155:PRINT
     @A(I),W;:V(I)=W
1168 IF RR<>0 THEN 1208
1170 IF R=2 GOSUB1155:PRINT@A(IJ),W;:V
     (IJ)=W:GOSUB1155:PRINT@A(I-1),W;:
     V(I-1)=W
1175 IF R=1 GOSUB1155:PRINT@A(IJ),W;:V
     (IJ)=W
1180 IF R=4 GOSUB1155:PRINT@A(I-1),W;:
     V(I-1)=W
1185 IF R=5 GOSUB1155:PRINT@A(IJ),W;:V
     (IJ)=W:GOSUB1155:PRINT@A(I+2),W;:
     V(I+2)=W:GOSUB1155:PRINT@A(IJ+2),
     W;:V(IJ+2)=W
1190 IF R=6 GOSUB1155:PRINT@A(I-1),W;:
     V(I-1)=W:GOSUB1155:PRINT@A(IJ),W;
     :V(IJ)=W
1195 IF R=7 GOSUB1155:PRINT@A(IJ),W;:V
     (IJ)=W:GOSUB1155:PRINT@A(1),W;:V(
     1)=W
1200 IF R=8 GOSUB1155:PRINT@A(IJ+1),W;
     :V(IJ+1)=W
1205 IF R=9 GOSUB1155:PRINT@A(I+1),W;:
     V(I+1)=W:GOSUB1155:PRINT@A(IJ),W;
     :V(IJ)=W
1208 PI=2:D1=I:BB=0:YU=0:GOSUB1500
1210 FOR I=1TO4:IF V(I)=0 GOSUB1155:PR
     INT@A(I),W;:V(I)=W:NEXT:ELSE NEXT
1215 PRINT@Z(G-1),T$;:PRINT@A(G-1),NU$
     ;
1220 GOTO660:REM USERS TURN
1250 II=1
```

154

```
1260 PRINT@A(MN(II)),"    ";:YU=V(MN(II
     ))+YU:V(MN(II))=0
1270 II=II+1
1280 IF II<>XI THEN1260
1290 GOSUB1000
1300 IF YU<9 THEN 808
1310 REM COMPUTER'S SCORE
1315 IF YU>9 THEN CS=YU+CS:YU=0
1320 GOTO1210
1325 REM USER TO INPUT AS COMPUTER
1330 INPUT Y
1335 IF I=4 AND Y<>D4 AND D4<>0 THEN G
     OSUB1380:GOSUB1000:GOTO692
1340 IF I=1 AND Y<>D1 THEN GOSUB1380:G
     OSUB1000:GOTO692
1345 IF I=2 AND Y<>D2 AND D2<>0 GOSUB1
     380:GOSUB1000:GOTO692
1350 IF I=3 AND Y<>D3 AND D3<>0 GOSUB1
     380:GOSUB1000:GOTO692
1355 IF Y=0 THEN 715:ELSE GOTO700
1380 REM WRONG INPUT FROM USER
1385 GOSUB1000
1390 PRINT"THE COMPUTER USED POSITIONS
     : ";
1395 IF D1<>0 PRINTD1;:IF D2<>0 PRINTD
     2;
1400 IF D3<>0 PRINTD3;:IF D4<>0 PRINTD
     4;
1405 GOSUB1050:RETURN
1410 REM TOTAL OF USERS INPUT
1415 IF E>9 GOSUB1000:PRINT"       SORRY
     ...YOU HAD TO GO OVER 9.":GOSUB10
     50:ER=E+ER:PI=0:GOTO1100
1420 IF E<9 THEN PI=0:GOTO1100
1422 GOTO725
1425 REM NEITHER CAN PLAY -- DRAW TWO
     NUMBERS
1430 ND=ND+1:IF ND=55 GOTO1550
1435 GOSUB270
1440 I=1:PRINT@Z(I),W;:X(I)=W
1445 ND=ND+1:IF ND=55 GOTO1550
```

```
1450 GOSUB270
1455 PRINT@A(I),W;:V(I)=W
1460 RETURN
1500 REM COMPUTER'S NUMBERS DRAWN
1505 IF R=1 THEN D2=IJ:RETURN
1510 IF R=2 THEN D2=IJ:D3=I-1:RETURN
1515 IF R=4 THEN D2=I-1:RETURN
1520 IF R=5 THEN D2=IJ:D3=I+2:D4=IJ+2:
     RETURN
1525 IF R=6 THEN D2=I-1:D3=IJ:RETURN
1530 IF R=7 THEN D2=IJ:D3=1:RETURN
1535 IF R=8 THEN D2=IJ+1:RETURN
1540 IF R=9 THEN D2=I+1:D3=IJ
1545 RETURN
1550 REM END OF RUN
1555 PRINT@512,;
1560 PRINT"THAT CONCLUDES THIS GAME...
     ......           "
1565 PRINT"FINISHING SCORE WAS: YOURS.
     ..";ER;" COMPUTER'S...";CS
1570 PRINT
1575 IF ER=CS THEN1595
1580 IF ER<CS THEN1590
1585 PRINT"YOU'VE LOST......";N$;" A W
     IN ? MAYBE NEXT TIME ???":GOTO160
     0
1590 PRINT"YOU'VE WON !! OUT-SMARTED Y
     OUR COMPUTER, VERY GOOD !!":GOTO1
     600
1595 PRINT"A TIE GAME...JUST AS WELL,
     NO ONE'S THE LOSER !!"
1600 PRINT
1605 PRINT"END OF RUN.........."
1610 GOTO1610
1620 REM INSTRUCTIONS
1625 PRINTTAB(10);"*** LOGIC DEDUCTION
     ***"
1630 PRINT
1635 PRINT"IN ORDER TO BEAT YOUR COMPU
     TER AT THIS GAME, YOU"
1640 PRINT"MUST HAVE THE LOWEST SCORE
     !!"
```

156

```
1645 PRINT"PLAYING THE GAME IS SIMPLE,
     JUST USE LOGIC."
1650 PRINT"YOU AND THE COMPUTER WILL H
     AVE 4 SQUARES, IN THESE"
1655 PRINT"SQUARES WILL BE NUMBERS FRO
     M 1 TO 9. BLOCK POSITIONS"
1660 PRINT"ARE 1, 2, 3, 4 -- FROM LEFT
     TO RIGHT."
1665 PRINT"WHICHEVER BLOCK NUMBERS YOU
     CHOOSE, THE COMPUTER"
1670 PRINT"MUST ALSO USE THE SAME ONES
     , IF YOUR TOTAL IS 9."
1675 PRINT"THE OBJECT IS TO GET THE CO
     MPUTER TO GO OVER 9"
1680 PRINT""THAT WAY THE TOTAL WILL GO
     ON ITS SCORE. "
1685 PRINT
1690 PRINT"PRESS ENTER";:INPUT X:CLS
1695 PRINT"EXAMPLE:"
1700 PRINT"IT'S YOUR TURN, YOU HAVE A
     5 IN POSITION 1 AND A"
1705 PRINT"4 IN POSITION 3. YOU ENTER
     POSITIONS (BLOCKS) 1"
1710 PRINT"& 4, YOUR TOTAL CAME TO 9 S
     O THE COMPUTER WILL"
1715 PRINT"ALSO HAVE TO USE POSITIONS
     1 & 4. IF THE COMPUTERS"
1720 PRINT"TOTAL AT THESE 2 BLOCKS ARE
     GREATER THAN 9, THAT"
1725 PRINT""TOTAL WILL GO ON ITS SCORE
     , LIKEWISE, IF LESS"
1730 PRINT"THAN 9 AND IT HAS ANOTHER N
     UMBER IN ANOTHER BLOCK"
1735 PRINT"THAT WILL MAKE IT 9, THE RU
     LES WILL BE REVERSED"
1740 PRINT"WHEN YOU PLAY, YOU'LL HAVE
     TO USE THE SAME BLOCK"
1745 PRINT"NUMBERS, NO MATTER WHAT THE
     TOTAL IS -- LESS THAN"
1750 PRINT"9,YOU'RE FINE -- MORE THAN 9
     AND THE TOTAL WILL GO"
```

```
1755 PRINT"ON YOUR SCORE."
1760 PRINT
1765 PRINT"PRESS ENTER";:INPUT X:CLS:P
     RINT
1770 PRINT"PLAY WILL CONTINUE UNTIL 54
      NUMBERS HAVE BEEN"
1775 PRINT"USED (1 THROUGH 9 -- 6 SETS
     )."
1780 PRINT"REMEMBER...THE ONE WITH THE
      LOWER SCORE WILL BE"
1785 PRINT"DECLARED THE WINNER !!"
1790 PRINT"ANOTHER POINT SHOULD ALSO B
     E MENTIONED NOW,"
1795 PRINT"ALL NUMBERS ARE DRAWN WITH
     THE RANDOM FUNCTION"
1800 PRINT"SO THERE IS NO WAY THE COMP
     UTER CAN CHEAT."
1805 PRINT
1810 PRINT"PRESS ENTER TO RUN THE GAME
     ";:INPUT X
1815 RETURN
```

EGGS OFF THE TABLE

This game gives you two tables and 25 square eggs—one at a time, of course. The object of the game is to slide the egg from one table to the next, without letting it fall between the tables and breaking (Fig. 7-3).

To slide the egg is simple, just input a number from 0 through 9, where 9 will be a distant slide. There is one sure-fire way to make just about every egg, but you should soon figure that one out. A game consists of 25 eggs. 1 point is given for each egg that makes it to the next table. See Fig. 7-4 for the flowchart.

Program Notes

Line 40 sets the counters and skips the instructions if game is played more than once.

Lines 250-320 draw the walls and tables. Line 270 is only read once through the game, so the distance between the tables can be changed.

Lines 330-370 provide a random function that selects either the right or left table for a starting point, then positions the egg.

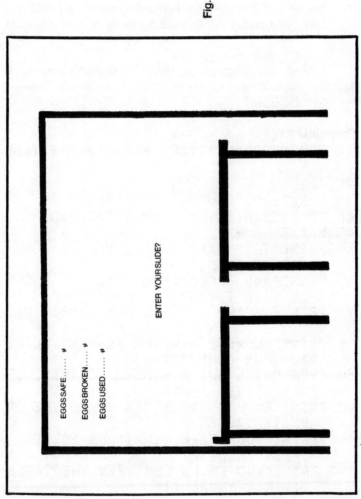

Fig. 7-3. Sample run of Egg Off the Table.

Variable LS=1 (line 350) keeps the egg moving in the same direction as the table selected.

Line 470 checks for egg slide (too little or too much) where line 490 prints a message and lets you try again.

Lines 500-550 slide the egg in the right direction according to the starting point.

Line 505 checks the distance between the tables. If your input is greater than 5 the computer will give you an extra amount to make up the large distance between the tables, but that doesn't mean you'll make it.

Line 570 checks the egg to see if it is still on a table.

Lines 610-655 let the egg fall to the floor and break in half.

Line 700 changes the distance between the tables (farther apart).

Line 710 counts the eggs used.

Line 800 and 810 check egg travel direction and tests if egg is safe on opposite table.

GOOD LUCK!!

Program Listing

```
10 REM PROGRAM TITLE: EGG OFF THE TABL
      E
20 CLS
30 PRINT@20,"EGG OFF THE TABLE"
40 TP=0:EB=0:EU=0:IF MM=1 THEN240
45 PRINT
50 PRINT"THIS GAME WILL GIVE YOU  SOME
      SQUARE EGGS."
60 PRINT"AND A COUPLE OF TABLES, ALL Y
      OU HAVE TO DO"
70 PRINT"IS INPUT A 'SLIDE' NUMBER FRO
      M 0-9 (0 THE"
75 PRINT"SLOWEST - 9 THE FASTEST SLIDE
      ). YOUR COMPUTER"
80 PRINT"WILL ADD A NUMBER TO THIS. IF
      IT SLIDES FAST"
90 PRINT"ENOUGH AND MAKES IT TO THE OP
      PSITE TABLE"
100 PRINT"YOUR FINE (THAT'S A POINT).
      IF IT SLIDES"
110 PRINT"AND FALLS (BETWEEN THE TABLE
      S), KER-PLUNK !!"
```

```
120 PRINT"THAT'S AN EGG OFF THE TABLE
    !!"
125 PRINT:GOSUB130:GOTO140
130 PRINT"PRESS ENTER TO BEGIN";:INPUT
    X:CLS:RETURN
140 PRINT
150 PRINT"ONE OTHER THING SHOULD BE ME
    NTIONED"
160 PRINT"BEFORE YOU GET STARTED."
210 PRINT"EACH TIME YOU MAKE A POINT,
    OR BREAK AN"
215 PRINT"EGG, THE TABLES WILL GET FAR
    THER APART."
220 PRINT"GAME IS 25 EGGS.":PRINT:GOSU
    B130
230 REM SET WALLS
240 REM DRAW TABLES
245 RANDOM:GOSUB250:GOTO260
250 FOR X=0TO47:SET(0,X):SET(1,X):SET(
    126,X):SET(127,X):NEXT
255 FOR Y=0TO127:SET(Y,0):NEXT:RETURN
260 REM USE TEMPORARY VARIABLES FOR TA
    BLES AND TWO LEGS
270 E=59:EE=65:L=53:LL=70:GOSUB280:GOT
    O330
280 FOR T=3TOE:SET(T,33):NEXT
290 FOR T=124TOEE STEP-1:SET(T,33):NEX
    T
300 FOR LE=34TO47:SET(6,LE):SET(7,LE):
    SET(L,LE):SET(L+1,LE)
310 SET(LL,LE):SET(LL+1,LE):SET(120,LE
    ):SET(121,LE):NEXT
320 RETURN
330 REM DRAW THE EGG AT A RANDOM SIDE
    (LEFT, RIGHT)
340 I=RND(2):ON I GOTO 350,360
350 EG=4:LS=1:GOTO370
360 EG=122
370 R=32:SET(EG,R):SET(EG+1,R)
375 GOSUB380:GOTO430
380 REM SET PRINT STATEMENTS
```

```
390 PRINT@70,"EGGS SAFE......";TP;
400 PRINT@134,"EGGS BROKEN....";EB;
410 PRINT@198,"EGGS USED......";EU;
420 RETURN
430 REM INPUT SLIDE / CHECK IT FOR < O
    R >
```

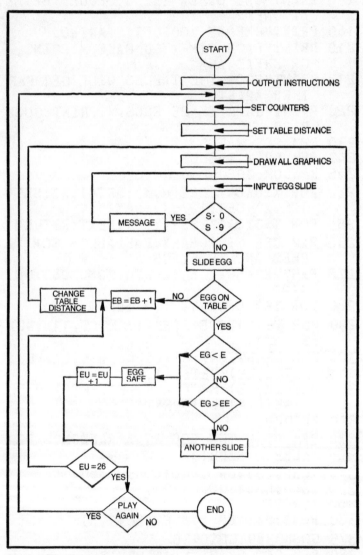

Fig. 7-4. Flowchart of Egg Off the Table.

```
435 GOSUB445:GOTO450
440 PRINT@262,;:RETURN
445 PRINT@398,;:RETURN
450 INPUT"        ENTER YOUR SLIDE";S
460 PRINT@422," ";:GOSUB250
470 IF S<0 OR S>9 THEN490
480 SS=S:GOTO500:REM GOOD ENOUGH
490 GOSUB440:PRINT"KEEP WITHIN LIMITS.
    ";:FOR XX=1TO1200:NEXT:GOSUB440:P
    RINT"                             ";:G
    OTO435
495 REM SLIDE THE EGG
500 IF S<=5 THEN SL=0:GOTO510
505 IF ABS(EE-E)>=26 THEN SL=(RND(35)+
    20):ELSE SL=2
510 IF LS=1 THEN540
520 RESET(EG,R):RESET(EG+1,R)
525 EG=((EG-S)-RND(SS)-RND(SL)):SET(EG
    ,R):SET(EG+1,R)
530 GOTO560
540 RESET(EG,R):RESET(EG+1,R)
550 EG=((EG+S)+RND(SS)+RND(SL)):SET(EG
    ,R):SET(EG+1,R)
560 REM CHECK IF STILL ON TABLE
570 IF POINT(EG,R+1)=0 THEN610
590 REM EGG SAFE?
600 GOTO800
610 REM EGG TO THE FLOOR
620 RESET(EG,R):RESET(EG+1,R)
630 R=R+1
640 SET(EG,R):SET(EG+1,R)
650 IF R<>47 THEN620
655 RESET(EG,R):SET(EG-1,R)
660 GOSUB445
670 PRINT"YOU'VE BROKEN THAT ONE.....T
    URKEY !!";
680 FOR XX=1TO1200:NEXT:EB=EB+1
690 REM ADD DISTANCE BETWEEN TABLES
700 E=E-1:EE=EE+1:L=L-1:LL=LL+1:LS=0
710 CLS:EU=EU+1:IF EU=26 THEN1000
720 GOSUB250:GOSUB280:GOTO330
800 IF LS=0 AND EG<E THEN840
```

```
810 IF LS=1 AND EG>EE THEN840
820 REM ANOTHER SLIDE
830 GOTO435
840 GOSUB445
850 PRINT"FANTASTIC !! YOU'VE MADE THA
    T ONE ACROSS !!";
860 FOR XX=1TO1200:NEXT
870 TP=TP+1:GOTO700
900 REM IF YOU WANT THE TABLES TO COME
    -UP
910 REM FARTHER APART BETWEEN BREAKS A
    ND
920 REM MAKING IT ACROSS CHANGE VARIAB
    LES
930 REM E,EE,L,LL IN LINE 700 TO A DIF
    FERENT
940 REM NUMBER, I.E. 2,3,4, ETC.
950 REM YOU CAN ALSO DELETE LINE 505 A
    ND
960 REM THE USER WOULD HAVE MORE THAN
970 REM ENOUGH TROUBLE GETTING AN EGG
980 REM ACROSS WHEN THE TABLES GET FAR
    THER
990 REM APART
1000 GOSUB445
1010 PRINT"        THAT'S";EU-1;"EGGS."
1020 FOR XX=1TO1200:NEXT:CLS:PRINT:PRI
     NT
1030 IF EB>TP THEN1060
1040 PRINT"YOU'VE CAME OUT WITH MORE E
     GGS SAFE THAN BROKEN !!"
1050 PRINT"WITH THE DISTANCE BETWEEN T
     HE TABLES, THAT'S TERRIFIC !!"
1055 GOTO1080
1060 PRINT"YOU'VE BROKEN";EB;"EGGS, TH
     ERE'S GOING TO BE A LOT"
1070 PRINT"OF MAD CHICKENS OUT THERE,
     WATCH OUT !!"
1080 PRINT
1090 PRINT"SHALL WE SLIDE SOME MORE EGG
     S";
1100 INPUT A$
```

```
1110 IF A$="YES" THEN MM=1:CLS:GOTO40
1120 PRINT"SEE IF YOU CAN FRY SOME SUN
     NY-SIDE-UP THEN !!!"
1130 END
```

WHICH KEY?

You might find it quite hard to beat this game without getting blown up. The computer draws 10 keys and a briefcase. You must select the key that opens it (Fig. 7-5). You are a secret agent. During your sleep someone broke into your room; much to your surprise instead of stealing your briefcase they've added several more keys to your collection.

Inside that case are some important papers and you need them now. But, you will have to choose which key will open the case, all of them are almost alike. If you select the right key you're fine, if not, the slightest pressure against the tumblers, from the wrong key, will set off an explosion!!!

All REM statements are included within the program, which should make it self-explanatory. See Fig. 7-6 for the flowchart.

Program Listing

```
10 REM PROGRAM TITLE: WHICH KEY ?
20 CLS:PRINTTAB(10),">>> WHICH KEY ? <
   <<"
30 PRINT:BW=0:DIM KK(12)
40 PRINT"YOU ARE A SECRET AGENT, YOU H
   AVE A"
50 PRINT"BRIEF CASE THAT CONTAINS SOME
    IMPORTANT"
60 PRINT"PAPERS, YOU NEED THESE PAPERS
    NOW."
70 PRINT"BUT YOU HAVE A SLIGHT PROBLEM
   , SOMEBODY"
80 PRINT"BROKE INTO YOUR ROOM WHILE YO
   U WERE ASLEEP"
90 PRINT"AND INSTEAD OF STEALING THE C
   ASE THEY'VE"
100 PRINT"SURPRISED YOU AND ADDED SEVE
    RAL KEYS TO"
110 PRINT"YOUR SET. YOU MUST FIGURE WH
    ICH IS THE"
```

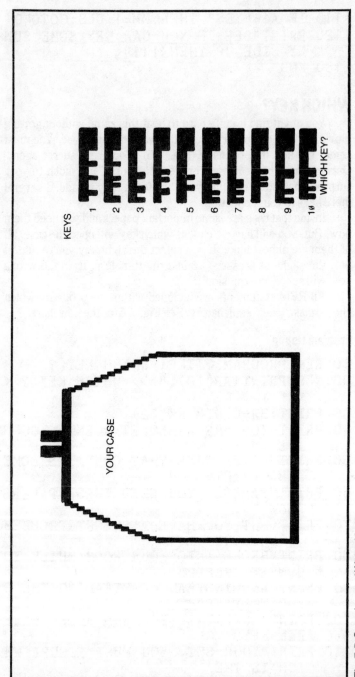

Fig. 7-5. Sample run of Which Key?

```
120 PRINT"RIGHT KEY TO GET THOSE PAPER
    S, AND,"
130 PRINT"BEWARE OF THE BOMB INSIDE TH
    AT IS TRIGGERED"
140 PRINT"BY THE PRESSURE AGAINST THE
    TUMBLERS CREATED"
150 PRINT"BY THE WRONG KEY.........."
160 PRINT"PRESS ENTER";:INPUT X:CLS
170 REM MAKE A SET OF 10 KEYS
180 REM PLACE THEM ON RIGHT SIDE OF VI
    DEO
190 A=106:B=170:K=1:RANDOM
200 FOR I=1TO10:K(I)=I:NEXT
210 PRINT@A-2,"KEYS";
220 I=1
230 PRINT@B,K(I);
240 KK(I)=B:I=I+1:B=B+64
250 IF I<>11 THEN230
260 REM DRAW THE KEYS
270 FOR V=93TO112
280 SET(V,6):SET(V,9):SET(V,12):SET(V,
    15)
290 SET(V,18):SET(V,21):SET(V,24):SET(
    V,27)
300 SET(V,30):SET(V,33):NEXT
310 A=184:Z=143:M=7:X=0
320 PRINT@A,CHR$(Z);:PRINT@A+1,CHR$(Z)
    ;:PRINT@A+2,CHR$(Z);
330 A=A+64:IF A<>824 THEN320
340 P=RND(105):IF P<93 THEN340
350 SET(P,M)
360 X=X+1:IF X<>5 THEN340
370 M=M+3:IF M<>37 THEN X=0:GOTO340:EL
    SE 500
380 PRINT@812,;
390 INPUT"WHICH KEY";KY
395 IF KY<1 OR KY>10 GOSUB380:GOTO390
400 PRINT@(KK(KY)+4),"              ";
    :KK(KY)=KY
410 GOSUB630:GOTO650
500 REM DRAW BRIEF CASE
510 X=10:Y=6
```

167

```
520 FOR C=YTOY+9:SET(X,C):X=X-1:NEXT
525 FOR C=10TO60:SET(C,Y):NEXT:PRINT@2
    05,"YOUR CASE";
530 X=60
540 FOR C=YTOY+9:SET(X,C):X=X+1:NEXT
545 FOR C=Y-3TOY:SET(33,C):SET(34,C):S
    ET(36,C):SET(37,C):NEXT
550 FOR C=Y+10TOY+30:SET(0,C):SET(X,C)
    :NEXT
560 FOR C=0TOX:SET(C,Y+30):NEXT
570 REM GET KEY NUMBER
580 FOR J=1TO10
590 I=RND(10):KE=I
600 NEXT
610 GOSUB380
620 GOTO390:REM GET KEY TO USE
630 REM SET PRINT @ AREA
640 PRINT@386,,::RETURN
650 PRINT"    KEY SELECTED - IN LOCK";
    :GOSUB660:GOTO670
660 FOR TT=1TO1200:NEXT:RETURN
670 GOSUB640
680 PRINT"ARE YOU READY TO TRY IT (Y/N
    )?";
690 A$=INKEY$:IF A$=""THEN690
700 IF A$="Y"THEN 750
710 GOSUB640:GOSUB660
720 PRINT"      SELECT ANOTHER KEY
        ";
730 GOSUB660
740 GOSUB380:GOTO390
750 KE=RND(10)
760 IF KY<>KE THEN800
770 GOSUB660:GOSUB640
775 REM RIGHT KEY
780 PRINT"     YOU'VE GOT IT OPEN !!!
        ";
790 GOTO920
800 GOSUB660
805 REM WRONG KEY
810 CLS:PRINTCHR$(23)
820 PRINT:PRINT:PRINT
```

```
830 Q$="BBBBBBBRRRRRRRROOOOOOOOOMMMMM
    M"
840 L=1
850 PRINTMID$(Q$,L,1);:FOR T=1TO50:NEX
    T
860 L=L+1
```

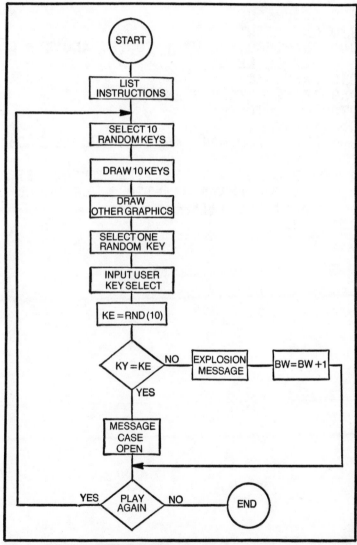

Fig. 7-6. Flowchart of Which Key?

```
870  IF L<>LEN(Q$) THEN850
875  PRINT:PRINT
880  PRINT"YOU'VE JUST BLOWN"
890  PRINT"YOURSELF AWAY !!!"
900  PRINT:BW=BW+1
910  PRINT"YOU WERE";ABS(KE-KY);"KEYs O
     FF."
920  GOSUB660
930  CLS:PRINT
940  PRINT"DO YOU WANT TO TRY ANOTHER S
     ET OF KEYS";
950  INPUT A$
960  IF A$<>"YES" THEN980
970  CLS:GOTO170
980  PRINT
990  PRINT"TOO MANY KEYS TO CHOOSE FROM
      ???"
1000 IF BW>0 THEN PRINT:PRINT"YOU WERE
     BLOWN AWAY";BW;"TIMES...I WOULD
     QUIT TOO !!!"
1010 END
```

Chapter 8
Seeking and Catching

TREASURE HUNT

This program will give you 10 possible treasure locations, but only one of them will actually hold the treasure. The computer rolls dice to get you closer and closer to a location. Print statements will keep you updated on the distance to the next location. If at anytime you want to stop at a location, press the space bar (the distance between you and location must be 10 or less). Then you'll soon know if you have located the treasure (Fig. 8-1).

But, there are a few strings attached. When the computer rolls the dice, if it rolls 1+1 you'll have to start over. If the computer rolls 6+6 you will end up in a bottomless pit. The computer will keep rolling dice until it comes up with 2+2, at which time you'll get out of the pit and resume your search.

Just remember, the only way you'll know your location is by watching the distance between you and location X n, where n is the next location. See Fig. 8-2 for the flowchart.

Program Notes

Lines 260-350 get the necessary data and set up the treasure map.

Line 370 sets your location.

Lines 380-410 selects one location for the treasure.

Line 420 updates your location and distance to next location.

Line 445 checks the dice for a 1+1 roll.

Line 450 gives you a slight break if your distance is less than 20.

Line 460 makes sure another location is brought up.

Line 490 checks dice for a 6+6 roll.

Lines 850 and 860 keep you in the pit until a 2+2 is rolled.

Lines 900-940 checks to see if you've found the treasure.

Lines 950-1020 give you a random print statement if you stop at the wrong location.

Line 1050 either makes you start over or lets you continue.

Program Listing

```
10 REM PROGRAM TITLE: TREASURE HUNT
15 CLS
20 PRINTTAB(10),"******* TREASURE HUNT
   *******"
30 PRINT
40 PRINT"THIS IS THE GAME OF TREASURE
   HUNT. YOU"
```

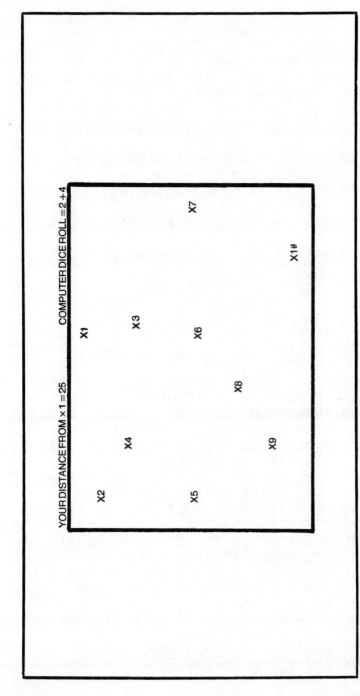

YOUR DISTANCE FROM ×1 = 25   COMPUTER DICE ROLL = 2 + 4

X1

X3

X6

X8

X2

X4

X5

X9

X7

X1Ø

Fig. 8-1. Sample run of Treasure Hunt.

```
50 PRINT"WILL HAVE A ROUTE TO TAKE, ON
      THIS ROUTE"
60 PRINT"WILL BE SOME X'S. AS THE OLD
      SAYING GOES"
70 PRINT"X MARKS THE SPOT, BUT IN THIS
      CASE IT MIGHT"
80 PRINT"MARK SOMETHING UNEXPECTED."
100 PRINT"DICE WILL DETERMINE YOUR MOV
      E,"
110 PRINT"IF YOU ROLL A ONE ON EACH DI
      CE YOU'LL"
120 PRINT"HAVE TO START OVER. IF YOU R
      OLL A SIX"
130 PRINT"ON BOTH DICE YOU'LL BE THROW
      N IN A BOTTOM-"
140 PRINT"LESS PIT AND THE ONLY WAY TO
      GET OUT IS"
150 PRINT
160 PRINT"PRESS ENTER";:INPUT X:CLS:PR
      INT
170 PRINT"TO ROLL A TWO ON BOTH DICE."
180 PRINT"THESE X'S WILL HAVE NUMBER L
      OCATIONS, IF"
190 PRINT"YOUR LOCATION IS 10 OR LESS
      FROM AN X LOCATION"
200 PRINT"AND YOU WANT TO STOP, PRESS
      THE SPACE BAR. OTHER-"
210 PRINT"WISE THE DICE WILL KEEP ROLL
      ING AND YOU'LL KEEP"
220 PRINT"MOVING. YOU'RE GOING TO FIND S
      OME OTHER SURPRISES"
230 PRINT"TO MAKE YOUR TRIP AS FRUSTRA
      TING AS POSSIBLE."
235 PRINT"NOTE: THE ONLY WAY YOU'LL KN
      OW WHERE YOU ARE AT"
236 PRINT"IS TO WATCH YOUR DISTANCE FR
      OM X....."
240 PRINT:SV=0
250 PRINT"PRESS ENTER TO BEGIN THE HUN
      T";:INPUT X:CLS
260 REM GET 10 LOCATIONS
270 FOR I=1TO10:X(I)=I
```

174

```
275 READ L(I):NEXT
280 REM DRAW THE TREASURE MAP
290 I=1:RANDOM
300 REM X LOCATION WILL BE DATA LIST
310 PRINT@L(I),CHR$(88);X(I);
320 I=I+1
330 IF I<>11 THEN300
340 FOR Y=0TO127:SET(Y,5):SET(Y,47):NE
    XT
350 FOR Y=0TO047:SET(0,Y):SET(127,Y):NE
    XT
360 REM SET YOUR STARTING LOCATION
370 YL=129
380 REM SELECT ONE TREASURE LOCATION
390 FOR TL=1TO10
400 JL=RND(10)
410 NEXT:TL=L(JL):XX=X(JL):TT=1
420 I=TT:YL=YL+(A+B):YD=ABS(L(I)-YL)
425 Q$=INKEY$:IF Q$=" "THEN900
430 PRINT@1,"YOUR DISTANCE FROM X";I;"
    =";YD;
440 PRINT@36,"COMPUTER DICE ROLL =";A;
    "+";B;
445 IF A=1 AND B=1 THEN800
450 IF YD<=20 THEN A=RND(3):B=RND(3):E
    LSE A=RND(6):B=RND(6)
460 IF YD<=5 THEN GOSUB1150:PRINT"STAR
    TING FOR THE NEXT LOCATION.";:FOR
    TM=1TO1200:NEXT:GOSUB1150:PRINT"
                                    "
    ;:TT=TT+1:IF TT=11 THEN1200:ELSE
    GOTO420
470 REM CHECK DICE FOR DOUBLE 6
490 IF A=6 AND B=6 THEN850
500 Q$=INKEY$:IF Q$=" " THEN900
510 FOR TM=1TO500:NEXT:GOTO420
800 PRINT@270,"LOOK AT THE DICE......"
    ;
810 PRINT@334,"YOU HAVE TO START OVER
    NOW, SORRY !!!";
820 FOR TM=1TO2000:NEXT:CLS:SV=SV+1
```

175

```
830 RESTORE:A=0:B=0:GOTO260
850 YD=YD:GOSUB1150:PRINT"YOU'RE IN THE
    BOTTOMLESS PIT !!";
855 IF A=2 AND B=2 THEN880
860 A=RND(6):B=RND(6):PRINT@36,"COMPUT
    ER DICE ROLL =";A;"+";B;
870 GOTO855
```

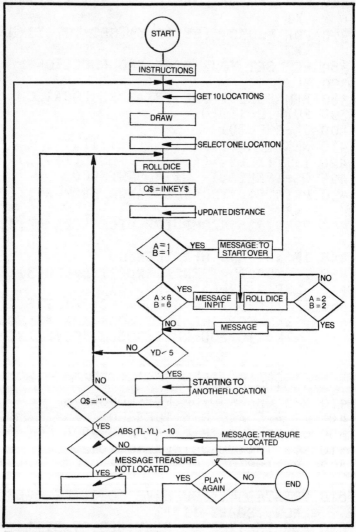

Fig. 8-2. Flowchart of Treasure Hunt.

176

```
880 GOSUB1150:PRINT"
                                    ";
890 GOTO420
900 REM CHECK DISTANCE TO TREASURE
910 IF ABS(TL-YL)>10 THEN950
920 GOSUB1150:PRINT"THAT'S THE TREASUR
     E !!!!";
930 FOR TM=1TO1200:NEXT:CLS
940 GOTO1200
950 GOSUB1150:PRINT"THIS ISN'T THE TRE
     ASURE !!!";
960 FOR TM=1TO1500:NEXT:GOSUB1150
970 AN=RND(5):ON AN GOTO980,990,1000,1
     010,1020
980 PRINT""YOU'VE BEEN BITTEN BY A SNAKE !
     !!";:GOTO1030
990 PRINT"BATS ARE SWARMING ALL OVER Y
     OU !!!";:GOTO1030
1000 PRINT"WARNING: STAY AWAY FROM THI
      S AREA !!";:GOTO1030
1010 PRINT"QUIT GETTING EXCITED, WRONG
      X !!!";:GOTO1030
1020 PRINT"YOU'VE FOUND SOME GREEN APP
      LES !!!";
1030 FOR TM=1TO1500:NEXT
1040 PRINT@595,"
                                     ";
1050 AM=RND(2):ON AM GOTO420,810
1100 DATA 160,200,291,337,455,484,503,
      667,788,948
1150 PRINT@595,;:RETURN
1200 PRINT:PRINT
1205 PRINT"   THAT IS ALL 10 LOCATIONS
      ."
1210 PRINT"   DO YOU WANT TO HUNT ANOT
      HER TREASURE NOW";
1220 INPUT A$
1230 IF A$="NO" THEN1250
1240 RESTORE:A=0:B=0:SV=0:CLS:GOTO260
1250 PRINT"COME ON COULDN'T YOU STAND
      ALL THE EXCITEMENT ???"
```

177

```
1260 IF SV>0 THEN FOR TM=1TO2000:NEXT:
     GOTO1280
1270 END
1280 PRINT"I CAN UNDERSTAND NOW, YOU H
     AD TO START OVER";SV;"TIMES !!"
1290 GOTO1270
```

RESET

This game table looks something like a pool table, but the resemblance stops there. You'll have 15 lighted blocks to reset, by entering numbers from 1 to 6. Entering a 1 will move your block down and to the right, entering a 2 will move your block down and to the left, and so on. All key closures will be explained in the program instructions.

Each time your block hits one of the set blocks, the block will be reset and you'll receive a point. If you have reset all the lighted blocks and your point count does not total 15, enter an 8 for the position, the computer will then set the block(s) you didn't receive a point for (Fig. 8-3).

Example: Your score = 12 and there are no blocks left to reset; enter an 8 and the computer will set another block (the one you missed or didn't get a point for). If you reset it your score will then total 13. Again enter an 8 for position, the computer will set another block. Keep this up until your total score (resets) total 15. Might sound a little complicated but you will soon get the point.

Program Notes

Some possible changes or additions might include adding more than 15 blocks to be reset. The total number of blocks set is determined lines 170 through 270.

If the user enters a 7 for a position, his block will flash. By omitting line 340 and deleting IF X=7 THEN 340 from line 410 the user will have to remember his/her block position.

The random variable QQ is used for the bouncing effect. If you do not want the blocks to bounce delete all the variables QQ. The user's block will then go from its starting point to the frame of the table (in its appropriate direction, for key closure).

Program Listing

```
5 REM PROGRAM TITLE: RESET
10 CLS:RANDOM:IF TT=1 THEN90
15 DIM A(100),Q(100),W(100)
```

178

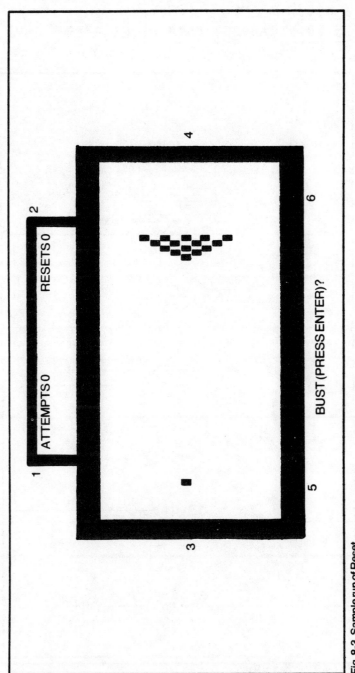

ATTEMPTS 0   RESETS 0

BUST (PRESS ENTER)?

Fig. 8-3. Sample run of Reset.

```
20 PRINT
25 PRINTTAB(25);"*** RESET ***"
30 PRINT
```

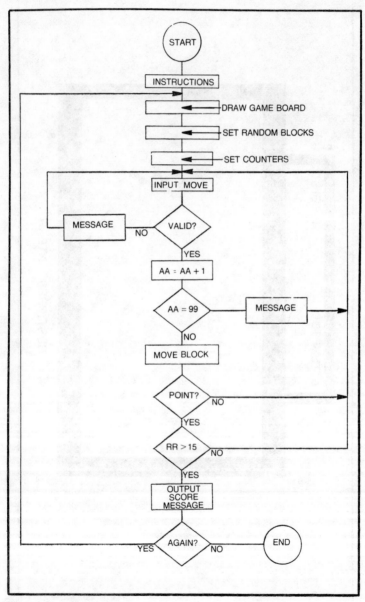

Fig. 8-4. Flowchart of Reset.

```
35 PRINT"THE OBJECT OF RESET IS TO DO
      JUST THAT, RESET AS"
40 PRINT"MANY SET BLOCKS AS YOU CAN IN
      THE LEAST AMOUNT OF"
45 PRINT"ATTEMPTS. YOU'LL RESET THESE
      BLOCKS WITH YOURS, BY"
50 PRINT"ENTERING, 1 - TO MOVE DOWN-RI
      GHT. 2 - TO MOVE DOWN-LEFT."
55 PRINT"3 - TO MOVE STRAIGHT-RIGHT. 4
      - TO MOVE STRAIGHT-LEFT."
60 PRINT"5 - TO MOVE UP-RIGHT. 6 - TO
      MOVE UP-LEFT. AND ENTER"
65 PRINT"A NUMBER 7 TO UPDATE YOUR LOC
      ATION (IT WILL FLASH)."
70 PRINT"IF AT ANY TIME YOU DO NOT REC
      EIVE A POINT FOR ONE YOU'VE"
75 PRINT"RESET, CONTINUE THE GAME. THE
      N AFTER YOU THINK ALL"
80 PRINT"BLOCKS ARE RESET BUT YOUR SCO
      RE IS LESS THAN 15, ENTER"
85 PRINT"A NUMBER 8 - HENCE, ALL BLOCK
      S YOU MISSED OR DIDN'T"
86 PRINT"RECEIVE A POINT FOR WILL BE S
      ET, THEN YOU'LL HAVE"
87 PRINT""A CHANCE TO RESET THEM....."
88 PRINT"PRESS ENTER TO ** R E S E T *
      *";:INPUT X$:CLS
90  G=9:P=33:R=19:V=79:RR=0:AA=0
100 FOR X=15TO110:SET(X,8):SET(X,7):SE
      T(X,30):SET(X,31):NEXT
110 FOR X=8TO30:SET(15,X):SET(16,X):SE
      T(17,X):SET(108,X):SET(109,X):SET
      (110,X):NEXT
130 FORX=2TO7:SET(29,X):SET(98,X):NEXT
140 FORX=29TO98:SET(X,2):NEXT
145 PRINT@75,"1";:PRINT@116,"2";:PRINT
      @390,"3";:PRINT@440,"4";:PRINT@71
      5,"5";:PRINT@756,"6";
150 FOR X=15TO23STEP2:SET(84,X):NEXT:F
      OR X=16TO22STEP2:SET(83,X):NEXT:F
      OR X=17TO21STEP2:SET(82,X):NEXT:F
```

181

```
        OR X=18TO20STEP2:SET(81,X):NEXT:S
        ET(80,19):SET(P,R)
155 GOTO280
160 REM BUST
170 B=80:BB=19:M=1
180 RESET(B,BB):RESET(B,B1):RESET(B,B2
        ):RESET(B,B3)
185 IF M>=2 THEN SET(X,Y):IF B=84THEN
        RESET(B,B3-2)
190 X=RND(100):IF X<19 OR X>100THEN190
200 Y=RND(28):IF Y<10 OR Y>28THEN200
220 IF A(X)=X OR A(Y)=Y THEN190
230 A(X)=X:A(Y)=Y:Q(M)=A(X):W(M)=A(Y):
        IF M>=16THEN RETURN
235 B=B+1:IF B=85THEN B=B-1
240 BB=BB+1:IF BB=24 THEN BB=BB-1
250 B1=BB-2:B2=B1-2:B3=B2-2
260 M=M+1
270 IF M<=16 THEN180:ELSE280
280 REM HIT Q TO BUST
290 GOSUB380:PRINT"BUST (PRESS ENTER)"
        ;
300 INPUT Z:GOSUB380
310 RESET(P,R)
320 P=P+1:SET(P,R)
330 IF POINT(V,R)THEN GOSUB160:ELSE GO
        TO310
340 GOSUB380:PRINT"FLASHING YOUR POSIT
        ION":Z=0
350 RESET(P,R):FOR I=1TO100:NEXT
360 SET(P,R):Z=Z+1
370 IF Z<>10THEN350:ELSE GOSUB380:GOTO
        390
380 PRINT@790,"
        ";:PRINT@790,;:RETURN
390 PRINT@81,"ATTEMPTS ";AA;:PRINT@102
        ,"RESETS ";RR;:GOSUB380:IFRR>=15T
        HEN1150:ELSE PRINT"FROM POSITION"
        ;
395 IF KA=0 AND AA=99 THEN1500
400 INPUT X:GOSUB1600:IF X=99 THEN980
```

```
401 GOSUB380:IF X=7 THEN340:ELSE IF X=
    8 THEN1350
402 GOTO1020
405 AA=AA+1
410 ON X GOTO 440,570,600,710,820,930
420 GOSUB380
440 RESET(P,R):R=R+1:P=P+1
450 SET(P,R):GOSUB1400
470 IF R<>28 AND P<=105 THEN440
480 IF P>=106 THEN390:ELSE QQ=RND(2):I
    F QQ=1 THEN820:ELSE 390
570 RESET(P,R):R=R+1:P=P-1
580 SET(P,R):GOSUB1400
590 IF P<>19 AND R<>28 THEN570
595 GOTO390
600 RESET(P,R):P=P+1
610 SET(P,R):IF POINT(P+1,R) THEN RESE
    T(P+1,R):RR=RR+1:GOTO1010
620 IF P<>106THEN600
630 IF R=28 OR R=29 THEN 390:ELSE QQ=R
    ND(2)
640 IF QQ=2 THEN 570:ELSE 390
710 RESET(P,R):P=P-1
720 SET(P,R):GOSUB1400
730 IF P<>19 AND R<>28 THEN710
740 IF R=10 OR R=29 THEN 390:ELSE QQ=R
    ND(2)
750 IF QQ=1 THEN820:ELSE 390
820 RESET(P,R):R=R-1:P=P+1
830 SET(P,R):GOSUB1400
840 IF R>=11 AND P<>106THEN820:ELSE 39
    0
930 RESET(P,R):P=P-1:R=R-1
940 SET(P,R):GOSUB1400
950 IF R>=11 AND P<>19THEN930
960 IF R>11 AND P>=18 THEN QQ=RND(2)
970 IF QQ=1 THEN570:ELSE 390
980 REM GIVING UP
990 PRINT@783,"GAVE UP -- YOU BIG CHIC
    KEN !!!";
1000 GOTO1250
1010 IF RR=M+1 THEN STOP:REM ALL RESET
```

183

```
1020 REM CHECK FOR MORE MOVEMENT
1050 IF X=1 AND R=28THEN1110:ELSE IF X
     =2 AND R=28THEN1110:ELSE IF X=2 A
     ND P=19THEN1110
1055 IF X=1 AND P=106THEN1110
1060 IF X=3 AND P=106 THEN1110
1065 IF X=4 AND P=19 THEN1110
1070 IF X=5 AND R=10 THEN1110
1080 IF X=5 AND P=106 THEN1110
1090 IF X=6 AND R<=10 THEN1110
1095 IF X=6 AND P=19 THEN1110
1100 GOTO405
1110 GOSUB380
1120 PRINT"INVALID START":FOR ZZ=1TO10
     00:NEXT
1130 GOTO390
1150 FOR ZZ=1TO1200:NEXT:CLS:PRINT
1160 IF AA<=15THEN1230
1170 IF AA>15 AND AA<=60THEN1200
1180 IF AA>60 AND AA<80THEN1210
1190 PRINT"YOUR SCORE SHOULDN'T EVEN B
     E MENTIONED,";AA;"ATTEMPTS !!":GO
     TO1250
1200 PRINT"THAT'S A REAL GOOD SCORE,";
     AA;"ATTEMPTS.":GOTO1250
1210 PRINT"A GAME WITH";RR;"RESETS. BU
     T YOUR SCORE HAS"
1220 PRINT"LEFT SOMETHING TO BE DESIRE
     D,";AA;"ATTEMPTS!!":GOTO1250
1230 PRINT"A PERFECT SCORE !!!!!"
1240 PRINT"WHAT'D YOU DO CHEAT ????"
1250 PRINT
1260 PRINT"DO YOU WANNA TRY AGAIN";
1270 INPUT A$
1280 IF A$="YES"THEN FOR I=1TO100:A(I)
     =0:NEXT:TT=1:GOTO10
1290 PRINT
1300 PRINT"END OF GAME......."
1310 GOTO1310
1350 GOSUB380
1360 PRINT"SETTING.........."
```

```
1370 FOR I=1TOM:IF Q(I) AND W(I)<>0 TH
     EN SET(Q(I),W(I)):ELSE NEXT
1380 FOR ZZ=1TO1000:NEXT:GOTO390
1400 IF POINT(P+1,R) THEN RESET(P+1,R)
     :RR=RR+1:ELSE IF POINT(P-1,R) THE
     N RESET(P-1,R):RR=RR+1:ELSE IF PO
     INT(P,R+1) THEN RESET(P,R+1):RR=R
     R+1:ELSE IF POINT(P,R-1) THEN RES
     ET(P,R-1):RR=RR+1
1440 RETURN
1500 PRINT@910,"TO GIVE-UP ENTER 99 FO
     R A POSITION";
1510 FOR ZZ=1TO1200:NEXT
1520 PRINT@910,"
                       ";
1530 KA=1
1540 GOTO390
1600 IF X<>1 AND X<>2 AND X<>3 AND X<>
     4 AND X<>5 AND X<>6 AND X<>7 AND
     X<>8 AND X<>99 THEN1620
1610 RETURN
1620 GOSUB380
1630 PRINT@783,"SORRY.....THAT NUMBER
     ISN'T LISTED";
1640 FOR ZZ=1TO1000:NEXT
1650 PRINT@783,"
                       ";
1660 GOSUB380
1670 GOTO390
```

UNBELIEVABLE (COMPUTER TAG)

Unbelievable is just what you'll be thinking when you run this program. You will attempt to tag the computer's block before it can tag yours. The computer's block must be hit on the left side, likewise, the computer must hit yours on its left side.

The computer's block will move randomly about the screen. To move yours around, use the 4 arrow keys. If you try to stall in one area too long, you will be deducted 1 point for delay of game. A games comprises 100 points.

If at any point you become confused as to whose block is whose, press one of the arrow keys to get your block out in the open. See Fig. 8-5 for the flowchart.

Program Notes

By changing variable C in line 220, the blocks can be just about any shape you wish (within the range of the computer). The program was put together with both blocks being the same shape to make the game more difficult.

If you don't feel the computer needs a break, delete line 315. That argument starts the computer's block right next to yours, but if you are fast enough, you can tag the computer first. Change the numeral 10 in lines 350 and 360 if you want your block to jump farther left or right, but keep it an even number.

The argument in line 375 checks to see if you are trying to stall the game. You can add a line like this for the computer, but, after you've run the game once, you'll know it won't be necessary. The speed of the computer's block is controlled at line 275. If you feel the computer's block needs a speed change, this is the place to make it.

GOOD LUCK!!

Program Listing

```
50 REM PROGRAM TITLE: UNBELIEVABLE (CO
     MPUTER TAG)
100 REM THIS PROGRAM WILL SET A RANDOM
110 REM BLOCK ON THE SCREEN AND THE COM
     PUTER
120 REM WILL MOVE IT RANDOMLY. YOU MUS
     T
130 REM CHASE THIS BLOCK, IF AND WHEN
     YOU
140 REM HIT IT YOU WILL SCORE A POINT
150 REM A TOTAL OF 100 POINTS IS GAME
160 REM YOU MUST HIT THE COMPUTER'S BL
     OCK - LEFT SIDE
170 REM TO SCORE / THE COMPUTER MUST H
     IT THE LEFT SIDE
180 REM OF YOUR BLOCK FOR IT TO SCORE
190 REM YOUR MOVES WILL DETERMINE THE
     COMPUTER'S
200 REM MOVES, PROVIDING A RANDOM NUMB
     ER IS GENERATED, SELECTED BY THE
     COMPUTER (OF COURSE)
204 CLS:GOSUB1000:REM INSTRUCTIONS
```

```
205 CLS
210 REM SET YOUR AREA AND COMPUTER'S A
    REA
220 GX=66:C=143:YP=0:CP=0
230 C$=CHR$(C)
235 A=RND(959):IF A<=64 THEN235
250 REM PRINT @ WILL BE USED FOR BLOCK
255 IF A<=64 OR A>=959 THEN PRINT@A,"
    ";:GOTO235
260 PRINT@A,C$;
275 FOR KL=1TO115:NEXT:REM IF LOOP ISN
    'T FAST ENOUGH FOR MOVEMENT LOWER
    IT !!
280 PRINT@A," ";:PRINT@GX," ";
285 REM SPICE COMPUTER'S MOVES
290 S=RND(10)
300 J=RND(10)
305 REM TOTAL COMPUTER'S MOVE
310 A=((A+S)-J)
315 CM=RND(5):IF CM=3 THEN A=(GX-RND(C
    M)):PRINT@A,C$;:REM A BREAK FOR Y
    OUR COMPUTER
320 P=PEEK(15340)
330 IF P=8 THEN GX=GX-64:REM FOR MOVE
    - UP
340 IF P=16 THEN GX=GX+64:REM FOR MOVE
    - DOWN
350 IF P=32 THEN GX=GX-10:REM FOR MOVE
    - LEFT
360 IF P=64 THEN GX=GX+10:REM FOR MOVE
    - RIGHT
365 REM THE NUMBER 10 CAN BE CHANGED I
    N LINES 350,360 FOR A SHORTER LEF
    T - RIGHT JUMP / BUT KEEP IT AN E
    VEN NUMBER
370 IF GX<=66 OR GX>=1020 THEN GX=66:R
    EM YOUR MOVE WITHIN LIMITS
375 REM CHECK FOR USER DELAY IN GAME
380 IF P<>8 AND P<>16 AND P<>32 AND P<
    >64 THEN P=0
390 PRINT@GX,C$;
```

```
395 IF GX+1=A THEN500:REM FOR YOUR POI
    NT
400 IF A+1=GX THEN550:REM FOR COMPUTER
     POINT
405 IF P=0 THEN PX=PX+1:IF PX=50 THEN4
    20:REM NO DELAY IN GAME !!
410 REM CONTINUE GAME IF SCORE <> 100
415 GOTO255
```

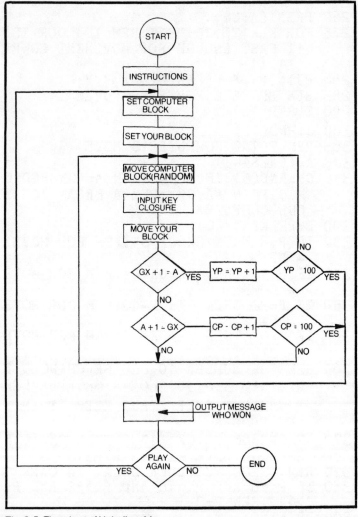

Fig. 8-5. Flowchart of Unbelievable.

```
420 REM USER LOSES 1 POINT FOR WAITING
425 PRINT@460,"ONE POINT LOST FOR DELA
    Y IN GAME !!";
430 FOR KL=1TO1200:NEXT
440 PRINT@460,"
                        ";
445 PRINT@GX," ";
450 PX=0:GX=64
455 REM USER LOSES ONE POINT FOR DELAY
     IN GAME
460 YP=YP-1:IF YP<=0 YP=0
470 GOSUB700:GOTO255
500 PRINT@87,"YOUR TAG !!";
510 FOR KL=1TO1000:NEXT
520 PRINT@87,"          ";
530 YP=YP+1:IF YP=100 THEN800
540 GOTO255
550 PRINT@85,"COMPUTER'S TAG !!";
560 FOR KL=1TO1000:NEXT
570 PRINT@85,"              ";
580 CP=CP+1:IF CP=100 THEN800
590 GOTO255
700 REM PRINT TOTAL SCORES THUS FAR
710 PRINT@897,"YOUR POINTS =";YP;
720 PRINT@934,"COMPUTER's POINTS =";CP
    ;
725 FOR KL=1TO500:NEXT
730 IF YP<CP PRINT@465,"YOU'RE FALLING B
    EHIND, DUMMY !!";
740 IF YP>CP PRINT@465,"YOU'RE BEATING Y
    OUR COMPUTER !!";
745 IF YP=CP PRINT@465,"KEEPING IT EQU
    AL ??";
750 FOR KL=1TO1500:NEXT
760 PRINT@460,"
              ";
770 PRINT@897,"                        ";
780 PRINT@934,"
        ";
790 RETURN
800 CLS
```

189

```
810 PRINT:PRINT
820 PRINT"THAT's THE GAME....."
830 IF YP<CP THEN860
840 IF YP>CP THEN870
850 IF YP=CP THEN880
860 PRINT"POOR YOU.....YOU'VE LOST TO
    YOUR COMPUTER !!":GOTO890
870 PRINT"AND WHO SAID COMPUTERS ARE
    SMART??" :GOTO890
880 PRINT"A TIE GAME ? TRY TO BEAT THE
    COMPUTER NEXT TIME."
890 PRINT
900 PRINT"ARE YOU READY TO GO AT IT AG
    AIN";
910 INPUT A$
920 IF LEFT$(A$,1)="Y" THEN205
925 PRINT
930 PRINT"HAVE YOU DEVELOPED BLISTERS
    ON YOUR FINGERTIPS ??"
940 PRINT
950 PRINT"END OF RUN....."
960 END

1000 PRINT
1010 PRINT"THIS GAME IS CALLED UNBELIE
     VABLE (COMPUTER TAG)."
1020 PRINT"YOU WILL BE USING ALL FOUR
     ARROW KEYS TO MOVE"
1030 PRINT"AROUND THE SCREEN, THAT PART
      IS EASY."
1040 PRINT"TO SCORE A POINT (100 POINT
     S IS GAME) YOU MUST"
1050 PRINT"HIT THE COMPUTER'S BLOCK ON
      THE LEFT SIDE"
1060 PRINT"LIKEWISE, FOR THE COMPUTER
     TO SCORE IT MUST HIT"
1070 PRINT"YOUR BLOCK ON THE LEFT SIDE
     , ANYTHING ELSE AND"
1080 PRINT"NO POINTS WILL BE GAINED."
1090 PRINT
1100 PRINT"PRESS ENTER.....";
1110 INPUT A$:CLS:PRINT
```

```
1120 PRINT"IF YOU DO NOT MOVE YOUR BLO
     CK WITHIN A CERTAIN"
1130 PRINT"AMOUNT OF TIME, YOU WILL LO
     SE ONE (1) POINT."
1140 PRINT"ALL THE COMPUTER'S MOVES WI
     LL BE RANDOMLY"
1150 PRINT"SELECTED, SO IF YOU FIND YO
     URSELF LOSING TO"
1160 PRINT"YOUR COMPUTER, DON'T HIT IT
     . IT MUST BE"
1170 PRINT"FASTER THAN YOU. IT CAN ONL
     Y MOVE ITS BLOCK"
1180 PRINT"ONE DIRECTION (A LARGE ONE)
     , YOU CAN MOVE ALL"
1190 PRINT"OVER THE SCREEN. JUST REMEMB
     ER, ONLY USE THE"
1200 PRINT"FOUR ARROW KEYS - UP - DOWN
     - LEFT - RIGHT."
1210 PRINT
1220 PRINT"PRESS ENTER TO START.....";
1230 INPUT A$
1240 RETURN
```

WATCH YOUR SCREEN

Blink your eyes while playing this game and you'll either lose some valuable points or end up in the gutter. It's a fast-paced game. You will notice 12 blocks, inside these blocks are numbers that range from 50 to 500. These numbers represent points.

To collect these points you will only use the space bar. Your block will be the flashing one, located at the lower left corner of the video display (this is the starting position). It will constantly be moving from left to right, to move it up merely press the space bar. It will then move up one line, press the space bar again and it will move up another line, and so on. To collect points, your block must hit one of the point blocks just right. You will receive points for that hit and the block will be reset (Fig. 8-6).

If at anytime you have the misfortune to land in the gutter, you'll lose all points that you've collected up to that point. If you manage to get to the top of the video without landing in the gutter, you can either press the space bar again (to return to beginning position) or just wait and the computer will automatically drop your block one line at a time once it reaches the right side of the video.

This might sound complicated but you'll soon catch on.

The game is over when all blocks have been reset. The computer will then print you a final message which ends the game. The total possible number of points are 2650. See Fig. 8-7 for the flowchart.

Program Notes

Some variations you might want to try are:

Changing the point system; you might want to raise or lower it.

Use a different key (to move your block) other than the space bar, line 340.

Have the player's block move even faster by lowering variable TP in line 120.

Change the ending messages for total points received in lines 1290-1330.

Your imagination is the only thing that is holding you back!

Program Listing

```
5 REM PROGRAM TITLE: WATCH YOUR SCREEN
10 CLS:PRINT@20,"** WATCH YOUR SCREEN *
   *"
15 PRINT:PRINT:RANDOM
20 PRINT"AND THAT'S WHAT YOU MUST DO T
   O WIN. A TOTAL OF"
25 PRINT"2650 POINTS CAN BE WON BUT YO
   U MUST STAY OUT OF"
30 PRINT"THE 'GUTTER'. LANDING THERE W
   ILL RETURN YOUR POINTS"
35 PRINT"TO ZERO."
40 PRINT"YOU WILL SEE BLOCKS ON THE SC
   REEN, EACH BLOCK WILL"
45 PRINT"HAVE A DIFFERENT NUMBER IN IT
   , THAT IS THE POINTS."
50 PRINT"YOUR BLOCK WILL LOOK LIKE THI
   S :  "CHR$(140)
55 PRINT"EACH TIME YOU WANT TO MOVE UP
   , PRESS THE <SPACE BAR>."
60 PRINT"WHEN YOUR BLOCK REACHES THE R
   IGHT OF THE SCREEN, IT"
65 PRINT"(YOUR BLOCK) WILL DROP ONE LI
   NE. WHEN YOU ARE AT THE"
```

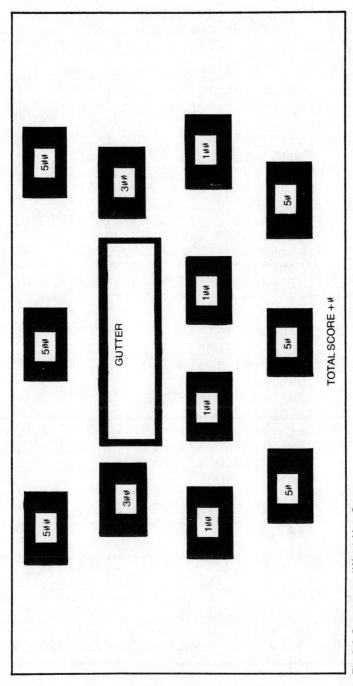

Fig. 8-6. Sample run of Watch Your Screen.

```
70 PRINT"TOP OF THE VIDEO AND YOU WANT
      TO RETURN DOWN, PRESSING"
72 PRINT:PRINT"(PRESS ENTER)";:INPUT X
      $:CLS:PRINT
75 PRINT"THE SPACE BAR WILL RETURN YOU
      TO THE BEGINNING POSITION"
80 PRINT"(BOTTOM OF VIDEO - LEFT CORNE
      R)."
85 PRINT"EACH TIME A BLOCK IS CORRECTL
      Y HIT, YOU WILL GAIN THOSE"
90 PRINT"POINTS AND THE BLOCK WILL BE
      RESET. GAME IS ALL BLOCKS"
95 PRINT"RESET.....GOOD LUCK !!"
96 PRINT"(P.S. YOUR BLOCK WILL AUTOMAT
      ICALLY MOVE RIGHT BY A"
97 PRINT"RANDOM NUMBER SELECTED BY THE
      COMPUTER)."
98 PRINT"PRESS ENTER ";CHR$(34);"TO WA
      TCH YOUR VIDEO";CHR$(34);:INPUT X
      $:CLS
100 CLS:DIM A(13)
105 FOR I=1TO12:READ A(I):NEXT
110 DATA 71,96,121,268,308,455,473,487
      ,505,655,673,691
115 GOSUB120:GOSUB225:GOTO320:REM SET
      TARGETS
120 Y=2:A=500:B=300:C=100:D=50:TP=300
130 FOR X=10TOX*2+7:SET(X,Y):SET(X+50,
      Y):SET(X+100,Y):NEXT
140 Y=Y+1
150 IF Y<>7 THEN130
160 PRINT@A(1),A;:PRINT@A(2),A;:PRINT@
      A(3),A;
170 Y=11
180 FOR X=20TOX*2-3:SET(X,Y):SET(X+80,
      Y):NEXT
190 Y=Y+1
200 IF Y<>16 THEN180
210 PRINT@A(4),B;:PRINT@A(5),B;
215 FOR Y=11TO17:SET(41,Y):SET(96,Y):N
      EXT
```

194

```
220 FOR X=41TO96:SET(X,11):SET(X,17):N
    EXT:PRINT@288,"GUTTER";:RETURN
225 Y=20
230 FOR X=10TOX*2+7:SET(X,Y):SET(X+35,
    Y):SET(X+64,Y):SET(X+100,Y):NEXT
```

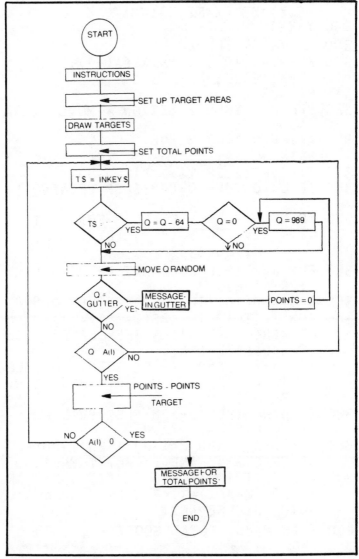

Fig. 8-7. Flowchart of Watch Your Screen.

```
240 Y=Y+1
250 IF Y<>25 THEN230
260 PRINT@A(6),C;:PRINT@A(7),C;:PRINT@
    A(8),C;:PRINT@A(9),C;
270 Y=29
280 FOR X=20TOX*2-3:SET(X+5,Y):SET(X+4
    1,Y):SET(X+77,Y):NEXT
290 Y=Y+1
300 IF Y<>34 THEN280
310 PRINT@A(10),D;:PRINT@A(11),D;:PRIN
    T@A(12),D;
315 RETURN
320 REM SET YOUR POSITION - MOVE IT RA
    NDOM
330 A$=CHR$(140):Q=898
335 PRINT@Q,A$;
340 T$=INKEY$:IF T$=" "THEN380
350 IF Q<=0 THEN Q=898:ELSE PRINT@Q,A$
    ;
355 IF Q<=512 THEN356:ELSE FOR JJ=1TOT
    P:NEXT:PRINT@Q," ";:PRINT@256,"
        ";:GOTO360
356 FOR JJ=1TOTP-200:NEXT:PRINT@Q," ";
    :PRINT@256,"           ";
360 Q=Q+RND(10):IF Q>=1012 THEN Q=898
365 FOR I=1TO12:IF ABS(Q-A(I)-1)>=0 AN
    D ABS(Q-A(I)-1)<3 THENGOSUB600:GO
    TO340:ELSE NEXT
370 IF Q>=277 AND Q<=303 THEN 1100:ELS
    E IF Q>=341 AND Q<=367 THEN 1100:
    ELSE GOTO400
380 IF Q<=0 THEN Q=898:ELSE PRINT@Q,"
    ";:Q=Q-64
385 IF Q>=277 AND Q<=303 THEN 1100:ELS
    E IF Q>=341 AND Q<=367 THEN 1100
390 FOR I=1TO12:IF ABS(Q-A(I)-1)>=0 AN
    D ABS(Q-A(I)-1)<3 THEN GOSUB600:G
    OTO340:ELSE NEXT
400 PRINT@988,"TOTAL SCORE +";P;:GOTO3
    40
600 REM SCORE + AREA
```

```
610 REM AND RESET BLOCK HIT
620 REM AND CHECK REMAINING BLOCKS
630 REM END IF ALL ARE RESET
700 IF A(I)=71 OR A(I)=96 OR A(I)=121
    THEN Y=2:GOTO900
710 IF A(I)=268 OR A(I)=308 THEN Y=11:
    GOTO930
720 IF A(I)=455 OR A(I)=473 OR A(I)=48
    7 OR A(I)=505 THEN Y=20:GOTO960
730 IF A(I)=655 OR A(I)=673 OR A(I)=69
    1 THEN Y=29:GOTO990
740 PRINT@256,"SCORE";
750 FOR I=1TO12:IF A(I)<>0 THEN Q=Q-64
    :RETURN:ELSE NEXT
760 GOTO1200
900 FOR X=10TOX*2+7:IF A(I)=71 THEN RE
    SET(X,Y):NEXT:GOTO910:ELSE IF A(I
    )=96 THEN RESET(X+50,Y):NEXT:GOTO
    910:ELSE IF A(I)=121 THEN RESET(X
    +100,Y):NEXT
910 Y=Y+1:IF Y<>7 THEN900
920 A(I)=0:P=P+A:GOTO740:REM SCORE/RET
    URN
930 FOR X=20TOX*2-3:IF A(I)=268 THEN R
    ESET(X,Y):NEXT:GOTO940:ELSE IF A(
    I)=308 THEN RESET(X+80,Y):NEXT
940 Y=Y+1:IF Y<>16 THEN930
950 A(I)=0:P=P+B:GOTO740:REM SCORE/RET
    URN
960 FOR X=10TOX*2+7:IF A(I)=455 THEN R
    ESET(X,Y):NEXT:GOTO970:ELSE IF A(
    I)=473 THEN RESET(X+35,Y):NEXT:GO
    TO970:ELSE IF A(I)=487 THEN RESET
    (X+64,Y):NEXT:GOTO970:ELSE IF A(I
    )=505 THEN RESET(X+100,Y):NEXT
970 Y=Y+1:IF Y<>25 THEN960
980 A(I)=0:P=P+C:GOTO740:REM SCORE/RET
    URN
990 FOR X=20TOX*2-3:IF A(I)=655 THEN R
    ESET(X+5,Y):NEXT:GOTO1000:ELSE IF
    A(I)=673 THEN RESET(X+41,Y):NEXT
```

```
       :GOTO1000:ELSE IF A(I)=691 THEN R
       ESET(X+77,Y):NEXT
1000  Y=Y+1:IF Y<>34 THEN990
1010  A(I)=0:P=P+D:GOTO740:REM SCORE/RE
      TURN
1100  REM IN GUTTER / SCORE RETURNS TO
      ZERO
1110  G=0
1120  PRINT@988," * IN GUTTER *      ";:F
      OR JJ=1TO100:NEXT
1130  PRINT@988,"                    ";:F
      OR JJ=1TO50:NEXT
1140  G=G+1
1150  IF G<>15 THEN1120
1160  P=0
1170  GOSUB215:GOTO320
1200  REM END OF GAME
1210  GOSUB215
1220  PRINT@281,"* * END OF GAME * *";
1230  PRINT@988,"TOTAL SCORE +";P;
1235  PRINT@832,;
1240  IF P>=0 AND P<=500 THEN1290
1250  IF P>=501 AND P<=1000 THEN1300
1260  IF P>=1001 AND P<=1500 THEN1310
1270  IF P>=1501 AND P<=2000 THEN1320
1280  IF P>2001 THEN1330
1290  PRINT"TRY AGAIN - WITH YOUR EYES
      CLOSED, YOUR SCORE MIGHT IMPROVE
      !!":GOTO1340
1300  PRINT"HAVE YOU ANY GLASSES ? YOU
      MIGHT HELP YOUR SCORE WITH THEM !
      !":GOTO1340
1310  PRINT"ALMOST HALF ? THAT'S NOT RE
      ALLY THAT BAD.....":GOTO1340
1320  PRINT"BETTER THAN HALF !! A REAL
      GOOD SCORE, FOR A BEGINNER ?":GOT
      O1340
1330  PRINT"NOW THAT IS A GREAT SCORE !
      !!"
1340  FOR J=1TO3000:NEXT
1350  CLS:PRINT
1360  PRINT:PRINT
```

```
1370 PRINT"*** GOODBYE FOR NOW ***"
1380 PRINT
1390 PRINT
1400 END
```

MAZE GAME

This is a two-level maze game, but naturally there is a catch to that. You can't proceed to the level II maze until you complete 5 rounds without error, in the level I maze. Movement through both level I and level II will be from left to right. You control your block with the four arrow keys.

With level I maze, you must connect your block with the flashing block, located on the right side of the display. With level I you can scrape the top or bottom of your block on any part of the maze, if you find it difficult to get through. But hitting the front or back of your block will count as a hit (Fig. 8-8A).

With the level II maze you will find that navigating through it will be much different than level I. You cannot scrape any part of the block on any part of the maze, to do so will count as a hit. If you go the wrong way you might get in a trap (Fig. 8-8B).

When you hit any part of the maze, the computer automatically RESETS your block and moves it in the opposite direction, when it does this you might become trapped because your block will be bouncing back and forth from one hit area to another. If this happens the only way you can escape is to *hold down* the appropriate arrow key for the direction you wish to go, do this while the computer is printing your TOTAL HITS, and keep holding it down until you're out of the trap.

As with level I, you must complete 5 rounds with level II to win. To complete a round with level II just enter the area titled HOME AREA, the computer will receive your entry and start you on another round (if 5 haven't been completed). See Fig. 8-9 for the flowchart.

Program Notes

If you wish you could change the total number of rounds required to move from level I to level II to a random value. And, with a little experimentation, the set-up for level I maze can be changed to suit your needs. Speed isn't a factor here, as the player will find enough difficulty just trying to reach the HOME AREA with the level II maze.

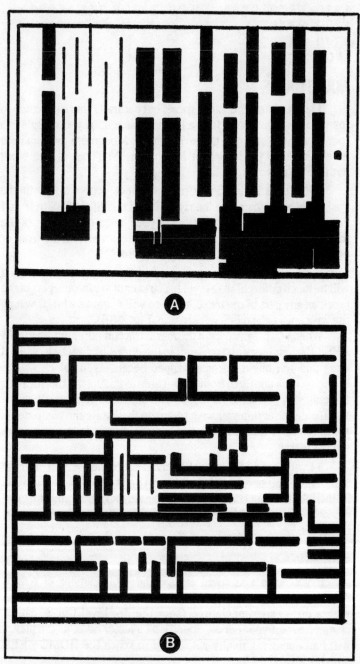

Fig. 8-8. Sample run of Maze Game.

Program Listing

```
5 REM PROGRAM TITLE: MAZE GAME
10 REM THIS MAZE GAME HAS TWO LEVELS O
    F
20 REM DIFFICULTY. THE FIRST LEVEL MUS
    T BE RUN
30 REM WITHOUT ERROR FIVE TIMES BEFORE
    THE
40 REM NEXT LEVEL WILL BE INTRODUCED.
    PART
50 REM OF THE MAZE WILL BE DRAWN AT RA
    NDOM.
60 REM MOVEMENT THROUGH THE MAZE WILL
    BE A LITTLE
70 REM FASTER WITH LEVEL II.
80 REM GOTO INSTRUCTIONS
90 GOSUB1200
100 REM DRAW LEVEL I
101 R=0:RR=1:H=0:H1=0:H2=0:H3=0:L=1:RA
    NDOM
105 CLS
110 XX=RND(17):XY=RND(5):YY=RND(19):F=
    XY
115 IF YY<=5 THEN YY=10
120 X=10:IF XX<=15 XX=15
130 SET(X,XY):SET(XX+3,XY+3):SET(XX+8,
    XY+2):SET(XX+12,XY):SET(XX+16,XY+
    4):SET(XX+20,XY+2):RESET(XX+42,XY
    ):RESET(XX+43,XY):RESET(XX+45,XY+
    1):RESET(XX+46,XY+1):SET(X+30,XY+
    3)
131 SET(X+39,XY+3):SET(X+62,XY+4):SET(
    X+70,XY):SET(X+80,XY+2):SET(X+89,
    XY):SET(X+98,XY+3)
135 SET(X+52,XY):IF R=2 THEN RESET(XX+
    18,XY+2):RESET(XX+21,XY+2)
140 X=X+1
150 IF X<>XX THEN130
160 XY=XY+1
170 IF XY<YY THEN120:ELSE IF R=1 THEN2
    00
```

```
175 IF R=2 THEN250
180 XY=XY+2:YY=YY+15:R=1
190 GOTO120
200 R=2
210 XY=XY+2:YY=YY+8
220 X=X+2
230 XX=X+10
240 GOTO130
250 REM DRAW FRAME
300 FOR J=0TO127:SET(J,F):SET(J,XY+4):
    NEXT
310 FOR J=FTOXY+4:SET(0,J):SET(127,J):
    NEXT
320 REM PLAY LEVEL I
330 GOTO5000
400 REM LEVEL II MAZE
410 REM THIS PART OF THE MAZE WILL
420 REM NOT USE ANY RANDOM NUMBERS
430 REM FOR SET-UP
440 REM DRAW FRAME
445 CLS:RR=1
450 FOR X=0TO127:SET(X,0):SET(X,42):SE
    T(X,47):NEXT
460 FOR X=0TO47:SET(0,X):SET(127,X):NE
    XT
470 REM SET VARIABLE LIST
480 A=23:B=50:D=0:F=20:E=42
490 REM DRAW MAZE
500 FOR Q=DTOA:SET(Q,D+2):NEXT
510 FOR Q=DTOA-2:SET(Q,D+5):SET(Q,D+8)
    :NEXT
520 FOR Q=A+3TO123:SET(Q,D+5):NEXT:RES
    ET(66,D+5):RESET(67,D+5):FOR Q=82
    TO84:RESET(Q,D+5):NEXT:RESET(102,
    D+5):RESET(103,D+5)
530 FOR Q=DTOA+4:SET(Q,D+12):NEXT:FOR
    Q=11TO13:RESET(Q,D+12):NEXT
540 FOR Q=6TO11:SET(A+3,Q):SET(A+4,Q):
    SET(B+18,Q):SET(B+19,Q):NEXT
550 FOR Q=31TO62:SET(Q,D+11):NEXT
560 FOR Q=9TO11:SET(63,Q):SET(64,Q):NE
```

202

```
XT:FOR Q=6TO8:SET(85,Q):SET(86,Q)
    :NEXT
570 FOR Q=B+18TOB+51:SET(Q,D+11):NEXT
580 FOR Q=12TO14:SET(B-7,Q):NEXT
590 FOR Q=B-7TOB+15:SET(Q,D+14):NEXT
600 FOR Q=DTOD+33:SET(Q,A-7):NEXT
610 FOR Q=A+14TOB+29:SET(Q,A-7):NEXT
```

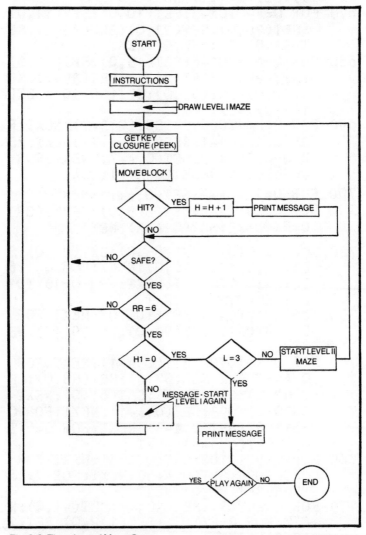

Fig. 8-9. Flowchart of Maze Game.

```
620 FOR Q=B+28TOB+59:SET(Q,A-8):NEXT
630 FOR Q=9TO14:SET(B+55,Q):SET(B+56,Q
    ):NEXT:FOR Q=8TO14:SET(B+72,Q):SE
    T(B+73,Q):NEXT
640 FOR Q=B+63TOB+73:SET(Q,A-8):NEXT
650 FOR Q=D+3TOA+16:SET(Q,A-3):NEXT
660 FOR Q=17TOA+3:SET(B-10,Q):SET(B-9,
    Q):SET(B-1,Q):NEXT
670 FOR Q=A-2TOA+3:SET(10,Q):SET(11,Q)
    :SET(20,Q):SET(21,Q):SET(30,Q):SE
    T(31,Q):SET(57,Q):NEXT
680 FOR Q=A+1TOA+6:SET(15,Q):SET(16,Q)
    :SET(25,Q):SET(26,Q):SET(35,Q):SE
    T(36,Q):SET(53,Q):SET(107,Q):SET(
    108,Q):NEXT
690 FOR Q=D+4TOD+108:SET(Q,A+7):NEXT:F
    OR Q=17TOA+1:RESET(Q,A+7):NEXT:FO
    R Q=81TO83:RESET(Q,A+7):NEXT:FOR
    Q=98TO100:RESET(Q,A+7):NEXT
700 FOR Q=19TOA+1:SET(Q,A+7):NEXT
710 FOR Q=20TOA+6:SET(B-5,Q):NEXT:FOR
    Q=BTOB+13:SET(Q,A-3):NEXT
720 FOR Q=16TO18:SET(85,Q):SET(86,Q):S
    ET(95,Q):SET(96,Q):NEXT:FOR Q=116
    TO123:SET(Q,17):NEXT:FOR Q=104TO1
    23:SET(Q,A-4):NEXT
730 FOR Q=19TOA+3:SET(103,Q):NEXT:FOR
    Q=A-4TOA-2:SET(90,Q):SET(91,Q):NE
    XT
740 FOR Q=67TO102:SET(Q,A-1):NEXT:FOR
    Q=A-3TOA-2:SET(67,Q):SET(68,Q):SE
    T(69,Q):SET(80,Q):SET(81,Q):NEXT
750 FOR Q=61TO93:SET(Q,A+1):NEXT:FOR Q
    =61TO87:SET(Q,A+3):NEXT:FOR Q=61T
    O81:SET(Q,A+5):NEXT
760 FOR Q=97TO102:SET(Q,A+3):NEXT:FOR
    Q=90TO96:SET(Q,A+5):NEXT:FOR Q=26
    TO28:SET(97,Q):NEXT
770 FOR Q=29TO34:SET(90,Q):SET(91,Q):N
    EXT:FOR Q=27TO31:SET(112,Q):SET(1
    13,Q):NEXT
```

```
780 FOR Q=DTO127:SET(Q,34):NEXT:FOR Q=
    23TO25:RESET(Q,34):NEXT:FOR Q=109
    TO111:RESET(Q,34):NEXT:RESET(42,3
    4):RESET(43,34):RESET(54,34):RESE
    T(55,34):RESET(92,34):RESET(93,34
    ):FOR Q=64TO66:RESET(Q,34):NEXT
790 FOR Q=35TO38:SET(26,Q):SET(27,Q):N
    EXT:FOR Q=DTOA+11:SET(Q,38):NEXT
800 FOR Q=B+22TO94:SET(Q,38):NEXT:FOR
    Q=103TO127:SET(Q,38):NEXT:FOR Q=1
    12TO127:SET(Q,36):NEXT
810 FOR Q=112TO127:SET(Q,A+9):NEXT:FOR
    Q=38TO41:SET(38,Q):SET(39,Q):SET
    (47,Q):SET(48,Q):SET(59,Q):SET(60
    ,Q):SET(72,Q):SET(73,Q):SET(98,Q)
    :SET(99,Q):NEXT
820 FOR Q=35TO39:SET(67,Q):SET(68,Q):S
    ET(69,Q):NEXT:FOR Q=107TO123:SET(
    Q,A):NEXT:FOR Q=36TO38:SET(B+2,Q)
    :SET(B+3,Q):SET(B+4,Q):SET(B+5,Q)
    :NEXT
830 REM TOTAL RUNS THROUGH MAZE = 5
840 REM HITS PER RUN AND TOTAL HITS WI
    LL BE PRINTED
845 A$="HOME AREA"
850 PRINT@884,A$;
855 TT=16242:POKE TT,32
860 B=2
870 W=40
880 GOTO5050
1000 GOSUB6050
1010 CLS:PRINT
1020 PRINT"THAT IS THE END OF LEVEL i
     AND II MAZE GAME."
1030 H3=H1+H2
1040 PRINT"YOUR ERRORS FOR BOTH LEVELS
      TOTALED";H3
1050 IF H3<=10 THEN1080
1060 IF H3>=20 THEN1090
1070 PRINT"AND THAT'S NOT A BAD SCORE
     AT ALL !!":GOTO1100
```

```
1080 PRINT"ONLY";H3;"HITS, THAT'S FANT
     ASTIC !!":GOTO1100
1090 PRINT"COULDN'T LOCATE THE RIGHT K
     EYs HUH ???"
1095 PRINTH3;"ERRORS ??? COULD YOU MAK
     E IT THROUGH A SHOE BOX ??"
1100 PRINT
1110 PRINT"READY TO TRY 'MAZE' AGAIN";
1120 INPUT A$
1130 IF A$<>"YES" THEN 1150
1140 GOTO101
1150 PRINT"SEE YOU NEXT TIME....."
1160 END

1200 CLS:PRINT
1210 PRINTTAB(15),"MAZE GAME"
1220 PRINT
1230 PRINT""THIS IS A MAZE GAME WHIC
     H YOU'LL CONTROL"
1240 PRINT"A BLOCK THROUGH A MAZE WITH
      THE FOUR ARROW"
1250 PRINT"KEYS ON YOUR KEYBOARD. THER
     E ARE TWO LEVELS"
1260 PRINT"OF DIFFICULTY TO THIS GAME,
      MEANING YOU CAN'T"
1270 PRINT"GO TO THE LEVEL II MAZE UNT
     IL 5 ROUNDS HAVE"
1280 PRINT"BEEN COMPLETED, WITHOUT ERR
     OR, IN LEVEL I."
1290 PRINT"WITH THE LEVEL I MAZE YOUR
     BLOCK CAN 'SCRAPE'"
1300 PRINT"ANYTHING ON ITS  TOP OR BOT
     TOM, BUT DON'T TRY"
1310 PRINT"THIS WITH LEVEL II, ANY HIT
     , TOP, BOTTOM, FRONT"
1320 PRINT"OR BACK WILL COUNT AS A 'HI
     T'."
1330 PRINT
1340 PRINT"PRESS ENTER";:INPUT A$
1350 CLS:PRINT
1360 PRINT"NOW, TO COMPLETE A ROUND FO
     R LEVEL I, YOUR BLOCK"
```

206

```
1370 PRINT"MUST 'HIT' THE FLASHING BLO
     CK ON THE RIGHT SIDE"
1380 PRINT"OF THE VIDEO. TO COMPLETE A
     ROUND IN LEVEL II"
1390 PRINT"ALL THAT IS NEEDED TO BE DO
     NE IS ENTER THE AREA"
1400 PRINT"TITLED 'HOME AREA', THE COM
     PUTER WILL RECEIVE"
1410 PRINT"YOUR ENTRY AND A ROUND WILL
     BE COMPLETED."
1420 PRINT
1430 PRINT"PRESS ENTER TO START LEVEL
     I";
1440 INPUT A$
1450 RETURN
5000 REM SET STARTING AREA FOR MOVEMEN
     T
5005 REM FOR LEVEL I
5010 B=4
5020 W=RND(XY-3):C=W-3
5030 IF W<=8 THEN 5020
5040 SET(B,W)
5050 T=PEEK(15340)
5053 IF L=2 THEN5060
5055 RESET(123,C):RESET(124,C)
5060 IF T=8 THEN W=W-1:RESET(B,W+1)
5070 IF T=16 THEN W=W+1:RESET(B,W-1)
5080 IF T=32 THEN B=B-1:RESET(B+1,W)
5090 IF T=64 THEN B=B+1:RESET(B-1,W)
5095 IF L=2 THEN5600
5100 IF B<=3 THEN B=4:GOTO5050
5110 IF B>=126 THEN B=125:GOTO5050
5120 IF W<=F THEN W=F+1:GOTO5050
5130 IF W>=XY+3 THEN W=W-1:GOTO5050
5140 SET(B,W):SET(123,C):SET(124,C)
5145 IF B<=110 THEN5170
5150 IF POINT(123,C+1) OR POINT(123,C-
     1) THEN5400
5160 IF POINT(122,C) THEN5400
5170 IF POINT(B-1,W) THEN5250
5180 IF POINT(B+1,W) THEN5250
```

```
5190 GOTO5050
5250 IF F>=3 THEN Q=RND(2):ON Q GOTO 5
     270,5280
5260 IF XY<=42 THEN5290
5270 PRINT@20,"SORRY, YOU'VE HIT !!";:
     GOTO5285
5280 PRINT@20,"THAT'S A HIT, BUSTER !!
     ";
5285 GOSUB6050:PRINT@20,"
                          ";:H=H+1:GOTO
     5330
5290 PRINT@980,"LET'S WATCH THE PATTER
     N !!";
5300 GOSUB6050
5310 PRINT@980,"
              ";
5320 H=H+1
5325 REM MOVE BLOCK AWAY FROM HIT AREA
5330 IF POINT(B+1,W) THEN RESET(B,W):B
     =B-1:GOTO5040
5340 IF POINT(B-1,W) THEN RESET(B,W):B
     =B+1:GOTO5040
5400 IF F>=3 THEN 5420
5410 IF XY<=42 THEN 5430
5420 PRINT@20,"THAT'S IT, YOU'RE SAFE!!
     ";:GOSUB6050:GOTO5450
5430 PRINT@980,"YOU'RE SAFE - FOR THIS
      ROUND !!";
5440 GOSUB6050:GOTO5460
5450 PRINT@20,"
          ";:GOTO5470
5460 PRINT@980,"
                 ";
5470 RR=RR+1:H1=H:RESET(B,W):RESET(123
     ,C):RESET(124,C):IF RR<>6 THEN548
     0
5475 GOTO5490
5480 GOTO5000:REM ANOTHER ROUND
5490 IF H1<>0 THEN 5510
5500 L=L+1:IF L=2 THEN PRINT@980,"BEGI
     NNING LEVEL II MAZE.....";:GOSUB6
     050:GOTO400:REM LEVEL II MAZE
```

```
5505 GOTO1000:REM END / PLAY AGAIN
5510 PRINT@963,"YOUR HITS TOTAL +";H1;
     "YOU CAN'T GO TO THE NEXT LEVEL..
     .";
5520 FOR KL=1TO2000:NEXT
5525 PRINT@963,"

     ";:H=0:RR=1
5530 GOTO5000

5600 IF B<=0 THEN B=1:GOTO5050
5610 IF B>=127 THEN B=126:GOTO5050
5620 IF W<=0 THEN W=1:GOTO5050
5630 IF W>=41 THEN W=40:GOTO5050
5640 SET(B,W)
5645 REM CHECK FOR HITS / ALL SIDES OF
     BLOCK
5650 IF POINT(B+1,W) THEN 5700
5660 IF POINT(B-1,W) THEN 5710
5670 IF POINT(B,W-1) THEN 5720
5680 IF POINT(B,W+1) THEN 5730
5685 IF B<=99 THEN 5695
5690 IF PEEK(TT)=136 THEN 5900:REM HOM
     E AREA
5695 GOTO5050
5696 REM MOVE BLOCK AWAY FROM HIT AREA

5700 RESET(B,W):B=B-1:GOTO5740
5710 RESET(B,W):B=B+1:GOTO5740
5720 RESET(B,W):W=W+1:GOTO5740
5730 RESET(B,W):W=W-1
5740 SET(B,W):H=H+1
5750 PRINT@24," THAT IS A HIT !! ";
5760 GOSUB6050
5770 PRINT@24,"                 ";
5780 PRINT@20," TOTAL HITS SO FAR =";H
     ;
5790 GOSUB6050

5800 PRINT@20,"                        "
     ;
5810 FOR Q=30TO100:SET(Q,0):NEXT
5820 GOTO5050
```

209

```
5900 PRINT@20," FANTASTIC YOU'RE HOME SA
     FE !! ";
5910 FOR KL=1TO1500:NEXT:H2=H+H2
5920 PRINT@20,"
          ";
5930 PRINT@23," TOTAL HITS SO FAR =";H
     2;
5940 GOSUB6050
5950 PRINT@23,"
       ";
5960 RR=RR+1
5970 IF RR<>6 THEN 5990
5980 GOTO1000:REM END / PLAY AGAIN
5990 PRINT@23," THIS WILL BE ROUND #";
     RR;
6000 GOSUB6050
6005 FOR Q=30TO100:SET(Q,0):NEXT
6010 REM GOTO ANOTHER ROUND
6020 H=0:RESET(B,W):GOTO830
6050 FOR KL=1TO1500:NEXT
6060 RETURN
```

Chapter 9
Gambling and Guessing

BY THE NUMBER

The playing field for this game will be 14 rows of underscores with 15 underscores in each row as shown in Fig. 9-1. You will place a bet to any amount. The computer will then set the playing field and at random points place numbers on these underscores. As it places numbers it will total the amount.

If the computer draws a 1, you'll have to start over, and lose the amount you've bet on that draw. The object of the game is to win at least $5,000.00 and get the rows to zero.

Each time the computer is finished placing numbers (and didn't draw a 1) you will be asket to press ENTER, doing so the computer will either divide your total random number by 2 or leave it as it stands. If your total random number is equal to or greater than 50 you will have one less row of underscores on the next draw. Watch out though. The computer has a tendency to start you over when least expected. See Fig. 9-2 for the flowchart.

Program Notes

Instead of underscores, you could use any character you choose by changing A$ in line 260.

You could raise or lower the target amount of $5,000.00 by changing variable TW in line 1020. Also instead of having the user start over with the computer drawing a 1, you could have the user input a number right after the bet, and, if the computer draws that number the user would have to start over. Be sure to change lines 345 & 350 for this approach.

At any rate, if any changes are made be sure to change the instructions to fit the program. Good luck, you'll need it trying to get the 14 cursor lines to 0.

Program Listing

```
50 REM PROGRAM TITLE:  BY THE NUMBER
100 CLS:GOSUB700:REM INSTRUCTIONS
170 DIM A(15),X(210)
180 REM KEEP NUMBERS WITHIN RANGE OF R
    OWS
190 REM DELETE ROWS AS L DECREASES
200 REM GET BET / SET PLAYING FIELD /
    SET COUNTERS
210 GOSUB215:T$="$**######.## DOLLARS"
    :GOTO220
```

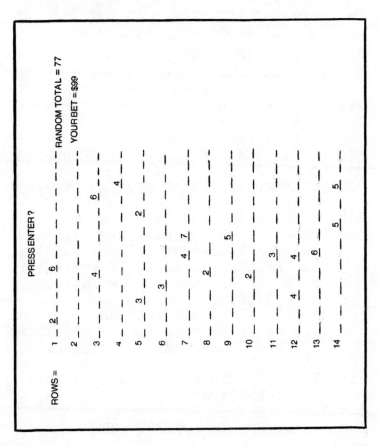

Fig. 9-1. Sample run of By the Number.

```
215 PRINT@24,"PLACE BET";:INPUT B:CLS:
    RETURN
220 FOR I=1TO14:READ A(I):NEXT:A=1:L=1
    5:M=210:BB=0:TT=0:TD=0
230 DATA 80,144,208,272,336,400,464
240 DATA 528,592,656,720,784,848,912
245 PRINT@A(1)-12,"ROWS =";
250 I=1:D=0:E=15:X=1
260 J=A(I):A$=CHR$(95):REM AREAS FOR U
    NDERSCORE CHR$(95)
265 PRINT@J-6,I;:REM UNDERSCORE WILL B
    E WITH PRINT @ STATEMENT
270 PRINT@J,A$;
280 X(X)=J:X=X+1:D=D+1:J=J+2:REM J+2 F
    OR SPACE BETWEEN NUMBERS / UNDERS
    CORE, D FOR NUMBER OF UNDERSCORES
    , X(X) FOR NUMBER PLACEMENT
290 IF D<>E THEN270
300 I=I+1:D=0:E=15:REM I+1 FOR PRINT @
    , RESET D - E FOR ANOTHER ROW
310 IF I<>L THEN260:REM L FOR AMOUNT O
    F ROWS (14)
315 TD=TD+1:REM DRAWS + 1
320 FOR I=1TOM:REM PLACEMENT OF NUMBER
    S
325 R=RND(10):REM RATE NUMBERS ARE PRI
    NTED
330 A=RND(9):IF R<>1 THEN 355
340 PRINT@X(I)-1,A;:AA=A+AA:PRINT@110,
    "RANDOM TOTAL=";AA;:IF B>=1E+04 T
    HEN PRINT@174,"YOUR BET =";:PRINT
    @238,"$";B;:ELSE PRINT@174,"YOUR
    BET= $";B;
345 IF A=1 AND AA<=10 THEN CN=A:GOTO40
    5:ELSE IF A=1 AND AA>=11 AND AA<=
    20 THEN 400:REM A=1 <=10 START OV
    ER
350 IF AA>=11 AND AA<=20 AND A=1 THEN
    AA=AA-RND(10)
355 NEXT
360 REM GOTO TOTAL OUTPUT SUB
```

```
370 GOSUB500
380 REM CHECK TO DELETE ONE LINE
390 IF AA>=50 THEN M=M-15:L=L-1:IF L=0
    THEN1000:REM M FOR PRINT @ - L F
    OR LINES LEFT
395 BB=B+BB:AT=AA+AT:AA=0:REM UPDATE C
    OUNTERS
398 CLS:GOSUB215:GOTO245
400 GOTO600:REM FOR INPUT OF NUMBER TO
    MATCH COMPUTER
405 PRINT@26,"START OVER";:Z=0
410 PRINT@X(I)-1,CN;:FOR K=1TO100:NEXT
412 PRINT@X(I)-1,"  ";:FOR K=1TO050:NEX
    T
415 Z=Z+1:IF Z<>10 THEN410
420 REM START OVER WITH '1'
425 PRINT@X(I)-1,CN;:FOR K=1TO1200:NEX
    T:L=15:M=210
430 N=N+1:NN=N*10:NN=-NN:REM FOR MINUS
    OF TOTAL AMOUNT
440 QQ=B:Q=-QQ+NN:AA=0:AT=0:CLS:GOSUB5
    10
450 CLS:GOSUB215:GOTO245
500 REM PRINT OUTPUT
505 PRINT@24,"PRESS ENTER";:INPUT B$:C
    LS
510 PRINT@82,"TOTAL DRAWS =";TD;
520 PRINT@146,"TOTAL  ONES  DRAWN =";N;
530 PRINT@210,"TOTAL RANDOM NUMBERS :"
    ;AT;
540 PRINT@274,"THIS RANDOM NUMBER :";A
    A;
545 IF AA<=0 THEN TT=Q+TT:AT=0:GOTO547
    :REM FOR MINUS AMOUNT
546 Q=0:TT=TT+(AA/RND(2))+B+Q-TD:REM F
    OR + AMOUNT
547 PRINT@402,"TOTAL EARNINGS + BET =
    ";
550 PRINT USING T$;TT:REM T$ FOR DOLLA
    R PRINT-OUT AMOUNT
555 PRINT@530,"STOP / CONTINUE (S/C)";
560 INPUT X$
```

```
570 IF X$="C" THEN RETURN
580 GOTO1000:REM WIN / LOSE MESSAGE -
    STOP / CONT
600 REM GET RANDOM NUMBER NUMBER FOR C
    OMPUTER
610 CN=RND(5):REM FOR COMPUTER NUMBER
620 PRINT@19,"ENTER A NUMBER (1-5)";
```

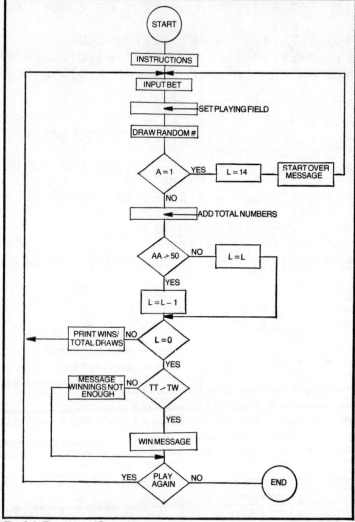

Fig. 9-2. Flowchart of By the Number.

```
630 INPUT NU
635 PRINT@19,"
        ";
640 IF NU=CN THEN AA=RND(51):GOSUB500:
    CLS:GOTO380
650 GOTO405:REM START OVER, LINES =15
700 REM INSTRUCTIONS
710 CLS:PRINT
720 PRINT@20,"** BY  THE  NUMBER **"
730 PRINT
740 PRINT"IS A GAME WHERE YOU'LL BE PL
    AYING AGAINST THE COMPUTER'S"
750 PRINT""RANDOM NUMBER GENERATOR. AND
      IT ISN'T YOUR ORDINARY NUMBER''
760 PRINT"GAME. FIRST YOU'LL BE ASKED
    TO PLACE A BET, WHICH CAN"
770 PRINT"BE ANYWHERE BETWEEN 0 AND 10
    0,000 (OR MORE). THE COMPUTER"
780 PRINT"WILL THEN PRINT 14 ROWS OF "
    ;CHR$(95);" AND AT RANDOM"
790 PRINT"PLACES, NUMBERS WILL BE PLAC
    ED AT THESE UNDERSCORES. IF"
800 PRINT"YOUR TOTAL AMOUNT IS LESS TH
    AN OR EQUAL TO 10 AND THE"
810 PRINT"COMPUTER DRAWS A 1 (ONE), YO
    U'LL HAVE TO START OVER"
820 PRINT"AND YOU'LL BE IN THE HOLE FO
    R THE AMOUNT YOU'VE BET."
830 PRINT
840 PRINT"PRESS ENTER";:INPUT X$:CLS:P
    RINT
850 PRINT"IF YOUR RANDOM TOTAL IS >=11
    AND <=20 AND THE COMPUTER"
860 PRINT"DRAWS A 1 (ONE) THAT RANDOM
    TOTAL WILL LESSEN BY 10."
870 PRINT"EACH TIME THE COMPUTER IS FI
    NISHED PLACING NUMBERS"
880 PRINT"YOUR TOTAL RANDOM AMOUNT WIL
    L BE DIVIDED BY 2, IF THE"
890 PRINT"TOTAL AMOUNT EXCEEDS 50 THE
    NEXT PRINT-OUT WILL CONTAIN"
```

217

```
900  PRINT"ONE LESS ROW. SO.....THE OBJ
     ECT OF THE GAME IS TO"
910  PRINT"GET THE ROWS TO 0 (ZERO) AND
     HAVE YOUR TOTAL WINNINGS"
920  PRINT"OF ATLEAST $ 5000.00. THAT'S
     THE ONLY WAY YOU CAN WIN."
922  PRINT:PRINT"PRESS ENTER";:INPUT X$
     :CLS:PRINT
930  PRINT
940  PRINT"BY THE WAY.....WHEN THE RAND
     OM TOTAL IS <=10 AND THE"
950  PRINT"COMPUTER DRAWS A 1, AS WAS S
     AID YOU'LL HAVE TO START"
960  PRINT"OVER AND BE IN THE HOLE FOR
     THAT AMOUNT, YOU'LL ALSO"
970  PRINT"BE DEDUCTED 10 (IN INCREMENT
     S OF 10) FOR EACH TIME YOU"
980  PRINT"HAVE TO START OVER, ALSO YOU
     R TOTAL WINNINGS WILL BE"
990  PRINT"DEDUCTED ONE POINT FOR EACH
     DRAW YOU TAKE."
991  PRINT"(THERE ARE OTHER SURPISES, B
     UT YOU'LL SEE THEM SOON)."
995  PRINT:PRINT"PRESS ENTER TO GET THE
     SHOW ON THE ROAD";:INPUT X$:CLS:
     RETURN
1000 REM CHECK IF TT>=1000 (TOTAL WINN
     INGS)
1010 REM AND PLAY AGAIN OR STOP
1020 TW=4999:REM COMPUTER TARGET AMOUN
     T
1030 FOR KL=1TO1200:NEXT:CLS
1040 PRINT:PRINT
1050 IF TT<=TW THEN1100
1060 PRINT"YOUR TOTAL WINNINGS EXCEED
     $";TW;"(TARGET AMOUNT)."
1065 IF L<>0 THEN PRINT"BUT ";:GOTO110
     5
1070 PRINT"AND YOU'VE OUTWITTED THE CO
     MPUTERS RANDOM GENERATOR,"
```

```
1080 PRINT"BY DELETING ALL ROWS, SO YO
     U'VE WON THIS GAME !!"
1090 GOTO1150
1100 PRINT"THIS ISN'T LAS VEGAS - BUT
     YOU HAVE LOST....."
1105 IF L<>0 THEN PRINT""YOU WERE SUPPOSED
     TO DELETE ALL LINES FIRST !! '':GOTO1150
     ":GOTO1150
1110 PRINT"YOU DID IN FACT DELETE ALL
     ROWS, BUT YOUR TOTAL"
1120 PRINT"WINNINGS DID NOT MEET OR EX
     CEED THE TARGET AMOUNT"
1130 PRINT"OF $";TW+1;". MAYBE YOU SHO
     ULD TRY 'GO FISH', AFTERALL"
1140 PRINT"THAT GAME DOESN'T INVOLVE R
     ANDOM NUMBERS....."
1150 PRINT
1160 PRINT"ARE YOU READY TO BATTLE THE
      RANDOM GENERATOR AGAIN"
1170 PRINT"AND PLAY ";CHR$(34);"BY  TH
     E NUMBER";CHR$(34);" ONCE MORE...
     .."
1180 PRINT"(ALL YOU HAVE TO DO IS WIN
     ";:PRINT USING T$;TW+1;
1185 PRINT")."; 
1190 INPUT X$
1200 IF X$="YES" THEN1230
1210 IF X$="NO" THEN1240
1220 PRINT:PRINT"THAT IS A YES / NO QU
     ESTION !!";:GOTO1190
1230 PRINT:PRINT"AND DELETE ALL LINES.
     ....":FOR KK=1TO1000:NEXT
1235 CLS:RESTORE:GOTO210
1240 PRINT:PRINT
1250 PRINT"MAYBE NEXT SPRING ?????"
1260 END
```

SOLITAIRE FOR TWO

This solitaire game lets you and your computer both play. You must use a combination of your cards (8 of them on the playing field) along with a draw card to total 15. The draw card *must* be used. Cards are valued as follows: aces count as 1, jacks count as 11, queens count as 12, and the king counts as 13. All other cards are face value (Fig. 9-3).

Each time you are able to enter a total of 15, it goes on your total score. Don't let the computer outsmart you! See Fig. 9-4 for the flowchart.

Program Notes

Lines 110-280 draw the cards.

Lines 300-330 are the graphics for the draw card.

Lines 340-400 set the areas for your cards.

Lines 410-470 set areas for the computer's cards.

Lines 480-540 establish a deck of 52 cards, suit and value.

Line 550 deletes cards as drawn.

Line 555 is the counter for the deck of cards, when variable CU reaches 52 a PRINT statement will be printed on the video "LAST CARD.....

Line 556 ends the game (end of deck).

Lines 660-760 set the strings for value and the suit for cards drawn.

Lines 840-860 are the arguments that determine who will go first.

Lines 1000-1145 input whether you can play; if yes, the input is the number of cards that will be used.

Lines 1200-1270 contain the arguments to see if computer is able to score.

Lines 1300-1390 are print messages for won, lost and play again.

Lines 1400-1435 draw your cards and place the cards drawn at the right.

Lines 1500-1640 clear (blank) the cards.

Lines 1650-1690 draw the cards for computer and place them at the right positons for the variable used.

Lines 1700-1970 are the instructions.

Program Listing

```
10 REM PROGRAM TITLE: SOLITAIRE FOR TW
   O
20 CLS:DEFINT E,J,T
30 DIM Q(53),S(53),I(12),X(52),Y(52)
40 GOSUB1700:GOTO560
100 RANDOM
110 REM USERS CARDS
```

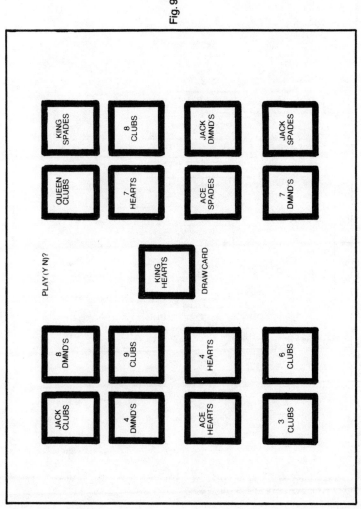

Fig. 9-3. Sample run of Solitaire for Two.

```
120 REM VARIABLES
130 A=10:X=0:U=19:YX=(U*3)-A:P=12
140 FOR M=XTOU:SET(M,1):SET(M,9)
150 SET(M,13):SET(M,21):SET(M,25):SET(
    M,33)
155 SET(M,37):SET(M,45)
160 NEXT:GOSUB200
170 X=U+4:U=(X+(A*2))
```

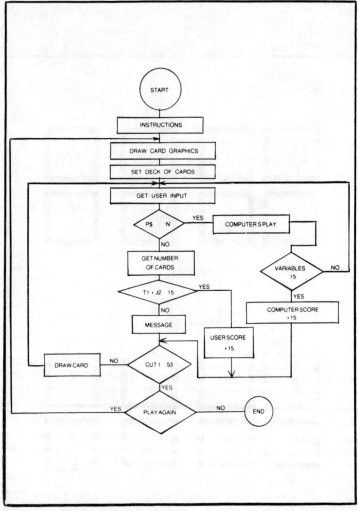

Fig. 9-4. Flowchart of Solitaire for Two.

```
180 IF X<>YX THEN140
190 IF R=1 R=0:GOTO300:ELSE 260
200 REM VERTICAL FOR CARDS
210 Y=2:N=8
220 FOR M=YTON:SET(X,M):SET(U,M):NEXT
230 Y=N+6:N=Y+6
240 IF Y<>(A*5) THEN220
250 RETURN
260 REM COMPUTER'S CARDS
270 X=(X*2)-A:U=(U*2)-31:YX=(YX*3)-A
280 R=1:GOTO140
300 REM DRAW CARD
310 FOR X=54TO73:SET(X,19):SET(X,27):N
    EXT
320 FOR Y=20TO26:SET(54,Y):SET(73,Y):N
    EXT
330 PRINT@667,"DRAW CARD";
340 REM CARD AREA FOR USER
350 U=67:W=130:J=1:L=1091
360 U(J)=U:W(J)=W:J=J+1
370 U=U+256:W=W+256:IF J=9 THEN410
380 IF U<>L THEN360
390 U=79:W=142:L=1103
400 GOTO360
410 REM CARD AREA FOR COMPUTER
420 C=109:V=172:J=1::L=1133
430 C(J)=C:V(J)=V:J=J+1
440 C=C+256:V=V+256:IF J=9 THEN480
450 IF C<>L THEN430
460 C=121:V=184:L=1207
470 GOTO430
475 CLS
480 REM ONE DECK OF CARDS
490 FOR K=1TO52:Q(K)=K:NEXT:E=K/4:S=K:
    S1=1:CU=0:RETURN
500 Z=RND(S)
510 IF Q(Z)=0 THEN500
520 T=(Q(Z)-1)/E:REM SUIT
530 J=Q(Z)-T*E:REM VALUE
540 J1=T:J2=J
550 Q(Z)=0:REM CARD USED
```

```
555 CU=CU+1:IF CU+1=52 GOSUB580:PRINT"
        LAST CARD...";:GOSUB596
556 IF CU+1=53 THEN GOSUB580:PRINT"   E
    ND OF GAME.....";:GOTO1300
558 RETURN
560 GOSUB100
570 GOTO600
580 PRINT@23,"                    ";
590 PRINT@23,;:RETURN
595 FOR TI=1TO2550:NEXT:RETURN
596 FOR TY=1TO1500:NEXT:RETURN
600 REM USERS CARD PLACEMENT
610 GOSUB580
620 PRINT"   YOUR CARD AREAS";
630 FOR I=1TO8:PRINT@U(I),I;:NEXT:GOSU
    B595:GOSUB580
640 FOR I=1TO8:PRINT@U(I)," ";:NEXT
650 FOR I=1TO8:A(I)=U(I):Z(I)=W(I):NEX
    T:I=1:V=1:II=1
660 A$="ACE":K$="KING":Q$="QUEEN":J$="
    JACK"
670 GOSUB500
680 IF J2=1 PRINT@A(I),A$;:J2=1:GOTO72
    0
690 IF J2=11 PRINT@A(I),J$;:J2=11:GOTO
    720
700 IF J2=12 PRINT@A(I),Q$;:J2=12:GOTO
    720
710 IF J2=13 PRINT@A(I),K$;:J2=13:GOTO
    720:ELSE PRINT@A(I),J2;
720 IF R=3 THEN X(II)=J2:ELSE Y(II)=J2
730 IF J1=0 PRINT@Z(I),"CLUBS";:GOTO76
    5
740 IF J1=1 PRINT@Z(I),"SPADES";:GOTO7
    65
750 IF J1=2 PRINT@Z(I),"DMND'S";:GOTO7
    65
760 IF J1=3 PRINT@Z(I),"HEARTS";
765 IF R=2 RETURN:ELSE IF R=1 R=2:GOTO
    820
770 I=I+1:II=II+1:V=V+1:IF I<>9 THEN67
    0
```

224

```
780 IF V=17 THEN810
790 FOR I=1TO8:A(I)=C(I):Z(I)=V(I):NEX
    T:I=1:II=1:R=3
800 GOTO670
810 A(I)=478:Z(I)=541:R=1:II=I:GOTO670
    :REM DRAW CARD
820 REM WHO GOES FIRST ?
825 M=8
830 GOSUB580
840 IF Y(M)=X(M) THEN870
850 IF Y(M)>X(M) THEN880
860 IF Y(M)<X(M) THEN890
870 M=M-1:GOTO830
880 PRINT" YOU GO FIRST.....";:GOTO100
    0
890 PRINT" I GO FIRST.....";:GOSUB596:
    GOTO1200
900 PRINT@A(II),"       ";:PRINT@Z(II),"
    ";
910 RETURN
1000 REM USER GOES FIRST
1010 GOSUB596
1020 LL=0:GOSUB580
1030 PRINT"    PLAY (Y/N) ?";
1040 P$=INKEY$:IF P$=""THEN1040
1045 IF P$="N"THEN B=B+1:IF B=2 B=0:GO
     SUB900:GOSUB500:GOSUB680::GOTO120
     0:ELSE GOTO1200
1050 B=0:GOSUB580
1060 PRINT" NUMBER OF CARDS ?";
1070 N$=INKEY$:IF N$=""THEN1070
1080 N=VAL(N$):GOSUB580
1090 PRINT"  CARD NUMBERS ?";
1100 K=1:T1=0
1110 M$=INKEY$:IF M$=""THEN1110
1120 T(K)=VAL(M$):T1=Y(T(K))+T1:K=K+1
1130 IF K<=N THEN1110
1140 IF T1+J2<>15 THEN1150
1145 FOR I=1TO8:A(I)=U(I):Z(I)=W(I):NE
     XT:T2=T1+J2+T2:GOSUB1500:GOTO1400
1150 GOSUB580:PRINT"INCORRECT TOTAL...
     ";:GOSUB596
```

```
1155 GOSUB580
1200 REM COMPUTER'S TURN
1205 GOSUB580:GOSUB595
1210 B=0:K=1:T3=0:H=0:KK=1
1220 IF J2+X(K)=15 THEN M1=1:GOSUB1560
     :GOTO1650
1225 IF J2+X(H)=15 THEN M1=1:GOSUB1580
     :GOTO1650
1230 IF J2+X(K)+X(H)=15 THEN M1=2:GOSU
     B1590:GOTO1650
1235 IF J2+X(H+2)+X(H+4)=15 THEN M1=2:
     GOSUB1600:GOTO1650
1240 K=K+1:IF K=9 AND H=9 THEN 1270
1250 IF K=9 THEN H=H+1:K=KK
1260 GOTO1220
1270 B=B+1:IF B=2 B=0:GOSUB900:GOSUB50
     0:GOSUB680:GOTO1020:ELSE GOTO1020
1300 REM WIN - LOSE
1305 FOR KL=1TO2500:NEXT
1310 CLS:PRINT
1315 IF T6=T2 THEN1330
1320 IF T6<T2 THEN1340
1325 IF T6>T2 THEN1355
1330 PRINT"LOOKS LIKE A TIE -- TURKEY
     !! YOUR TOTAL POINTS"
1335 PRINT"ARE, ";T2;" AND MINE ARE ";
     T6;".":GOTO1365
1340 PRINT"YOU'VE WON THIS ONE !! BUT
     DON'T BE TO SURE ABOUT"
1345 PRINT"THE NEXT GAME, I MIGHT DECI
     DE TO STACK THE DECK !!"
1350 GOTO1365
1355 PRINT"SORRY TURKEY !!! YOU'VE LOS
     T THIS GAME, HOW'S YOUR"
1360 PRINT"ADDING MACHINE WORKING ?? U
     SE IT NEXT TIME !!"
1362 PRINT"YOUR TOTAL POINTS WERE: ";T
     2;" MINE: ";T6;"."
1365 FOR KL=1TO5000:NEXT:PRINT
1370 PRINT"SHALL WE TRY ANOTHER GAME O
     F IT";
1375 INPUT I$
```

226

```
1380 IF RIGHT$(I$,1)="S" THEN T2=0:T6=
     0:CLS:GOSUB100:GOTO600
1385 PRINT:PRINT"END OF RUN.........."
1390 GOTO1390
1400 REM DRAW CARD(S)
1405 I=1
1410 A(I)=A(T(I)):Z(I)=Z(T(I)):GOSUB50
     0
1415 Y(T(I))=J2:GOSUB680
1420 I=I+1:IF I<=N THEN1410
1425 GOSUB500:II=9
1430 A(I)=A(II):Z(I)=Z(II):GOSUB680
1435 IF LL=1 THEN1020:ELSE 1200
1500 REM CLEAR CARD USED
1510 I=1
1520 PRINT@A(T(I))","        ";:PRINT@Z(T
     (I))","         ";
1530 I=I+1
1540 IF I<=N THEN1520
1550 GOSUB900:RETURN
1560 REM CLEAR COMPUTER CARD
1570 PRINT@C(K)","        ";:PRINT@V(K)","
          ";:T6=J2+X(K)+T6:GOTO1610
1580 PRINT@C(H)","        ";:PRINT@V(H)","
          ";:T6=J2+X(H)+T6:GOTO1610
1590 PRINT@C(K)","        ";:PRINT@C(H)","
          ";:PRINT@V(K)","        ";:PRI
     NT@V(H)","        ";:T6=J2+X(K)+X(H)
     +T6:GOTO1610
1600 PRINT@C(H+2)","        ";:PRINT@C(H+
     4)","        ";:PRINT@V(H+2)","
     ";:PRINT@V(H+4)","        ";:T6=J2+X
     (H+2)+X(H+4)+T6:UU=1
1610 REM
1620 PRINT@A(II)","        ";:PRINT@Z(II)
     ","        ";
1630 FOR I=1TO8:A(I)=C(I):Z(I)=V(I):NE
     XT
1640 RETURN
1650 REM DRAW FOR COMPUTER
1660 I=K:M2=1
```

227

```
1665 IF UU=1 UU=0:K=H+2:H=H+4
1670 A(I)=C(K):Z(I)=V(K):GOSUB500
1675 X(K)=J2:GOSUB680:IF M2=M1 THEN168
     5
1680 M2=M2+1:K=H:GOTO1670
1685 LL=1:M1=0
1690 GOTO1425
1700 CLS
1710 PRINTTAB(15);"<SOLITAIRE FOR TWO>
     "
1730 PRINT"SOLITAIRE FOR TWO IS DESIGN
     ED FOR YOU AND YOUR"
1740 PRINT"COMPUTER. EACH OF YOU WILL
     HAVE EIGHT CARDS DRAWN"
1750 PRINT"FROM THE DECK (1 DECK - 52
     CARDS). THE OBJECT OF"
1760 PRINT"THE GAME IS TO USE THE DRAW
      CARD WITH A COMBINATION"
1770 PRINT"OF YOUR CARDS TO TOTAL 15.
     ACE'S COUNT AS 1 - KING'S"
1780 PRINT"COUNT AS 13 - QUEEN'S COUNT
      AS 12 - JACK'S COUNT AS"
1790 PRINT"11 AND ALL OTHER CARDS ARE
     FACE VALUE. THE CARDS YOU"
1800 PRINT"USE WILL DETERMINE THE POIN
     TS YOU HAVE GAINED WHEN"
1810 PRINT"THE DECK RUNS OUT, EITHER Y
     OU OR YOUR COMPUTER WILL"
1820 PRINT"WIN BY THE MOST POINTS GAIN
     ED."
1825 PRINT"(NOTE: WHEN YOUR ASKED <NUM
     BER OF CARDS ?> THIS MEANS"
1828 PRINT"TO ENTER THE AMOUNT OF YOUR
      CARDS YOU'LL USE ALONG"
1829 PRINT"WITH THE <DRAW CARD> )."
1830 PRINT
1840 PRINT"PRESS ENTER";:INPUT XX:CLS:
     PRINT
1850 PRINT"THIS GAME USES THE INKEY$ F
     UNCTION, SO ALL YOUR"
1860 PRINT"ENTRYS WILL NOT REQUIRE THE
      USE OF 'ENTER'. THE"
```

228

```
1870 PRINT"VALUE OF THE 8TH CARD WILL
     DETERMINE WHICH OF"
1880 PRINT"YOU WILL GO FIRST, IN CASE
     OF A TIE THE 7TH CARD"
1890 PRINT"WILL BE USED, ETC., ETC."
1900 PRINT"THE COMPUTER WILL PRINT YOU
     R CARD POSITIONS AT THE"
1910 PRINT"BEGINNING OF THE RUN, REMEM
     BER THESE POSITIONS --"
1920 PRINT"EACH TIME IT'S YOUR TURN, Y

     OU ONLY GET ONE CHANCE"
1930 PRINT"TO ENTER THE CORRECT CARD(S
     )."
1940 PRINT
1950 PRINT"PRESS ENTER TO BEGIN RUN";:
     INPUT XX
1960 CLS
1970 RETURN
```

PYRAMID (SOLITAIRE)

Beware... This game could become habit forming!

To win, all numbers must be deleted from the pyramid, but, you might find this a little difficult to do (Fig. 9-5). Numbers can only be deleted from the pyramid if their sum equals 13. And, you can only go through the deck once! See Fig. 9-6 for the flowchart.

Good luck!

Program Notes

Lines 70-495 draw the pyramid and set the PRINT @ areas for cards.

Lines 500-750 set a deck of cards, select the cards at random and print their value at the correct location of the pyramid.

Lines 760-945 accept your input. If you desire more cards from the pyramid the program will branch to lines 1500-1660.

Lines 960-1030 check total amount of all cards entered, blanks them out and draws more cards (if any are left in deck).

Lines 1260-1380 check input of card to see if it is still covered.

Lines 2000-2570 are the instructions.

Program Listing

```
10 REM PYRAMID (SOLITAIRE)
15 GOSUB2000:DEFINT N,F
```

```
20 CLS:DIM A(50),C(52),H(52),F(52),Q(5
   2)
70 RANDOM:REM THE CARDS (GRAPHIC)
80 B=24:E=10:F=120:J=37:K=42:M=24:ML=0
   :R=0
90 FOR X=ETOF:SET(X,J):SET(X,K)
100 IF X=B THEN X=X+2:B=B+16
110 NEXT:M=M+8:IF M=80 THEN200
120 B=M
130 E=E+8:F=F-8:K=J-1:J=K-5
140 GOTO90
200 REM VERTICAL LINES FOR CARDS
220 E=38:F=41:J=10:K=24:B=123:M=10
230 FOR Y=ETOF:SET(J,Y):SET(K,Y):NEXT
240 J=K+3:K=K+16:IF J=B THEN M=M+8:IF
    M=66 THEN350 ELSE260
250 GOTO230
260 F=E-3:E=E-6:B=B-8
270 J=M:K=J+14:GOTO230
350 FOR X=4TO17:SET(X,7):SET(X,12):NEX
    T
360 FOR Y=8TO11:SET(4,Y):SET(17,Y):NEX
    T
380 REM CARD PLACEMENT
390 A(0)=95:A(1)=219:A(2)=227
400 C=343
410 FOR I=3TO5:A(I)=C:C=C+8:NEXT
420 C=467
430 FOR I=6TO9:A(I)=C:C=C+8:NEXT
440 C=591
450 FOR I=10TO14:A(I)=C:C=C+8:NEXT
460 C=715
470 FOR I=15TO20:A(I)=C:C=C+8:NEXT
480 C=839
490 FOR I=21TO27:A(I)=C:C=C+8:NEXT:A(2
    8)=196
495 GOSUB700:REM CARD AREA FOR INPUT F
    ROM USER
500 REM CARDS -- ONE DECK
510 FOR I=1TO52:C(I)=I:NEXT:C=(I-1)/4:
    M=C*4:K=1:GOTO550
520 K=RND(52):IF C(K)=0 THEN520
```

230

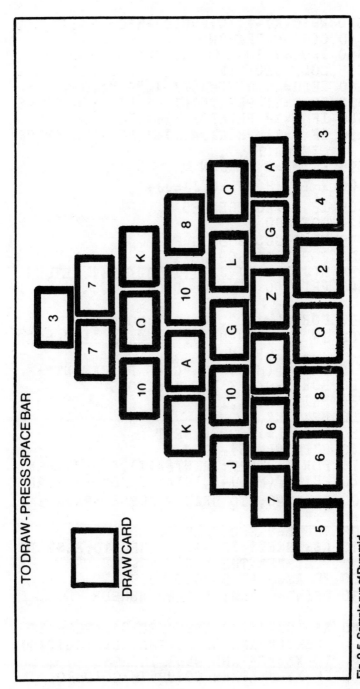

TO DRAW - PRESS SPACE BAR

DRAW CARD

Fig. 9-5. Sample run of Pyramid.

231

```
530 N=(C(K)-1)/C:F=C(K)-N*C
540 C(K)=0:RETURN
550 I=0:JJ=1
555 GOSUB520:G=F
560 IF G=1 PRINT@A(I)+1,"A ";:GOTO595
570 IF G=11 PRINT@A(I)+1,"J ";:GOTO595
580 IF G=12 PRINT@A(I)+1,"Q ";:GOTO595
590 IF G=13 PRINT@A(I)+1,"K ";:ELSE PR
    INT@A(I),G;
595 IF ML=2 RETURN
600 I=I+1:H(JJ)=G:JJ=JJ+1
605 IF I<>28 THEN555
610 GOTO800
615 ML=2:GOSUB555:G=F
620 FORKK=1TO500:NEXT
630 H(JJ)=G:JJ=JJ+1:IF JJ<>M+1 RETURN
640 PRINT@0,"END OF DECK...............
    .";
650 FOR KL=1TO2000:NEXT:GOTO1700
700 IF DD=1 THEN780:REM CARD PLACEMENT
    -- FOR INPUT
710 PRINT@(M*5)-10,"CARD PLACEMENT";
720 FOR I=0TO27:FOR KK=1TO015
730 PRINT@A(I),I;
740 NEXT KK,I
750 FOR KL=1TO2000:NEXT
760 PRINT@(M*5)-10,"                ";
770 FOR I=0TO27:PRINT@A(I)," ";:NEXT
780 PRINT@(M*5)-9,"DRAW CARD";:RETURN
800 PRINT@0,"TO DRAW - PRESS SPACE BAR
    .";
805 IF ML=0 G=0:ELSE G=F
810 A$=INKEY$:IF A$="" THEN810:ELSE IF
    A$="E" THEN830
820 IF A$=" "THEN GOSUB615
830 PRINT@0,"ENTER CARD NUMBER
    ";
840 X$=INKEY$:IF X$=""THEN840:ELSE IF
    X$="E" AND WE<>1 THEN L=G:GOTO940
842 IF X$="E" AND WE=1 THEN960
845 IF X$=" "THEN GOSUB615:GOTO830
```

232

```
850 V=VAL(X$):V=V*10
860 Z$=INKEY$:IF Z$=""THEN860
870 S=VAL(Z$)
880 SC=V+S:L=H(SC+1):GOSUB1260:IF RY=1
    THEN RY=0:GOTO800
885 IF A(SC)=0 THEN1050
890 PRINT@0,"WITH CARD DRAWN ?
    ";
900 Q$=INKEY$:IF Q$="" THEN900
905 IF Q$="C" GOSUB1500:GOTO890
910 IF Q$="D" THEN960
920 IF Q$="E" AND WE<>1 THEN940:ELSE L
    L=LL-G:ND=1:GOTO962
930 GOTO890
```

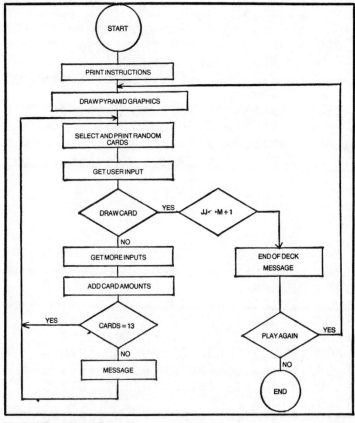

Fig. 9-6. Flowchart of Pyramid.

```
940 IF L<>C THEN GOSUB1200:GOTO800
945 GOSUB1260:IF RY=1 RY=0:GOTO800
947 PRINT@0,"CORRECT AMOUNT.....";:GOS
    UB1000:GOTO800:REM FOR KINGS ONLY
950 PRINT@0,"CORRECT AMOUNT.....";:GOS
    UB1000
955 IF ND=1 ND=0:GOTO800:ELSE GOSUB615
    :GOTO830:REM DRAW ANOTHER -- IF A
    NY
960 LL=L+G+LT+LF
962 IF LL<>C THEN GOSUB1200:GOTO800
965 GOSUB1260:IF RY=1 RY=0:GOTO800
970 GOTO950:REM ANOTHER CARD
1000 FOR KK=1TO1200:NEXT
1010 PRINT@A(SC),"    ";:IF WE=1 PRINT@
     A(SW),"    ";
1012 IF WD=1 PRINT@A(SL),"    ";
1020 A(SC)=0:IF WE=1 THEN A(SW)=0
1025 IF WD=1 THEN A(SL)=0
1030 LL=0:L=0:G=0:LT=0:LF=0:WE=0:WD=0
1040 RETURN
1050 PRINT@39,"CARD USED - TRY AGAIN."
     ;:GOSUB1220:GOTO830
1200 REM INCORRECT AMOUNT
1210 PRINT@0,"INCORRECT TOTAL -- NOT";
     C;
1220 FOR KK=1TO1500:NEXT
1230 PRINT@0,"
     ";
1235 PRINT@39,"
     ";
1240 LL=0:L=0:G=0:LT=0:LF=0
1250 RETURN
1260 IF SC=0 THEN1330
1270 IF SC>=1 AND SC<=2 THEN1340
1280 IF SC>=3 AND SC<=5 THEN1350
1290 IF SC>=6 AND SC<=9 THEN1360
1300 IF SC>=10 AND SC<=14 THEN1370
1310 IF SC>=15 AND SC<=20 THEN1380
1320 RETURN
1330 IF A(SC+1)+A(SC+2)<>0 THEN1400
```

234

```
1335 GOTO1390
1340 IF A(SC+2)+A(SC+3)<>0 THEN1400
1345 GOTO1390
1350 IF A(SC+3)+A(SC+4)<>0 THEN1400
1355 GOTO1390
1360 IF A(SC+4)+A(SC+5)<>0 THEN1400
1365 GOTO1390
1370 IF A(SC+5)+A(SC+6)<>0 THEN1400
1375 GOTO1390
1380 IF A(SC+6)+A(SC+7)<>0 THEN1400
1390 RETURN
1400 PRINT@39,"CARD COVERED - TRY AGAI
     N.";
1410 GOSUB1220
1430 RY=1
1440 RETURN
1500 REM MORE CARDS FROM PYRAMID
1510 PRINT@0,"MAKE ANOTHER SELECTION
        ";
1540 W$=INKEY$:IF W$=""THEN1540
1550 W=VAL(W$):W=W*10
1560 R$=INKEY$:IF R$=""THEN1560
1570 U=VAL(R$)
1580 SW=W+U:LZ=H(SW+1):LT=LZ:IF A(SW)=
     0 THEN1050
1590 WE=1
1600 LL=L+G+LT
1610 PRINT@0,"ANOTHER CARD (Y/N)?
     ";
1615 W$=INKEY$:IF W$=""THEN1615
1620 IF W$="N" THEN RETURN
1625 PRINT@0,"MAKE ONE OTHER SELECTION
        ";
1630 D$=INKEY$:IF D$=""THEN1630
1635 UL=VAL(D$):UL=UL*10
1640 Z$=INKEY$:IF Z$=""THEN1640
1645 UZ=VAL(Z$)
1650 SL=UL+UZ:LY=H(SL+1):LF=LY:IF A(SL
     )=0 THEN1050
1655 LL=L+G+LT+LF:WD=1
1660 RETURN
1700 REM WON - LOST - PLAY AGAIN
```

235

```
1710 FOR I=0TO27:IF A(I)=0 THEN R=R+1:
     NEXT:ELSE R=R:NEXT
1715 IF R>=28 THEN1770
1730 CLS:PRINT
1740 PRINT"YOU HAVE LOST THIS BATTLE O
     F SOLITAIRE."
1750 PRINT"MAYBE A COUPLE OF COURSES I
     N ADDITION WOULD HELP ??"
1760 GOTO1800
1770 CLS:PRINT
1780 PRINT"REALLY GOOD !!!"
1790 PRINT"YOU'VE WON THIS HAND OF SOL
     ITAIRE !!!"
1800 PRINT
1810 PRINT"ARE YOU READY TO TACKLE A F
     RESH DECK OF CARDS";
1820 INPUT I$
1830 IF I$="YES" THEN DD=1:CLS:GOTO70
1840 PRINT
1850 PRINT"END OF PROGRAM.........."
1860 END
2000 CLS
2010 PRINTTAB(10);"PYRAMID (SOLITAIRE)
     "
2020 PRINT
2030 PRINT"THIS CARD GAME MUST BE FOLL
     OWED TO THE LETTER."
2040 PRINT"OTHERWISE, YOU'LL FIND YOUR
     SELF LOSING EVERY GAME."
2050 PRINT"THE OBJECT OF THE GAME IS S
     IMPLE, DELETE ALL CARDS"
2060 PRINT"IN THE PYRAMID BEFORE THE R
     EMAINING CARDS IN THE"
2070 PRINT"DECK RUN OUT (YOU CAN ONLY
     GO THROUGH THE DECK"
2080 PRINT"ONE TIME). TO DELETE CARDS
     -- ADD THEM TOGETHER"
2085 PRINT"TO TOTAL 13."
2090 PRINT"FACE CARDS ARE, ACE - 1, KI
     NG - 13, QUEEN - 12"
2100 PRINT"JACK - 11. ALL OTHER CARDS
     ARE FACE VALUE."
```

236

```
2110 PRINT
2120 PRINT"PRESS ENTER TO CONTINUE INS
     TRUCTIONS";
2130 INPUT I$
2140 CLS:PRINT
2150 PRINT"CARDS ARE ENTERED BY THEIR
     PLACEMENT AREA, ONLY !!"
2160 PRINT"00 BEING THE TOP OF THE PYR
     AMID AND 27 BEING THE"
2170 PRINT"LAST CARD OF THE PYRAMID. A
     LWAYS ENTER LEADING"
2180 PRINT""ZEROS WHERE NECESSARY."
2190 PRINT"START AT THE BOTTOM OF THE
     PYRAMID AND WORK YOUR"
2200 PRINT"WAY UP, CARDS MUST BE UNCOV
     ERED BEFORE YOU CAN"
2210 PRINT"USE THEM. THAT IS, BEFORE Y
     OU CAN USE CARD 15,"
2220 PRINT"CARDS 21 & 22 MUST BE OUT O
     F THE WAY."
2230 PRINT"REMEMBER THE FOLLOWING KEYS
     :"
2240 PRINT"SPACE BAR TO DRAW A CARD."
2250 PRINT"YOU WILL HAVE THE FOLLOWING
      QUESTIONS / COMMENTS:"
2260 PRINT"<TO DRAW - PRESS SPACE BAR.
     >"
2270 PRINT"IF YOU WANT ANOTHER CARD, D
     O JUST THAT. IF THERE"
2280 PRINT"ARE CARDS IN THE PYRAMID TH
     AT TOTAL 13, PRESS 'E'."
2285 PRINT"PRESS ENTER";:INPUT X:CLS:P
     RINT
2290 PRINT"<ENTER CARD NUMBER>, WILL T
     HEN APPEAR, ENTER 1"
2300 PRINT"CARD FROM PYRAMID, OR PRESS
      SPACE BAR TO DRAW ANOTHER CARD."
2310 PRINT"<WITH CARD DRAWN ?> IF YOU
     HAVE ANOTHER CARD FROM"
2320 PRINT"THE PYRAMID YOU WANT TO USE
     , PRESS 'C'."
```

```
2330 PRINT"<MAKE ANOTHER SELECTION> WI
     LL APPEAR. THEN YOU"
2340 PRINT"CAN ENTER ANOTHER CARD FROM
      THE PYRAMID."
2350 PRINT"<ANOTHER CARD (Y/N)? > BY E
     NTERING 'Y' YOU CAN"
2360 PRINT"ADD STILL ANOTHER CARD FROM
      THE PYRAMID, AS LONG"
2370 PRINT"AS YOUR TOTAL UP TO THIS PO
     INT DOESN'T EXCEED 13."
2380 PRINT"<WITH CARD DRAWN ?> WILL AP
     PEAR AGAIN. IF YOU"
2390 PRINT"USE ALL THE CARDS FROM THE
     PYRAMID PLUS THE"
2400 PRINT"CARD THAT WAS DRAWN, PRESS
     'D' -- OTHERWISE PRESS"
2410 PRINT"'E' TO USE CARDS ONLY FROM
     THE PYRAMID."
2420 PRINT
2430 PRINT"PRESS ENTER (AGAIN)";:INPUT
      X:CLS:PRINT
2440 PRINT"ANYTIME YOU ENCOUNTER A  K
     (KING), JUST PRESS 'E'."
2450 PRINT"DRAWN CARDS WILL ADVANCE AU
     TOMATICALLY WHEN THE"
2460 PRINT"'DRAW CARD' IS USED TO TOTA
     L 13."
2470 PRINT"ALL THESE INSTRUCTIONS MIGH
     T SOUND LIKE YOU'RE IN"
2480 PRINT"FOR SOMETHING OUT OF THIS W
     ORLD, BUT AFTER A FEW"
2490 PRINT"HITS AND MISSES YOU'LL SOON
      CATCH ON."
2500 PRINT
2510 PRINT"NOTE: ALL FUNCTIONS ENTERED
      INCLUDING CARDS, WILL"
2520 PRINT"USE THE INKEY$ FUNCTION --
     SO DON'T PRESS ENTER"
2530 PRINT"UNLESS OTHERWISE REQUESTED
     !!!"
2540 PRINT
```

```
2550 PRINT"PRESS ENTER (FINALLY) TO BE
     GIN";
2560 INPUT X
2570 RETURN
```

TEN (SOLITAIRE)

This solitaire game is quite a bit different from pyramid. Cards
with this solitaire game must match both in value and color. Play
red on red, black on black (Fig. 9-7).

As with pyramid, you'll only be allowed to go through the deck
once, so use your head. This game also uses the INKEY$ function,
so don't press enter, unless directed to do so. See Fig. 9-8 for the
flowchart.

Program Notes

Lines 70-350 get the 52 cards for one deck, set the suit, value
print 10 cards, face up and then draw one more for you.

Lines 550-970 get your input. They check for use of the draw
card or for two cards from the playing field. They add the values and
ensure that the colors are equal. This routine set the positions used
for another card drawn.

Lines 1200-1320 are PRINT messages.

Lines 1400-1690 are the instructions.

Lines 1700-1860 are closing messages and contain argument
for another RUN of the game.

Program Listing

```
10 REM PROGRAM TITLE: TEN (SOLITAIRE)
20 CLS:DEFINT Q,W:DIM M(52),D(52),B(12
   ),T(12),F(52)
30 RANDOM
40 GOSUB1400:GOTO350
70 REM PRINT THE CARDS - 10 TOTAL - FA
   CE UP
80 A=9:L=120:V=L-92:AY=24:LY=AY+9:Y=36
   :YY=Y+9
90 FOR H=ATOL:SET(H,AY):SET(H,LY):SET(
   H,Y):SET(H,YY)
100 IF H=V THEN FOR F=AYTOLY:SET(H-20,
    F):SET(H,F):NEXT:FOR G=YTOYY:SET(
    H-20,G):SET(H,G):NEXT:H=H+2:V=V+2
    3
```

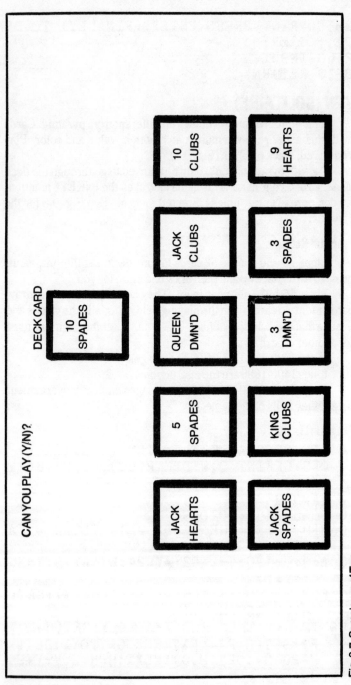

CAN YOU PLAY (Y/N)?

DECK CARD

10 SPADES	

JACK HEARTS	5 SPADES	QUEEN DMN'D	JACK CLUBS	10 CLUBS
JACK SPADES	KING CLUBS	3 DMN'D	3 SPADES	9 HEARTS

Fig. 9-7. Sample run of Ten.

```
110 NEXT
115 FOR H=54TO74:SET(H,AY-12):SET(H,LY
    -12):NEXT
118 FOR H=AY-12TOLY-12:SET(54,H):SET(7
    4,H):NEXT
120 PRINT@220,"DECK CARD";:RETURN
130 REM CARDS - ONE DECK - 13 OF EACH
    SUIT
140 FOR I=1TO52:M(I)=I:NEXT:P=(I-1)/4:
    I=1:J=1:S=1:TC=0:RETURN
150 C=RND(52)
```

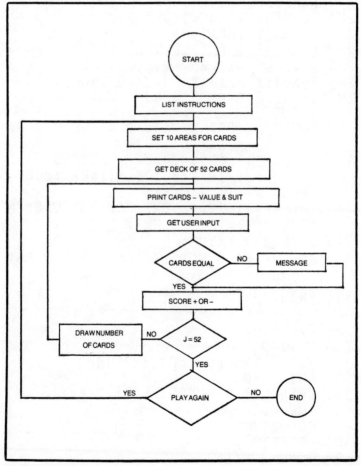

Fig. 9-8. Flowchart of Ten.

```
160 IF M(C)=0 THEN 150
165 IF J=52 GOSUB310:PRINT"LAST CARD..
       ........":GOSUB340
170 Q=(M(C)-1)/P:F=Q
180 W=M(C)-Q*P:DC=W
185 M(C)=0
190 RETURN
200 C$="CLUBS"
210 S$="SPADES"
220 D$="DMN'D"
230 H$="HEARTS"
240 REM CARD LOCATIONS
250 LC=584:X=1:XX=1:GOTO260
255 IF X=11 THEN294
260 LL=LC+62:B(X)=LL:T(X)=LC
280 LC=LC+11.7:LE=LE+11.7
285 X=X+1:XX=XX+1:IF XX<=5 THEN260
290 IF XX=6 THEN LC=840
292 GOTO255
294 GOSUB310:PRINT"CARD PLACEMENT AREA
      S."
295 T(X)=351:B(X)=414:FOR I=1TO10:IF I
      <>10 PRINT@T(I),"0";I;:NEXT:ELSE
      PRINT@T(I),I;:NEXT
296 FOR KL=1TO2000:NEXT:FOR I=1TO10:PR
      INT@T(I),"   ";:NEXT
298 GOSUB310:RETURN
300 REM PRINT @ FOR STATEMENTS - QUEST
      IONS
310 PRINT@0,"
                            ";
320 PRINT@0,;
330 RETURN
340 FOR U=1TO1200:NEXT:RETURN
350 GOSUB310
360 PRINT"10 CARDS WILL BE DRAWN FROM
      DECK."
370 GOSUB340
380 GOSUB70
390 GOSUB200:E=1
400 GOSUB140:GOTO520
```

```
420 IF DC=1 PRINT@T(E),"ACE";:GOTO455
430 IF DC=11 PRINT@T(E)-1,"JACK";:GOTO
    455
440 IF DC=12 PRINT@T(E)-1,"QUEEN";:GOT
    O455
450 IF DC=13 PRINT@T(E)-1,"KING";:ELSE
    PRINT@T(E),DC;:
455 D(I)=DC
460 IF F=0 PRINT@B(E),C$;:F(S)=0:GOTO5
    00
470 IF F=1 PRINT@B(E),S$;:F(S)=0:GOTO5
    00
480 IF F=2 PRINT@B(E),D$;:F(S)=5:GOTO5
    00
490 IF F=3 PRINT@B(E),H$;:F(S)=5
500 IF E>=11 RETURN
510 E=E+1:RETURN
520 GOSUB150:GOSUB420:IF TE=53 THEN540
530 IF J<=10 THEN J=J+1:I=I+1:S=S+1:GO
    TO520
540 GOSUB310
550 PRINT"CAN YOU PLAY (Y/N) ?"
560 A$=INKEY$:IF A$=""THEN560
565 IF A$="N" AND J+1=53 GOTO1700:REM
    END COMMENTS
570 IF A$="N" THEN GOSUB1000:E=11:GOSU
    B1090:GOTO540
580 GOSUB310
590 PRINT"WITH CARD FROM DECK (Y/N) ?"
600 A$=INKEY$:IF A$=""THEN600
610 IF A$="N" THEN800
620 GOSUB310
630 PRINT"ENTER ONE CARD FROM PLAYING
    FIELD."
640 PT=1
650 GOTO860
665 IF ABS(D(J)-D(C2))>0 GOSUB1250:GOT
    O540
670 IF ABS(F(J)-F(C2))>1 GOSUB1290:GOT
    O540
680 GOTO910
```

243

```
800 REM ENTER CARDS FROM PLAYING FIELD
810 GOSUB310
820 PRINT"ENTER 2 CARDS (01 THROUGH 10
    ) ?"
830 A1$=INKEY$:IF A1$=""THEN830:ELSE P
    RINT@64,A1$;
840 A2$=INKEY$:IF A2$=""THEN840:ELSE P
    RINT@65,A2$;
850 C1=VAL(A1$+A2$):IF C1<1 OR C1>10 G
    OSUB1200:GOTO810
860 A3$=INKEY$:IF A3$=""THEN860:ELSE P
    RINT@67,A3$;
870 A4$=INKEY$:IF A4$=""THEN870:ELSE P
    RINT@68,A4$;
880 C2=VAL(A3$+A4$):IF C2<1 OR C2>10 G
    OSUB1200:IF PT=1 THEN620:ELSE810
884 IF C1=C2 GOSUB310:PRINT"QUIT TRYIN
    G TO CHEAT !!!":GOSUB340:IF PT=1
    THEN620:ELSE810
885 IF PT=1 THEN665
890 IF ABS(D(C1)-D(C2))>0 GOSUB1250:GO
    TO540
900 IF ABS(F(C1)-F(C2))>1 GOSUB1290:GO
    TO540
910 GOSUB310
915 PRINT"         CORRECT !!!":TR=TR-1:GO
    SUB340
925 GOSUB1000:IF PT<>1 GOSUB1040:ELSE
    GOSUB1060
930 IF PT=1 THEN E=C2:GOSUB1090:GOTO94
    5
932 IF J+1<>53 THEN E=C1:GOSUB420
935 D(C1)=D(J):F(C1)=F(J)
940 E=C2:GOSUB1090:D(C2)=D(J):F(C2)=F(
    J)
945 IF PT=1 PT=0:D(C2)=D(J):F(C2)=F(J)
950 E=11:GOSUB1090
960 C1=0:C2=0
970 GOTO540
1000 REM CLEAR LAST CARD
1010 PRINT@T(E)-1,"          ";
```

244

```
1020 PRINT@B(E),"          ";
1030 RETURN
1040 PRINT@T(C1)-1,"          ";
1050 PRINT@B(C1),"          ";
1060 PRINT@T(C2)-1,"          ";
1070 PRINT@B(C2),"          ";
1075 TC=TC+1
1080 RETURN
1090 REM CARD ADVANCE
1100 IF J+1=53 RETURN
1110 J=J+1:I=I+1:S=S+1
1120 GOSUB150
1150 GOSUB420
1160 RETURN
1200 REM TRY A RIGHT CARD NUMBER
1210 GOSUB310
1220 PRINT"WATCH THE TYPING, THAT WAS
     1 THROUGH 10 !!"
1230 GOSUB340
1240 RETURN
1250 GOSUB310
1260 PRINT"THAT WAS TWO NUMBERS -- THE
     SAME ?  TRY AGAIN."
1270 GOSUB340
1280 RETURN
1290 GOSUB310
1300 PRINT"THAT'S RED ON RED -- BLACK
     ON BLACK ??!!"
1310 GOSUB340
1320 RETURN
1400 CLS
1410 PRINT@25,"TEN (SOLITAIRE)"
1420 PRINT
1430 PRINT"YOU MIGHT FIND THIS A SIMPL
     E GAME...BUT ALMOST"
1440 PRINT"IMPOSSIBLE TO WIN !!"
1450 PRINT"THE RULES ARE THIS: YOU WIL
     L HAVE A DECK OF 52"
1460 PRINT"CARDS. 10 OF THESE WILL BE
     PLACED FACE UP, THEN"
```

245

```
1470 PRINT"THE COMPUTER WILL DRAW THE
     FIRST CARD FOR YOU."
1480 PRINT"YOU WILL THEN BE ASKED IF Y
     OU CAN PLAY (CARDS"
1490 PRINT"THAT MATCH), IF NOT YOU'LL
     DRAW ANOTHER CARD FROM"
1500 PRINT"THE DECK. IF YOU CAN PLAY Y
     OU CAN EITHER USE THE"
1510 PRINT"CARD FROM THE DECK OR TAKE
     TWO OUT OF THE PLAYING"
1520 PRINT"FIELD."
1530 PRINT"NOW HERE'S THE CATCH: EACH
     CARD YOU ENTER (THROUGH"
1540 PRINT"THE INKEY$ FUNCTION -- ENTE
     R LEADING ZERO'S), THE"
1550 PRINT
1560 PRINT"PRESS ENTER TO CONTINUE";:I
     NPUT X:CLS
1570 PRINT
1580 PRINT"FACE VALUE AND THE COLOR (B
     LACK ON BLACK -- RED"
1590 PRINT"ON RED) MUST MATCH, OR NATU
     RALLY THE COMPUTER"
1600 PRINT"WILL GIVE YOU A SUITABLE ST
     ATEMENT."
1610 PRINT"AN EXAMPLE MIGHT BE:"
1620 PRINT"KING OF SPADES -- KING OF C
     LUBS THESE WOULD MATCH,"
1630 PRINT"BUT DON'T TRY TO ENTER CARD
     S OF UNMATCHED COLORS"
1640 PRINT"OR NUMBERS."
1650 PRINT"THE ONLY WAY YOU CAN WIN IS
      TO USE ALL CARDS IN THE"
1660 PRINT"DECK (WHICH YOU CAN ONLY GO
      THROUGH ONCE !!)."
1670 PRINT
1680 PRINT"PRESS ENTER TO BEGIN";:INPU
     T X
1690 CLS:RETURN
1700 REM CLOSING MESSAGE -- PLAY AGAIN
1710 GOSUB310
```

```
1720 IF TC<26 THEN1750
1730 PRINT"THIS IS REALLY HARD TO BELE
     IVE !! YOU'VE WON !!!"
1740 PRINT"WITH ALL";26;"SETS PAIRED O
     FF.":GOTO1770
1750 PRINT"SORRY CHARLIE...YOU HAVE LO
     ST THIS GAME."
1760 PRINT"PERHAPS YOU COULD IMPROVE Y
     OUR SCORE BY CHEATING ???"
1770 PRINT
1780 PRINT"ANOTHER DECK IS ALMOST READ
     Y, IF YOU WANT TO TRY AGAIN";
1790 INPUT I$
1800 IF LEFT$(I$,1)="Y" THEN1820
1810 GOTO1840
1820 C1=0:C2=0:RANDOM:CLS:GOTO350
1830 REM END OF PROGRAM
1840 PRINT
1850 PRINT"E N D.........."
1860 GOTO1860
```

SPINNING WHEEL

This program gives you the front view of a spinning roulette wheel. You'll be able to get a computer loan and have to pay it back out of your winnings. After you have paid it back, the object then will be to break the computer bank—the object of any gambling game.

All of this might sound simple, but getting the wheel to stop on a number you've chosen might prove to be something else (numbers range from 0 to 50), the wheel will start out fast then gradually slow down and stop.

The PRINT statements display throughout the program will let you know where you stand (Fig. 9-9). See Fig. 9-10 for the flowchart.

Program Notes

Lines 25-120 spin the wheel and flash the winning number.

Lines 125-540 are self-explanatory.

Lines 600-680 are the PRINT@ statements that keep you updated on your winnings (or losses).

Lines 690-710 receive your bet and check it to ensure that amount you can cover the bet.

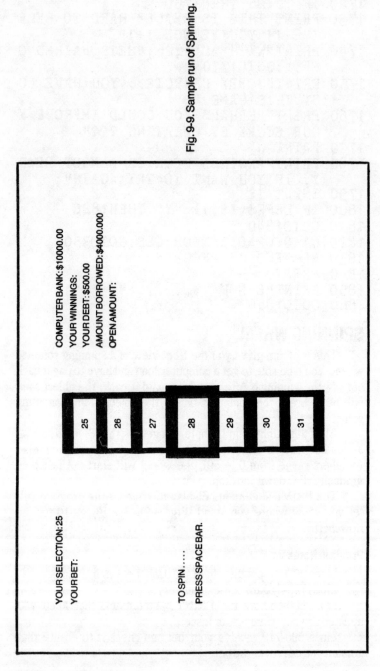

COMPUTER BANK: $10000.00
YOUR WINNINGS:
YOUR DEBT: $500.00
AMOUNT BORROWED: $4000.000
OPEN AMOUNT:

| 25 | 26 | 27 | 28 | 29 | 30 | 31 |

YOUR SELECTION: 25
YOUR BET:

TO SPIN.....
PRESS SPACE BAR.

Fig. 9-9. Sample run of Spinning.

Lines 717-880 change the variables for a spin that was lost. If winnings and amount borrowed equal 0, you will be asked if you want to borrow some more money.

Lines 900-960 handle a win and check to see if the computer bank has been broken.

Lines 1000-1670 handle DATA for PRINT @, PRINT messages and instructions.

Program Listing

```
10  CLS:GOSUB1500:J=0:D$="$$####.##":D
    IM K(100)
15  GOSUB440:GOSUB690
20  RANDOM:PRINT@0,"YOUR SELECTION:";II
    ;
22  PRINT@64,"YOUR BET:";USING D$;YB;
25  FOR X=50TO66:SET(X,1):SET(X,7):SET(
    X,13):SET(X,19):SET(X,24):SET(X,3
    0):SET(X,36):SET(X,42):NEXT
26  IF MR<>1 GOSUB1000:GOSUB600:ELSE GO
    SUB620
27  FOR Y=2TO41:SET(50,Y):SET(66,Y):IF
    Y>=19 AND Y<=24 SET(49,Y):SET(67,
    Y):NEXT:ELSE NEXT:GOSUB1200
28  P=1:I=RND(50):JJ=RND(25)
30  N=1
40  PRINT@A(N)+V,I;:PRINT@A(N+1)+V,I+1;
    :PRINT@A(N+2)+V,I+2;:PRINT@A(N+3)
    +V,I+3;:PRINT@A(N+4)+V,I+4;:PRINT
    @A(N+5)+V,I+5;:PRINT@A(N+6)+V,I+6
    ;
46  N=N+1:ELSE IF N<>8 THEN40
48  IF I=0 I=45
49  I=I-1
50  FOR T=1TOJ:NEXT:J=J+10:K(M)=I
60  IF J<=600+JJ THEN 30
70  X=0
80  PRINT@A(4),I+4;:FOR TY=1TO100:NEXT
90  PRINT@A(4),"    ";:FOR GY=1TO50:NEX
    T
100 FOR TY=1TO25:NEXT:X=X+1
110 IF X<>10 THEN80
```

```
120 PRINT@A(4),I+4;
125 PRINT@64,"WINNING NUMBER:";I+4;
130 IF II<>I+4 THEN720
140 PRINT@192,"FANTASTIC !!";:PRINT@25
    6,;
150 PRINT"YOU'VE WON THIS ONE.";:GOTO9
    00
160 PRINT@192,"SORRY......";:PRINT@256
    ,;
170 PRINT"AN OBSESSION MAYBE ?";
200 PRINT@320,"TRY AGAIN";
210 INPUT AN$
```

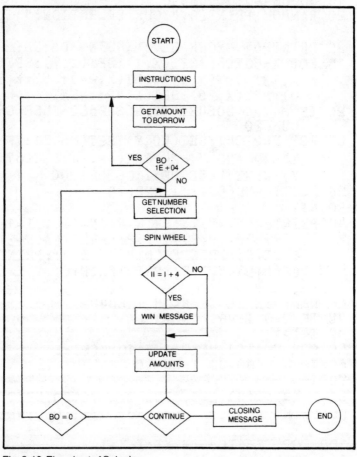

Fig. 9-10. Flowchart of Spinning.

```
220 IF AN$="YES" THEN CLS:GOTO250
240 GOTO1300
250 IF YW>BO AND PB<>1 THEN270
260 IF YW<=0 AND TL=BO THEN PB=0:PL=1:
    GOSUB450:ELSE IF YW=0 AND BO=0 TH
    EN PL=1:GOSUB450
265 GOTO850
270 PRINT"YOU HAVE WON ENOUGH TO REPAY
     THE AMOUNT"
280 PRINT"YOU'VE BORROWED, DO YOU WISH
     TO REPAY NOW"
290 PRINT"(IF YOU DON'T -- YOU CAN'T C
    ONTINUE PLAYING)";
300 INPUT AN$
310 IF AN$="YES" THEN YW=ABS(YW-BO):CM
    =CM+BO:BO=0:BA=0:PB=1:CLS:GOTO850
320 GOTO1300
440 IF MR=1 THEN500
450 PRINT"AMOUNT YOU WISH TO BORROW";
460 INPUT BO
470 IF BO>1E+04 PRINT"SORRY...CAN'T AD
    VANCE THAT AMOUNT.":FOR K=1TO1500
    :NEXT:CLS:GOTO450
480 IF PL=1 THEN BO=BO+BA:RETURN
490 BA=BO+BA
500 PRINT"ENTER A NUMBER (0-50)";
510 INPUT II
520 IF II<0 OR II>50 PRINT"DUMMY !! TH
    AT'S BETWEEN 0 AND 50, TRY AGAIN.
    ....":FOR KK=1TO1200:NEXT:GOTO500
540 RETURN
600 CM=1E+04
620 PRINT@35,"COMPUTER BANK:";USING D$
    ;CM;
630 PRINT@99,"YOUR WINNINGS:";USING D$
    ;YW;
640 PRINT 163,""YOU'REINDEBT: ";USINGD
    /;TL;
650 PRINT@291,"AMOUNT BORROWED:";USING
    D$;BO;
660 PRINT@355,"OPEN AMOUNT:      ";USING
    D$;YA;
```

251

```
680  RETURN
690  PRINT"ENTER YOUR BET -- UP TO";:IF
     YW>0 PRINTYW;:ELSE PRINTBO-TL;
695  INPUT YB

700  IF MR=1 AND YB>YA PRINT"IMPOSSIBLE
     !! YOU HAVEN'T GOT THAT MUCH...T
     RY AGAIN.":FOR KK=1TO1200:NEXT:GO
     TO690
710  YA=((BO-YB)+YW):IF YA<=0 YA=0
715  CLS:RETURN
717  REM LOSE ROUND
720  CM=CM+YB
730  TL=TL+YB
735  YW=YW-YB:IF YW<=0 YW=0
740  GOSUB620
750  GOTO160

850  MR=1
860  J=0
870  YY=0
880  GOTO15

900  REM WIN ROUND
910  IF TL<>0 THEN TL=TL-YB:YW=YW:CM=CM
     :GOTO935
920  YW=YW+YB
930  CM=CM-YB
935  IF TL<=0 TL=0
940  GOSUB620:IF CM<=0 AND BO=0 THEN110
     0
960  GOTO200
1000 FOR N=1TO7:READ A(N):NEXT
1010 DATA 91,219,347,475,603,731,859
1020 M=1:RETURN
1100 FOR KK=1TO1200:NEXT
1110 CLS:PRINT
1120 PRINT"YOU'VE DONE IT !!!!"
1130 PRINT""YOU'VE BROKEN THE COMPUTER'S
     BANK !!!"
1140 PRINT
1150 PRINT"SHALL WE TRY IT AGAIN";
1160 INPUT AN$
```

```
1170  IF AN$="YES" THEN PB=0:YW=0:MR=0:
      GOTO15
1180  GOTO1300
1200  PRINT@384,"TO SPIN.....";
1205  PRINT@448,"PRESS SPACE BAR.";
1210  S$=INKEY$:IF S$=" " THEN 1230
1220  GOTO1210
1230  PRINT@384,"                 ";
1240  PRINT@448,"                 ";
1250  RETURN
1300  FOR KK=1TO2000:NEXT
1310  CLS
1320  PRINT
1330  PRINT"THERE ALWAYS HAS TO BE ONE
      CHICKEN"
1340  PRINT"IN THE CROWD......YOU'VE BE
      EN ELECTED !!!!"
1350  IF YW>0 THEN1370
1360  PRINT"AND YOU DIDN'T WIN ONE THIN
       DIME !!":GOTO1380
1370  PRINT"YOU DID WIN A GRAND TOTAL O
      F";USING D$;YW
1380  PRINT
1390  PRINT"END OF PROGRAM.........."
1400  GOTO1400
1500  REM INSTRUCTIONS
1510  PRINT
1520  PRINTTAB(10);"S P I N N I N G   W
      H E E L"
1530  PRINT
1540  PRINT"STEP RIGHT UP, IF YOU'VE GO
      T THE GUTS,"
1550  PRINT"AND TRY TO WIN A FORTUNE WI
      TH THE SPINNING WHEEL."
1560  PRINT"THE OBJECT IS TO BREAK THE
      COMPUTER BANK AND"
1570  PRINT"TO PAY BACK ANY AMOUNT YOU'
      VE BORROWED. THE COMPUTER"
1580  PRINT"BANK WILL START OUT WITH $1
      0000.00, FOR EACH DOLLAR"
1590  PRINT"YOU WIN, THE COMPUTER BANK
      WILL DECREASE BY THAT"
```

```
1600 PRINT"AMOUNT. FOR EACH DOLLAR YOU
        LOSE THE COMPUTER BANK"
1610 PRINT"WILL INCREASE BY THAT AMOUN
        T. SO.....MAKE EACH"
1620 PRINT"BET COUNT. AND YOU SHOULDN'
        T ENCOUNTER ANY PROBLEMS."
1630 PRINT
1640 PRINT"PRESS ENTER TO BEGIN THE GA
        ME";
1650 INPUT AN$
1660 CLS
1670 RETURN
```

Glossary

Glossary
Computer Terms
For Level II Basic

address—a value specifying the location of a byte in memory.

alphanumerics—the set of letters A-Z, the numerals 0-9, various punctuation marks and special characters.

argument—the value supplied to a function and then operated on to derive a result.

array—a series of items, not necessarily arranged in a meaningful pattern, i.e. one or more dimension.

ASCII—American Standard Code for Information Interchange. An 8-bit character code.

assembler—a program that prepares a program in machine language from a program in symbolic language.

BASIC—Beginners All-purpose Symbolic Instruction Code.

baud—a unit of signaling speed in bits per second. LEVEL II operates at 500 bits per second.

binary number—a number system using two digits "0" and "1" represented in the base-two number system.

bit—abbreviation for binary digit, the smallest memory cell in a computer.

byte—the smallest memory that can be addressed in BASIC, consisting of eight consecutive bits.

decimal number—the number system that uses the numerals 0-9 and has a base of 10.

expression—a valid series of constants, variables and functions.

file—an organized collection of related DATA.

hexadecimal number—a number represented in the base-16 number system, using the digits 0 through 9 plus the letters A, B, C, D, E and F.

intrinsic function—a complicated function that may be built into the computers ROM and used directly in a BASIC statement.

logical expression—an expression which is either true or false. 1 means true, 0 means false.

machine language—written in binary-coded instructions and is used directly by the computer.

port—one of 256 channels through which DATA can be input to or output from a computer.

RAM—Random Access Memory. The memory available for writing programs or storing DATA.

ROM—Read Only Memory. The memory permanently stored in a computer that can only be read from.

routine—a set of computer instructions arranged in a sequence and used to direct the computer to carry out a certain operation.

statement—a complete instruction written in BASIC or a source language.

string—a sequence of alphanumeric characters. Limit 255.

subroutine—an instruction that can be accessed many times throughout a program by the computer.

variable—a quantity that can take on any of a given set of values.

variable name—the label by which a given variable is addressed.

Appendix A
TRS-80 Level II Summary˙

ENTER	carriage return and interpret command.
⟵	cursor backspace / delete last character typed.
⟶	move cursor to next tab stop. Tab stops are at positions 0, 8, 16, 24, 32, 40, 48, and 56.
SHIFT ⟵	move cursor to beginning of line; erase line.
SHIFT ⟶	converts display to 32 characters per line.
↓	linefeed.
:	statement delimiter, used between statements on same line.
CLEAR	clears display and returns to 64 characters per line.

EXECUTE MODE

BREAK	stops execution of program, LIST, etc.
ENTER	interpret DATA entered from keyboard with input command.
SHIFT @	pause of execution, freeze display on video screen during LIST.

ABBREVIATIONS

? use in place of PRINT.

. use in place of line number with LIST, EDIT, etc, of current line.

, use in place of REM.

RELATIONAL OPERATORS

SYMBOL	MEANING	EXPRESSIONS
<	less than	precedes
>	greater than	follows
=	equal to	equals
<= or =<	less than or equal to	precedes or equals
>= or =>	greater than or equal to	follows or equals
<> or ><	not equal to	does not equal

ORDER OF OPERATIONS

↑ (exponentiation)
/ (negation)
*, /
+, −

RELATIONAL OPERATIONS

NOT
AND
OR

GRAPHIC STATEMENTS

STATEMENT	FUNCTION	EXAMPLE
CLS	clear video display	CLS
RESET(X, Y)	turn off graphic block at location (X, Y)	RESET(A, W+1)
SET(X, Y)	turn on graphic block at location (X, Y) (where X is the horizontal co-ordinate and Y is the vertical co-ordinate on the video display)	SET (M, L*2)

ARITHMETIC FUNCTIONS   EXP*

FUNCTION	OPERATION	EXAMPLE
ABS(exp)	returns absolute value	ABS(N-I)
ATN (exp)	returns arctangent in radians	ATN (3*3)

260

CDBL (exp)	returns double-precision representation of exp	CDBL(2)
CINT (exp)	returns largest integer not greater than exp	CINT(J+B)
COS (exp)	returns the cosine of exp	COS(3*F)
CSNG (exp)	returns the natural exponential, exp	EXP(22.2)
FIX (exp)	returns the integer equivalent to truncated exp	FIX(B−B)
INT (exp)	returns largest integer not greater than exp	INT(Y−L)
LOG (exp)	returns logarithm of exp	LOG(44.3)
RND (0)	returns a pseudo-random number between 0.000001 and 0.999999 inclusive	RND(0)
RND(exp)	returns a pseudo-random number between 1 and int(exp) inclusive.	RND(10)
SGN (exp)	returns a −1 for negative exp; 0 for zero exp; +1 for positive exp	SGN(3+J)
SIN (exp)	returns a sine of exp	SIN(B/F)
SQR (exp)	returns square root of exp	SQR(2+2*J)
TAN (exp)	returns tangent of exp	TAN(G)

*EXP is any constant or numeric-valued expression.

Appendix B
Base Conversion

Binary	Octal	Hexadecimal	Decimal
00000000	000	00	0
00000001	001	01	1
00000010	002	02	2
000000011	003	03	3
00000100	004	04	4
00000101	005	05	5
00000110	06	06	6
00000111	007	07	7
00001000	010	08	8
00001001	011	09	9
00001010	012	0A	10
00001011	013	0B	11
00001100	014	0C	12
00001101	015	0D	13
00001110	016	0E	14
00001111	017	0F	15
00010000	020	10	16
00011000	030	18	24
00100000	040	20	32
00101000	050	28	40
00110000	060	30	48
00111000	070	38	56
01000000	100	40	64
01001000	110	48	72
01010000	120	50	80
01011000	130	58	88
01100000	140	60	96
01101000	150	68	104
01110000	160	70	112
01111000	170	78	120
10000000	200	80	128
10001000	210	88	136

Binary	Octal	Hexadecimal	Decimal
10010000	220	90	144
10011000	230	98	152
10100000	240	A0	160
10101000	250	A8	168
10110000	260	B0	176
10111000	270	B8	184
11000000	300	C0	192
11001000	310	C8	200
11010000	320	D0	208
11011000	330	D8	216
11100000	340	E0	224
11101000	350	E8	232
11110000	360	F0	240
11111000	370	F8	248
11111001	371	F9	249
11111010	372	FA	250
11111011	373	FB	251
11111100	374	FC	252
11111101	375	FD	253
11111110	376	FE	254
11111111	377	FF	255

Appendix C
BASIC Statements

AUTO	turn on automatic line numbering. Can be set for different increments.
CLEAR	set numerics to zero, strings to null.
CLEAR N	same as CLEAR but sets aside a certain amount of memory for strings (N).
CLOAD	load program from cassette player. If no filename is specified, the current program will be loaded.
CLOAD?	compares program on tape with program in memory. If programs are not equal "BAD" will be printed on video display.
CONT	continue after BREAK or STOP in execution.
CSAVE	saves current program on cassette tape, a filename should be used so that program can be compared with what is in memory.
DATA	hold DATA for access by READ statement.
DELETE	delete program line or lines specified by INPUT statement.
DIM	allocate storage for dimensional array with specified size per dimension.
EDIT	puts computer in EDIT mode for line specified.
END	end execution of program, returns computer to command mode.
ERROR	if an error is encountered in the program, the computer prints the offending line number and the error code for that line.
FOR – TO –	open a FOR-NEXT loop.
FOR–TO–STEP–	open a FOR-NEXT loop with optional STEP · If no step is specified an increment of one is used.
GOTO	branch to a specified line number in the program.
GOSUB	branch to a sub-routine beginning with the specified line number.
IF - THEN - ELSE	test expression; if true, execute the statement and jump to the next program line. If it's false, the ELSE statement will be executed.

INPUT	await input from keyboard.
INPUT #-1	input from cassette # 1.
LET (var-exp)	assigns the value of an expression to variable. The LET is optional with LEVEL II BASIC.
LIST	list all program lines, or a specified range of lines.
NEXT var.	close the FOR - NEXT loop. The variable may be omitted, or a variable list may be used to close nested loops.
NEW	deletes the entire program in memory and returns to command mode.
ON - GOTO	branches to a specified line number after evaluating the expression. Otherwise go to the next statement.
ON - GOSUB	same as ON - GOTO but branches to the appropriate GOSUB statement.
PRINT exp.	outputs to the video display the value of exp, which can be a string expression, a numeric, a constant or a list of items.
PRINT #-1	output to cassette # 1.
PRINT @	begins printing at a specified area on the video display; a PRINT modifier.
PRINT USING	PRINT format specifier, output exp in a form specified by a string field.
RANDOM	reseeds the RANDOM number generator.
REM	remark indicator. The rest of line is ignored.
READ	assigns values to specified variables starting with the current DATA element.
RESTORE	resets the data pointer to the first item in the first DATA statement.
RESUME	returns from the error routine to the line specified.
RETURN	branch to statement *following* last GOSUB executed.
RUN	execute the program. If no line is specified, execution begins with the program's lowest line number.
STOP	stop the program's execution and print a break message containing current line number. Program execution can resume with CONT.
SYSTEM	enter the monitor mode for loading a machine-language program from cassette tape player.
TAB	print modifier; begins printing at specified TAB area of the video display.
TROFF	turn off the line numbers trace.
TRON	turn on the line numbers trace (very useful when debugging).

STRING FUNCTIONS

FUNCTION	OPERATION
ASC	returns the ASCII code of first character in string argument.
CHR$	returns a one-character string defined by a code. If a control function is specified by code, that function is activated.
FRE	returns amount of memory available for string storage.

INKEY$	strobes the keyboard and returns a one-character string corresponding to the key pressed during strobe.
LEN	returns the numeric length of string.
LEFT$	returns the first n characters of a string (where n is a numeric expression).
MID$	returns the substring of a string with length n and starting at position
MID$ (cont)	m in a string (where n and m are numeric expressions).
RIGHT$	returns the last n characters of a string (where n is a numeric expression).
STR$	returns a string representation of an evaluated argument.
STRING$	returns a sequence of characters using the first character. PRINT STRING$ (50, "*"), for example, will print 50 asteriskson the video display.
VAL	returns a numeric value corresponding to a numeric-valued string, such as PRINT VAL (A$+W$).

Appendix D
ASCII Character Codes

CODE	CHARACTER	CODE	CHARACTER
32	SPACE	53	5
33	!	54	6
34	"	55	7
35	#	56	8
36	$	57	9
37	%	58	:
38	&	59	;
39	'	60	<
40	(	61	=
41	)	62	>
42	*	63	?
43	+	64	@
44	,	65	A
45	-	66	B
46	.	67	C
47	/	68	D
48	0	69	E
49	1	70	F
50	2	71	G
51	3	72	H
52	4		

CODE	CHARACTER
73	I
74	J
75	K
76	L
77	M
78	N
79	O
80	P
81	Q
82	R
83	S
84	T
85	U
86	V
87	W
88	X
89	Y
90	Z
91	↑ or [
92	↓
93	←
94	→
95	underscore

Appendix E
Standard Logic Gates and Functions

GATE	FUNCTION
OR GATE	produces an output whenever any one (or more) of its inputs are energized.
NOR GATE	an OR gate followed by an inverter to form a binary circuit which the output is logic 0 if any of the inputs are logic 1 and is logic 1 only if all inputs are logic 0.
AND GATE	produces an output of logic 1 only when all inputs are logic 1 and produces an output of logic 0 if any of the inputs are logic 0.
NAND GATE	a combination of a NOT function and an AND function. The output is logic 0 only if all inputs are logic 1; it is logic 1 if any input is logic 0
NOT CIRCUIT	called an inverter circuit, containing only one input and one output. The output of the gate is always the opposit of the input.
BUFFER GATE	a logic gate with a high output drive capability. Used when it is necessary to drive a large number of gate inputs from one gate function

Index

Index

r